Democracy in Retreat

A COUNCIL ON FOREIGN RELATIONS BOOK

Democracy in Retreat

The Revolt of the Middle Class and the Worldwide Decline of Representative Government

Joshua Kurlantzick

Yale UNIVERSITY PRESS
New Haven & London

Yale University Press books may be purchased in quantity for educational, business, or promotional use. For information, please e-mail sales.press@yale.edu (U.S. office) or sales@ yaleup.co.uk (U.K. office).

Set in Granjon type by Westchester Book Group, Danbury, Connecticut.
Printed in the United States of America.

Library of Congress Cataloging-in-Publication Data

Kurlantzick, Joshua, 1976–
    Democracy in retreat : the revolt of the middle class and the worldwide decline of representative government / Joshua Kurlantzick.
        p.   cm.
    Includes bibliographical references and index.
    ISBN 978-0-300-17538-7 (alk. paper)
    1. Democracy—Case studies.   2. Democratization—Case studies.   I. Title.
    JC423.K857 2013
    321.8—dc23

                                                                2012031764

A catalogue record for this book is available from the British Library.

This paper meets the requirements of ANSI/NISO Z39.48-1992 (Permanence of Paper).

10 9 8 7 6 5 4 3 2 1

THE COUNCIL ON FOREIGN RELATIONS

The Council on Foreign Relations (CFR) is an independent, nonpartisan membership organization, think tank, and publisher dedicated to being a resource for its members, government officials, business executives, journalists, educators and students, civic and religious leaders, and other interested citizens in order to help them better understand the world and the foreign policy choices facing the United States and other countries. Founded in 1921, CFR carries out its mission by maintaining a diverse membership, with special programs to promote interest and develop expertise in the next generation of foreign policy leaders; convening meetings at its headquarters in New York and in Washington, DC, and other cities where senior government officials, members of Congress, global leaders, and prominent thinkers come together with CFR members to discuss and debate major international issues; supporting a Studies Program that fosters independent research, enabling CFR scholars to produce articles, reports, and books and hold roundtables that analyze foreign policy issues and make concrete policy recommendations; publishing *Foreign Affairs,* the preeminent journal on international affairs and U.S. foreign policy; sponsoring Independent Task Forces that produce reports with both findings and policy prescriptions on the most important foreign policy topics; and providing up-to-date information and analysis about world events and American foreign policy on its website, www.cfr.org.

For Shira

Contents

Acknowledgments

This book could not have been written without the generous assistance and wise advice of many people.

At the Council on Foreign Relations, Richard N. Haass and James M. Lindsay read drafts of the work and offered critical and insightful comments. Elizabeth Leader, Marissa Clingen, David Silverman, Hunter Marston, and Shelby Leighton contributed important research and analysis. Susan Strange helped enormously at the National Archives. The CFR library offered essential abilities to find nearly anything, and Patricia Dorff and the CFR publications staff worked to bring it to publication. Elizabeth Economy offered essential guidance and mentorship. I am grateful to CFR's Civil Society, Markets, and Democracy Initiative for its support.

The Henry Luce Foundation and the Smith Richardson Foundation's generous grants allowed me to do the research and writing of the book; without their help, it would not have happened. At Smith Richardson, I am specifically grateful to Allan Song, while at Luce I am grateful to Helena Kolenda and Li Ling. The MacArthur Foundation also provided assistance to portions of the research, for which I am very grateful.

I am also indebted to all the democracy activists, advocates, and scholars who generously offered their time to speak with me, around the world—and sometimes at peril to themselves.

At Yale University Press, I am grateful to editor William Frucht for his guidance and thoughts in shaping the book, as well as to editor Jeffrey Schier for his line editing.

Shira provided not only counsel and advice throughout but also love. Without her this book would not have happened.

Throughout it all, Caleb remained the joy in my life.

Democracy in Retreat

I

Democracy Goes into Reverse

URING APRIL, the hottest month of the year in Thailand, all activity in Bangkok slows to a molasses pace. With temperatures rising to well over 100 degrees Fahrenheit, many residents leave town, heading north or to the islands east and south of the city, and the slow-moving flow of traffic releases a cloud of smog into the steaming air. In mid-April, the entire country shuts down for a week for the Thai New Year, leaving the few people still in the capital marveling at their sudden ability to drive across the city in minutes rather than hours.

But in the spring of 2010, Bangkok was anything but quiet. Tens of thousands of red shirted protesters descended upon the city to protest against the government, which they viewed as illegitimate and unsympathetic to the working class, and to call for a new election. They mostly hailed from poorer villages in the rural northeast, or from working class suburbs of Bangkok. At first, the protests seemed like a village street party. Demonstrators snacked on sticky rice and grilled chicken, and danced in circles to bands playing mor lam, a northeastern Thai music that, with its wailing guitars and plaintive, yodeling vocals, resembles an Asian version of Hank Williams. Amid a rollicking, almost joyous atmosphere, over 100,000 red shirts soon gathered around a makeshift stage in central Bangkok to demand the resignation of the government.

Within weeks, however, the demonstrations turned violent, leading to the worst bloodshed in Bangkok in two decades. On April 10, some demonstrators fired on police and launched grenades at the security forces. The troops cracked down hard, sometimes shooting randomly into the crowds.[1] By the end of the day, twenty-four people had been killed.

That was just a warm-up for late May. By that time, the red shirts had been camped out for weeks in the central business district, shutting down commerce and paralyzing traffic. The government and the armed forces, which had rejected the protesters' demands for an immediate election, decided to take a tougher line. Advancing into the red shirts' encampment, heavily armed soldiers created virtual free-fire zones, shooting at anyone who moved and reportedly posting snipers in buildings above the streets to take out red shirts. A prominent general who had joined the red movement was killed by a bullet to the forehead as he stood talking with a reporter from the *New York Times*.[2] The red shirts battled back, setting fire to the stock exchange, the largest mall in the city, and other symbols of elite privilege. On the evening of May 19, flames engulfed the Bangkok skyline, dwarfing the temples of the old city and the glass-and-steel high rises of the financial district.[3] By the end of May, most of the red shirts had gone home, but the battle had ended at a terrible cost. The clashes had resulted in the killing of over one hundred people, most of them civilians, and the government had declared a state of emergency in most provinces, giving it the equivalent of martial law powers to detain people without having to charge them with committing a crime.

Such violence has become increasingly common in a country that was once among the most stable in Southeast Asia and an example to other developing nations of democratic consolidation. Four years before the red shirt protests, a different group of protesters had launched Thailand into turmoil, gathering on the main green in the old city of Bangkok, near the Grand Palace, with its glittering spires inlaid with tiny gems. Then it was thousands of middle-class urbanites from Bangkok—lawyers, doctors, shopkeepers, and others—demanding the removal of Prime Minister Thaksin Shinawatra, a charismatic populist, mostly backed by the rural poor, who had been elected by large majorities but was clearly disdainful of democratic institutions.

Dressed in the yellow of Thailand's revered monarch, King Bhumibol Adulyadej, the middle-class protesters were led by a group with the Orwellian name People's Alliance for Democracy (PAD). Like the Democratic

People's Republic of Korea (North Korea) or the old German Democratic Republic, the PAD was neither democratic nor representative of many people. Its platform for change called for reducing the number of elected seats in Parliament, essentially to slash the power of the rural poor, who constitute the majority of Thais.[4] "The middle class—they disdain the rural masses and see them as willing pawns to the corrupt vote buyers," said one former U.S. ambassador to Thailand.[5]

Thaksin had used his power to eviscerate the civil service, silence the media, and allegedly disappear political opponents. He declared a "war on drugs" in which more than two thousand people were killed by the security forces, frequently with gunshots to the back of the head, and often despite the fact that they had no links to narcotics.[6] He also cracked down on dissent. In one horrific incident in October 2004, Thai security forces rounded up hundreds of young men in southern Thailand after demonstrations against the government at a local mosque. The security forces stacked them inside stifling, insufficiently ventilated trucks; eighty-five people died of suffocation.[7] On a daily basis Thaksin spread fear among potential critics. At the offices of the *Bangkok Post* its tough investigative reporters, who had survived on cheap whiskey and cigarettes through coups, street protests, and wars, were completely dispirited. One editor said they were scared even to touch stories related to Thaksin, for fear the prime minister's cronies would buy the paper and fire them.[8]

Still, Thaksin had been elected twice, and he dominated Thai politics largely because he was the most compelling, organized, and dynamic politician in the country. In a lengthy cable analyzing Thaksin's appeal—and released to the public by Wikileaks—Ralph Boyce, a former U.S. ambassador to Thailand who was no fan of Thaksin's repressive policies, admitted: "Thaksin's personality, sophisticated media presentation, focused populist message, and traditional get-out-the-vote organizing, combined to allow [Thaksin's party] to leave . . . its closest rival in the political dust . . . Thaksin . . . has no equal in Thailand on how to attract political attention."

In 2005 Thaksin trounced the Democrat Party, which was favored by most yellow shirts, and in 2006, when he called a new election, the Democrats simply refused to participate. By that time the Democrats, once the most powerful party in Thailand, had been reduced to a small rump in Parliament, holding less than one hundred out of the five hundred seats in total. Instead of contesting the 2006 election, then, the yellow shirts, who shared political leanings with the Democrat Party, tried to paralyze the country. They stormed Parliament and shut it down, trapping lawmakers and forcing some senior ministers to flee, James Bond–style, over a fence and into a nearby building. Later, they laid siege to the main international airport, throwing commerce into turmoil and severely damaging tourism, one of the country's main sources of foreign exchange.

After months of rallies, Thaksin's government was finally ousted in a coup in 2006, but this only led to more chaos. For nearly a decade now, Thailand has weathered one street protest after another, with both sides disdaining democratic institutions and refusing to resolve their differences at the ballot box instead of in the streets, often with bloody results. After Thaksin and, later, other pro-Thaksin parties were prevented from assuming power despite their electoral mandates, Thailand's working classes formed their own movement. They donned red clothing—Thaksin's color—in response to the yellow shirts. (The red shirts' official name was the United Front for Democracy Against Dictatorship.) Just as the yellow shirts had tried to create havoc and paralyze the economy, so too the red shirts attempted to destroy what was left of democratic culture and order. They laid siege to Parliament, forcing lawmakers loyal to the yellow shirts to flee. In April 2009, they stormed a meeting of Southeast Asian nations in the resort town of Pattaya, forcing many visiting Asian leaders to hide inside their hotel, and ultimately causing the meeting to be canceled, to the great embarrassment of the Thai government.[9] Finally, in the spring of 2010, the red shirts converged on Bangkok.

In July 2011, despite efforts by Thailand's middle classes and its military to prevent the red shirts from taking power, the red shirts' favored party, called Puea Thai, won national elections again, forming a majority in parliament. The electoral victory handed the prime ministership to Yingluck Shinawatra, the party's leader—and the youngest sister of former prime minister Thaksin. Soon, Thailand was boiling again, as Thaksin's opponents revolted against his sister's government, warning that if Thaksin returned to Bangkok—and to power—they might well riot in the streets again, shutting down the city once more.

In the late 1990s, the possibility of such a breakdown of democracy in Thailand seemed remote. After a massive popular demonstration of hundreds of thousands in Bangkok ousted a military regime in 1992, Thais believed they had finally created a stable democracy. At the *Bangkok Post,* young reporters often seemed downright jubilant. During the day, they crawled through traffic in their cars to research investigative pieces unthinkable under past dictatorships; at night, they often attended informal strategy sessions about how to make good on the promises written into the new, progressive constitution passed in 1997. That groundbreaking constitution guaranteed many new rights and freedoms, created new national institutions to monitor graft, and strengthened political parties at the expense of unelected centers of power—the palace, the military, big business, and the elite civil service—that together had run Thailand since the end of the absolute monarchy in the 1930s. It also set the stage for elections in 2001 that were probably the freest in Thailand's history. Meanwhile, the media utilized its new freedoms, along with new technologies like the Internet and satellite television, to explore formerly taboo topics like political corruption and labor rights.

By the early 2000s, many Thais felt great pride in their nation's democratic development. Outsiders noticed, too. "Thailand's freedom, openness, strength, and relative prosperity make it a role model in the region for what people can achieve when they are allowed to," U.S. Assistant Secretary of State James Kelly declared in 2002.[10] Besides Kelly, former Secretary of State Madeleine Albright and then Secretary of State Colin Powell, among others, heaped praise on Bangkok. Powell declared in 2002, "Thailand has lived up to our expectations in so many ways."[11] In its 1999 report, the international monitoring organization Freedom House ranked Thailand a "free" nation.[12]

Today, Thailand looks almost nothing like a model emerging democracy. The never-ending cycle of street protest, by both the middle class and the poor, paralyzes policy making, hinders economic growth, and deters investment at a time when authoritarian competitors like China and Vietnam are vacuuming up foreign capital. Few Thais now trust the integrity of the judiciary, the civil service, or other national institutions. Even the king, once so revered that Thais worshipped him like a god, has seen his impartiality questioned.[13] The Thai military now wields enormous influence behind the scenes, a dramatic reversal from the 1990s, when most Thais believed the military had returned to the barracks for good.[14] A once freewheeling media has become increasingly shuttered and servile. The government now blocks over one hundred thousand websites, more than in neighboring Vietnam.[15] Once-groundbreaking Bangkok newspapers now read like Asian versions of the old Pravda, lavishing praise on the red shirts or the yellow shirts depending on the paper's point of view.[16] The Thai government even began locking up Americans visiting the country who'd written blog posts about the Thai monarchy years earlier. Even after Thaksin's sister took the reins of power, little changed, with arrests and Web blocking continuing as before.

Many middle-class Thais, faced with the breakdown of their once-vibrant democracy, seem to believe their country is somehow singular—that its collapse is due to a coincidence of factors that are unique to the country and hard for a foreigner to understand: the end of the reign of Bhumibol, who'd long played a stabilizing role; the Asian financial crisis, which pushed the country toward populism; and the unfortunate rise of Thaksin, a man with little commitment to the rule of law. "We were just unlucky," a senior Thai government official said. "If we'd not had Thaksin, if His Majesty could have been more involved, like in 1992, things would have been much different. . . . It's a Thai situation." [17]

But democratic meltdowns like Thailand's have become depressingly common. In its annual international survey, the most comprehensive analysis of freedom around the globe, Freedom House, which uses a range of data to assess social, political, and economic freedoms in each nation, found that global freedom plummeted in 2010 for the fifth year in a row, the longest continuous decline in nearly forty years. At the same time, most authoritarian nations had become more repressive, stepping up their oppressive measures with little resistance from the democratic world. Overall, Freedom House reported, twenty-five nations went backward, in terms of freedom, in 2010 alone, while only eleven made any gains; among the decliners were critical regional powers like Mexico and Ukraine. This despite the fact that in 2011 one of the most historically authoritarian parts of the world, the Middle East, seemed to begin to change. The decline, Freedom House noted, was most pronounced among what it called the "middle ground" of nations, primarily in the developing world—nations that have begun democratizing but are not solid and stable democracies.[18] Indeed, the number of electoral democracies fell in 2010 to its lowest number since 1995.[19] "A 'freedom recession' and an authoritarian resurgence have clearly emerged as global trends," writes Freedom House's director of research, Arch Puddington. "Over the last four years, the dominant pattern has been one of growing restrictions on the fundamental freedoms of expression and association in authoritarian settings, and a failure to continue democratic progress in previously improving countries."[20] Freedom House also found an increasing "truculence" among authoritarian regimes. This truculence actually was only made stronger by the Arab Spring, which led autocratic regimes like China and Uzbekistan to crack down harder on their own populations. The International Federation for Human Rights, an organization that monitors abuses around the world, found in its late-2011 annual report that the Arab uprisings had little impact on a dire, deteriorating climate for human rights defenders worldwide.[21]

Indeed, in the fall of 2011 Russia, which along with China is one of the most powerful authoritarian nations, made clear that any hopes of change were just a mirage, as Prime Minister Vladimir Putin, who has dominated Russia for more than a decade, announced that, in a secret deal with President Dmitry Medvedev, Putin would once again assume the presidency in 2012 and potentially serve two more terms, which would keep him in control of the Kremlin until 2024, longer than some Soviet leaders had lasted. Putin had been constitutionally barred from serving another presidential term after his first two terms ended in 2008, and once Medvedev assumed the presidency some Russian liberals had hoped that he would introduce reforms, despite his history as a close confidante of Putin's. Indeed, in office Medvedev declared that Russia's criminal justice system needed to be overhauled, and that the country should open up its political system, but his announcement that he had secretly agreed with Putin to manipulate the presidency and prime ministership to put Putin back in power showed that he, too, was at heart hardly a democrat. When Russia's finance minister questioned the handoff of power from Medvedev back to Putin, he was summarily fired, in a clear message.

The stagnation of democracy predates this five-year period, Freedom House noted; since 2000 democracy gained little ground around the world, before sliding backward beginning in the mid-2000s. "Since they were first issued in 1972, the findings in *Freedom in the World* have conveyed a story of broad advances," Freedom House reported. "But freedom's forward march peaked around the beginning of the [2000s]."

Even as some democrats were celebrating the Arab Spring and hoping that, as in 1989, its revolutions might spread to other parts of the world, a mountain of other evidence supported Freedom House's gloomy conclusions. Another of the most comprehensive studies of global democracy, compiled by Germany's Bertelsmann Foundation, uses data examining democracies' ability to function, manage government, and uphold freedoms to produce what it calls the "transformation index." The overall goal of the index is to analyze the state and quality of democracy in every developing nation that has achieved some degree of freedom. To do so, Bertelsmann looks at a range of characteristics including the stability of democratic institutions, political participation, the rule of law, and the strength of the state, among other areas. And the most recent index found "the overall quality of democracy has eroded [throughout the developing world]. . . . The key components of a functioning democracy, such as political participation and civil liberties, have suffered qualitative erosion. . . . These developments threaten to hollow out the quality and substance of governance." The index concluded that the number of "highly defective democracies"—democracies with institutions, elections, and political culture so flawed that they no longer qualified as real democracies—had roughly doubled between 2006 and 2010. By 2010, in fact, nearly 53 of the 128 countries assessed by the index were categorized as "defective democracies."

Sixteen of these fifty-three, including regionally and globally powerful states like Russia and Kenya, qualified as "highly deficient democracies," countries that had such a lack of opportunity for opposition voices, problems with the rule of law, and unrepresentative political structures that they were now little better than autocracies. The percentage of "highly deficient democracies" in the index has roughly doubled in just four years. And in Africa, which had been at the center of the global wave of democratization in the late 1990s and early 2000s, the deterioration was most pronounced. Between 2008 and 2010, Bertelsmann found, sub-Saharan Africa was home to nine of the thirteen nations in the developing world that suffered the greatest deterioration in the quality of their political systems. Among these backsliders were Senegal, Tanzania, and Madagascar, which once were among the greatest hopes for democracy on the continent.

Even nations that have been held up as democratic models have regressed over the past five to ten years, according to both the Freedom House and the Bertelsmann studies. When they entered the European Union in the late 1990s and early 2000s, Hungary, Poland, the Czech Republic, and Slovakia were considered success stories and would join the older democracies of Western Europe as solid, consolidated democratic systems. But in their decade inside the EU, all of these new entrants actually have been downgraded repeatedly by Freedom House, showing that their democratic systems, election processes, and commitments to civil liberties have deteriorated.[22] Populist and far-right parties with little commitment to democratic norms gained steadily in popularity; public distaste for democracy in these supposed success stories skyrocketed, so much so that in one 2006 survey publics in Central Europe showed the most skepticism about the merits of democracy of any region of the world.[23] Hungary deteriorated so badly that its press freedoms reverted to almost Soviet-type suppression, with its government using harsh new laws and other attacks to silence the media.[24]

The third major international study of democracy, the Economist Intelligence Unit's (EIU) "index of democracy," only further confirmed the decline. The EIU's annual survey of the entire world analyzes democracy using categories for electoral process, pluralism, political participation, political culture, functioning of government, and civil liberties including press freedom and freedom of association. In its most recent study, it found that democracy was in retreat across nearly the entire globe. "In all regions, the average democracy score for 2010 is lower than in 2008," noted the report. In ninety-one of one hundred sixty-seven countries it studied, the democracy score had deteriorated in that time period, and in many others it had only remained stagnant. Of the seventy-nine nations that it assessed as having some significant democratic qualities, only twenty-six made the grade as "full democracies," while the other fifty-three were ranked only as "flawed democracies" because of serious deficiencies in many of the areas it assessed. "Democracy is in retreat. The dominant pattern in all regions . . . has been backsliding on previously attained progress," the survey concluded.

In some of the specific categories that it examined to assess democracy, such as media freedom, the EIU found that backsliding was even more severe than the broader decline in the democracy index. More than thirty nations, including regional powers—and onetime examples of democratization— like Russia, Hungary, Mexico, and Turkey, witnessed sharp increases in media and online repression between 2008 and 2010. The Economist Intelligence Unit's 2011 Democracy Survey, released roughly a year after the Arab uprisings began, had just as much gloom. As in 2010, it similarly found that "democracy has been under intense pressure in many parts of the world," and that the quality of democracy had regressed on nearly every continent in 2011.

Like Freedom House and the Bertelsmann Foundation, the EIU found that, with only a few exceptions, backsliding was occurring in nearly every developing region of the world. It found that authoritarianism was becoming more entrenched in Central Asia, democratization was being reversed in Africa, authoritarian populists were emerging in Latin America, and political participation was plummeting in the former Soviet states of Eastern and Central Europe, undermining the region's democratic transitions.

Assessing the data, and the severe reversals, the EIU was glum about the future, though it recognized that the Middle East had nowhere to go but up, given its long-entrenched authoritarianism. "The threat of backsliding now greatly outweighs the possibility of future gains [in democratization worldwide]," the survey concluded.

Old-fashioned coups also have returned. In Latin America, Asia, and even most of Africa, coups, which had been a frequent means of changing governments during the Cold War, had become nearly extinct by the early 2000s. But between 2006 and 2010 the military grabbed power in Guinea, Honduras, Mauritania, Niger, Guinea-Bissau, Bangladesh, Thailand, Fiji, and Madagascar, among other states.

In many other developing nations, such as Mexico, Pakistan, and the Philippines, the military did not launch an outright coup but managed to restore its power as the central actor in political life, dominating the civilian governments that clung to power only through the support of the armed forces. Freedom House, in fact, notes that the global decline in democracy in the past five years has been the result, in part, of weakening civilian control of militaries across the developing world. The civilian Thai prime minister in the late 2000s, Abhisit Vejjajiva, who took power in 2008, owed his survival in office to the military's backing, and senior army officers made clear to him, in private, that if they withdrew their support, his government could easily collapse. Unsurprisingly, the Thai military's budget more than doubled between 2006 and 2011, with much of the expenditures going toward tools to control Thailand's own population, rather than toward fighting potential foreign enemies. After Thaksin's sister became prime minister, the armed forces negotiated a deal with her that gave the military total control over its own budget, with little civilian authority—and which essentially preserved its ability to interfere in politics indefinitely. Philippine president Gloria Macapagal-Arroyo relied upon the armed forces to enforce a crackdown against opponents. According to several local human rights groups, more than a thousand left-leaning activists, opposition politicians, and other government opponents were killed between 2001 and 2010, and one comprehensive study found that "the [Philippine] military [is] an important veto actor in the competition among the country's political elites."[25]

"It's almost like we've gone back to the [Ferdinand] Marcos era," prominent rights activist and lawyer Harry Roque Jr. said as he waited in his office for the security forces to come and interrogate him.[26] "There's the same type of fear, the same abuses, the same attitude by the military that their actions will never face consequences." Within months of the election of Arroyo's successor, Benigno Aquino, in 2010, the Philippine military seemed ready to bolster its power even more. Several prominent former military officers reportedly launched a new movement called "Solidarity for Sovereignty," designed to step in if the president's government, as one of them put it, "self-destructed."[27]

Similarly, in Pakistan, though General Pervez Musharraf, who took power in a coup in 1999, eventually returned leadership to a civilian government nearly a decade later, Pakistan's army clearly had reestablished itself as the central power in policy making. After interludes of civilian control in the 1990s, the army has again "assumed control as well as oversight of public policy. . . . The military has carved out a role and position in the public and private sectors, including industry, business, agriculture, education and scientific development, health care, communications, and transportation," reported military analysts Siegfried Wolf and Seth Kane. In early 2010, when the Pakistani leadership held talks in Washington on the future of the bilateral relationship with the United States, there was no doubt about who was the key player on the Pakistani side: not civilian president Asif Ali Zardari but army chief of staff Ashfaq Kayani.[28] Similarly, after American Special Forces swooped into Pakistan in the spring of 2011 to kill Osama bin Laden, it was Kayani who essentially enunciated the Pakistani government's response to America.

Indeed, in another recent comprehensive study, this time of Asia, researchers from the Institute for Security and International Studies in Thailand concluded, "Any short-term prospects for civilian control in the young democracies of South and Southeast Asia are gloomy indeed." Yet support for democracy has become so tepid in many parts of the developing world that many of these coups or military interventions were cheered. After the coup against Thaksin in Thailand in 2006, many urban Thais openly celebrated.

"Academic contacts [of U.S. diplomats] could only be described as ebullient [about the coup,]" reported the American embassy in Bangkok in one cable written after the coup.

Across the Middle East, armed forces also have dominated the Arab Spring and Summer, putting the lie to the idea that the Arab uprising is going to bring democracy to the region. Instead, in the near term the Arab uprisings appear to be entrenching the power of militaries in the region, sparking massive unrest, scaring middle-class liberals into exodus, and potentially empowering Islamists. Protesters may have challenged leaders from Yemen to Egypt, but the loyalty of the military has determined whether these rulers stay in power, and during any transition the militaries have, by default, become the dominant—and sometimes only—national institutions. In Bahrain, the military's willingness to continue to support the regime of Sheikh Hamad bin Isa al-Khalifa allowed the royal family to crush protests, to enlist the support of armies from other Gulf states, including Saudi Arabia, and to maintain a tight grip on power after antigovernment protests flared in early 2011.

As in Bahrain, armies have used this power to ensure that they will remain at the center of politics for years to come, in part because middle classes in the region fear that the end of dictatorships like Hosni Mubarak's could usher in chaos, insecurity, and bloodshed if the military does not step in. Egypt's generals, write political analysts Jeff Martini and Julie Taylor, "are determined to . . . protect their privileged position. . . . The generals now hope to create a system of carefully shaped [institutions] that will preserve their power and reduce the chances that any single political group can challenge them." Indeed, they note, during Egypt's transition the generals have insisted the military be exempted from parliamentary scrutiny, enjoy power over an elected president, and maintain the legal right to intervene in politics under a broad array of circumstances.

By the summer and fall of 2011, as this book was being written, the Egyptian military increasingly demonstrated that it had no interest in giving up the power it had amassed over decades, and that it had learned how to use a political vacuum to bolster its own power, as it had many times in the country's past. In 2011, the Egyptian military controlled nearly every aspect of the country's supposed transition. It passed legislation outlining the terms of potential new elections without consulting with the public, a move that led some protesters to rally again, in central Cairo, to demand that the military remove itself from politics. The army also has expanded laws used to jail dissidents, imprisoning many who have criticized the military since the fall of the Mubarak regime, and has helped ensure that the armed forces' business interests, which are vast, will remain protected under any future Egyptian government. When liberal Egyptians, including some Christians, protested against the military's power in post-Mubarak Egypt in early October 2011, chanting, "The people want to bring down the field marshal," riot police and other armed security forces beat protesters mercilessly and ultimately opened fire, killing at least twenty-four people and wounding some two hundred.[29] Ultimately, the antiarmy sentiment grew so fierce that, in November, crowds gathering once again in Tahrir Square in downtown Cairo battled with riot police and other security forces, as they demanded that the military release its hold on power and ensure that, in the future, it could not dominate an elected government. Thousands, possibly even tens of thousands of demonstrators, packed into the square, which had been the site of the initial protests that toppled Mubarak nearly a year earlier. The security forces attacked the crowds with rubber bullets, tear gas, and batons, killing at least one person and injuring more than a thousand, according to press reports.[30] Though the military appeared to cede some ground after these protests, allowing the constitution to be altered to place the military formally under civilian control, it retained broad powers that seemed inimical to democracy, including, essentially, the right to overturn civilian governments if it desired.

Meanwhile, in the autumn of 2011 Islamists made significant gains nearly everywhere in the region. The first elections held, post-Arab Spring, in Tunisia, were a triumph for democracy in the Arab world. People across Tunisia waited patiently in long lines to vote, and monitors reported that polling was free, fair, and peaceful, which was hardly expected—anticipating chaos, Tunisia had deployed some forty thousand policemen at polling sites.[31]

Following the voting, many Tunisians took to public spaces to celebrate the fact they voted, despite difficulties in the year since they had toppled their autocrat: Tunisia's economy had weakened, partly because of the war next door in Libya, and in a freer political climate grievances about economic inequality increasingly bubbled to the surface in poorer parts of Tunisia. But in October 2011, Tunisians defied many predictions of a disastrous election. Overall, nearly 90 percent of eligible voters cast a ballot, a huge turnout. Because of quotas imposed in the electoral laws, some 30 percent of seats in the new parliament would go to women. Still, when the results came in, it was clear that Al Nahda, the main Islamist party, had won a sizable victory, mostly at the expense of the secular, liberal Progressive Democratic Party. Al Nahda's leadership, which openly styled themselves after Turkey's progressive Islamists, said all the right things about their commitment to building Tunisian democratic institutions, upholding individual freedoms, and separating mosque and state.[32] (Before the election, the transitional government had banned parties that theoretically did not demonstrate a commitment to democracy, and so prevented a more avowedly Islamist and Salafist party from even contesting the poll.)[33]

But unlike Turkey, where Islamists took decades to demonstrate their allegiance to the secular state, and today have been governing for more than ten years, in Tunisia, which was less than a year from autocratic rule, many middle- and upper-class Tunisians had doubts about Al Nahda's long-term commitment to the secular state. (Al Nahda had been banned under Tunisia's dictatorship.) Before the election, groups of activists allied with Al Nahda had stormed a private Tunisian television station, trying to close it down for showing what they deemed sacrilegious content; in the past, Al Nahda activists had attacked rivals by throwing acid in their faces, among other tactics.[34] And in the run-up to the election, hard-line Salafists clearly enjoyed something of a renaissance in Tunisia, making their presence felt throughout society. In June radicals attacked people attending a film in Tunis, and they also have attacked some artists whom they have deemed "un-Islamic."[35] Many liberal, middle-class Tunisians continued to express doubt about Al Nahda despite its leadership's vows to uphold democracy;

applications to leave Tunisia and gain passports more than doubled in 2011. These doubts boded poorly for the country's future, since these middle classes and elites would be critical for growth, development, and democratic consolidation.

Perhaps Al Nahda's success would be fleeting. A study released in early 2011 in the *Journal of Democracy* found that, by surveying parliamentary elections in twenty-one countries, Islamic parties tended to do best in the initial elections after the end of authoritarian rule, a period when they tended to be the most organized group in the country. Over time, as elections became more regular, their support tended to wane, and wound up averaging about 15 percent of the vote.[36] Islamist parties also tended to become more moderate over time, as they tried to appeal to less religious swing voters, in order to possibly gain enough votes to govern. Still, this study does not necessarily predict the future: Islamist parties in the post— Arab Spring countries tend to be better entrenched, better organized, and even more dominant than in places where they have competed in the past, such as Indonesia, where religious-oriented parties were hardly as powerful as a group like Egypt's Muslim Brotherhood or Salafists, who adopted a harder-line position than the Brotherhood. In the initial rounds of Egypt's parliamentary elections, held in December, the Brotherhood and the more extreme Salafists gained overwhelming victories, even in areas long considered some of the most liberal parts of Egypt, such as Cairo; liberal and secular parties generally placed very poorly, split among themselves and unable to sometimes garner even enough votes to make it into Parliament. The Islamists' dominance of the voting set them up in prime position to write Egypt's new constitution.

In Libya the death of Muammar Qadaffi led, in the short run, to chaos in Tripoli and other towns, and a clear rise in the power of Islamists in what was already the most religiously conservative country in north Africa. The post-Qadaffi interim leadership quickly brought up the possibility of legalizing polygamy in order to create a more pious nation, infuriating some Libyan women's groups.[37] They further suggested that sharia should be the basis of law in the new Libya, and many Libyans agreed that, in post-Qadaffi elections, Islamists would dominate, since as in Egypt they had built a strong underground organization in Libya during the authoritarian period. Youssef Sherif, a leading Libyan intellectual, told reporters, "Every day the Islamists grow stronger. When there is a parliament, the Islamists will get the majority."[38] Indeed, despite having worked through NATO to end Qadaffi's regime, many senior American officials essentially accepted that by ousting the Libyan dictator they were likely to empower an Islamist government, given Libya's religious conservatism—and they had little trust that Islamists in Libya would uphold a semblance of a secular state. Militias wielding Soviet-designed Kalashnikov assault rifles and rocket launchers roamed the country, often engaging in banditry to support themselves, and the weak transitional government had trouble disarming anyone.[39] One of the most powerful post-Qadaffi leaders to emerge, with his own group of armed backers, was a man who previously had led a hard-line organization linked to Al Qaeda.[40] As in Egypt, some Libyan liberals now are wondering whether the Libyan transitional government will turn into an autocracy of its own—or whether perhaps it actually should, since holding elections anytime soon could lead to more chaos or to an Islamist takeover.[41]

The strengthening of military rule in many developing nations has been disastrous for reform, despite the militaries' contention that they are the only institutions standing in the way of civil strife or Islamist rule. Indeed, human rights groups such as Amnesty International found that, since the winter of 2010–11, human rights abuses actually have increased in nearly every Middle Eastern nation, including Syria, Egypt, and Bahrain, where at least five hundred people were detained for protesting between February and September 2011.[42]

Despite the fact that militaries could hardly be called agents of reform, middle classes in many developing nations, both in the Middle East and in other parts of the world, often continued to support the armed forces as potential antidotes to popular democracy—democracy that might empower the poor, the religious, and the less educated. In this way, Egyptian liberals' concerns about the fruits of democracy were not unique. Overall, in fact, an analysis of military coups in developing nations over the past twenty years, conducted by my research associate Daniel Silverman and myself, found that in nearly 50 percent of the cases, drawn from Africa,

Latin America, Asia, and the Middle East, middle-class men and women either agitated in advance for the coup or, in polls or prominent media coverage after the coup, expressed their support for the army takeover.

Although the uprisings in the Middle East have led to unrest, civil strife, and renewed military rule, they have had little impact on other parts of the world—a sharp contrast to 1989, when the revolts in Eastern Europe helped catalyze change in other parts of the Soviet Union, as well as in China. Picking up from the Tunisian uprising, a small group of Chinese liberals in early 2011 attempted to launch their own "jasmine revolution," beginning with an online manifesto calling for protests. But their numbers likely never exceeded a few hundred people, and the Chinese government quickly quashed their movement, closing down websites and arresting organizers. More important, these protests gained little traction with the Chinese public, which knew relatively little about the demonstrations in the Middle East and, as we will see later, is far more satisfied with their country's leadership than Egyptians or Tunisians were with theirs. In sub-Saharan Africa, too, the Arab uprisings ultimately had minimal impact; protests broke out in places from Malawi to Burkina Faso to Uganda, but none succeeded in toppling rulers; in response to the uprisings, the militaries in many of these African countries were able to further entrench their power. In Zimbabwe, the military has come to dominate the power structure of Robert Mugabe's regime, making him and his allies even more indebted to the armed forces. Overall, concluded Northwestern University's Richard Joseph in a survey of the current state of politics in sub-Saharan Africa, "the electoral authoritarian regime," not democracy, has become the most prevalent political system in Africa—a system that includes not only Mugabe but some of the other most entrenched autocrats, such as Angola's Jose Eduardo dos Santos, who has ruled his country since 1979.[43]

In addition to these studies showing the return of coups, opinion polling from many developing nations shows not only that the quality of democracy is declining but also that public views of democracy are deteriorating as well. The international public opinion group Program on International

Policy Attitudes uses extensive questionnaires to ask people in a range of Latin American, African, Asian, and Middle Eastern nations about their views on democracy, as compared with other potential political systems. The regular "Afrobarometer" survey of the African continent has found declining levels of support for democracy throughout much of sub-Saharan Africa; in Nigeria, the largest nation on the continent, support for democracy has plummeted over the past decade. In several polls only 16 percent of Russians said that it was "very important" that their nation be governed democratically. Even in Kyrgyzstan, which despite its flaws remains the most democratic state in Central Asia, one comprehensive Gallup poll found that a majority of the population did not believe that a political opposition is very or somewhat important, and a sizable plurality said democracy was not important to their country. Shortly after Kyrgyzstan's presidential elections in the fall of 2011, this disinterest in democratic politics became clear: losing candidates and their supporters massed in public areas around the country, trying to use protests to bring down the supposed victor.[44]

"Latinobarómetro" polls and studies of South America showed similar dissatisfaction with democracy. In Ecuador, Guatemala, Paraguay, Colombia, Peru, Honduras, and Nicaragua, either a minority or only a tiny majority of people think democracy is preferable to any other type of government. Overall, in the most recent Latinobarómetro survey, only a small majority of people across Latin America supported democracy as a political system, and less than 40 percent said they were satisfied with the way that democracy works in practice in their country.[45] In most countries in Latin America, these figures have either remained stagnant or slumped from where they were a decade ago. Many Latin Americans now say they do not even have a functioning democracy at all.[46] Meanwhile, in Pakistan, roughly 60 percent of respondents in a comprehensive regional survey said that the country should be ruled by the army, one of the highest votes of support for military rule in the world.

The global economic crisis, which continued to hit Europe hard in 2010 and 2011, only weakened public support for democracy in new democracies in Central and Eastern Europe. A comprehensive study of Central and Eastern Europe by the European Bank for Reconstruction and Development

(EBRD), released in 2011, found that the crisis had severely lowered people's support for democracy.[47] "The more people were personally hit by the crisis, the more they turned away from democracy," it found.[48] Support for democracy had declined, since 2006, in all of the new European Union nations except Bulgaria. In some of these countries, such as the Slovak Republic and Hungary, support for democracy fell, in the EBRD's surveys, by as much as twenty percentage points compared to 2006. This decline provided an opportunity for stronger, even authoritarian, leaders. "Those who enjoyed more freedoms wanted less democracy and markets when they were hurt by the crisis," the EBRD report noted.[49]

Even in East Asia, one of the most economically vibrant and globalized regions of the world, polls show rising dissatisfaction with democracy. In fact, several countries in the region have developed what Asian democratization specialists Yu-tzung Chang, Yunhan Zhu, and Chong-min Park, who studied data from the regular "Asian Barometer" surveys, have termed "authoritarian nostalgia." "Few of the region's former authoritarian regimes have been thoroughly discredited," they write, noting that the region's average score for commitment to democracy, judged by a range of prodemocratic responses to surveys, has fallen in the most recent studies. An analysis of the Asian Barometer data by Park found that, even in South Korea, one of the supposed success stories of democracy in the developing world, the percentage of South Koreans saying that under certain circumstances an authoritarian government was preferable doubled between 1996 and 2006. "An upward trend is unequivocal," Park writes. "In times of crisis these halfhearted citizens may not be mobilized to defend democratic institutions and processes." Similarly, in Taiwan, another supposedly stable democracy, the Asian Barometer survey found that only 40 percent of respondents agreed that democracy was "preferable to all other kinds of government," a low figure. Only slightly more than 50 percent of Mongolians and Filipinos, two other supposedly vibrant democracies, thought democracy was preferable to all other kinds of government.

Even in developing nations where democracy has deeper roots, and seems to be stronger, disillusionment with its political processes, and with democratically elected leaders, has exploded in recent years, as these leaders have seemed unable to develop effective solutions for global and local economic crises, other than biting austerity measures. From Indians demonstrating in Delhi in support of hunger strikers attacking corruption in Indian politics, to Israelis camping in the streets of Tel Aviv in the biggest demonstrations in the country's history to protest their leaders' lack of interest in basic economic issues, to the Occupy movement across the United States and countries of Western Europe, people in even more established democracies are increasingly turning to street protests to make their points, since they believe they cannot be heard at the ballot box. They have become convinced, they say, that the democratic process has become so corrupted, so dominated by entrenched interests, and so disassociated from popular issues, that they can change their countries only through massive rallies, even if those protests use the street to bring down leaders fairly elected. "Our parents are grateful because they're voting," one young woman told reporters in Spain, where tens of thousands of young people also have launched full-time street protests against politicians' lack of interest in the country's long-term unemployment crisis, which has led to unemployment of nearly 40 percent for recent university graduates of both sexes. "We're the first generation to say that voting is worthless."

This democratic decline is not concentrated in one region or one continent, and, unlike previous waves of democracy regression such as those occurring in the 1920s and 1930s, today's decline includes a far wider array of nations, from more regions of the globe, and is much less likely to be stopped. More important, many of the countries that are regressing from democracy are regional powers, including Russia, Kenya, Thailand, Argentina, Senegal, the Philippines, Hungary, Venezuela, Mexico, Nigeria, and many others. Their examples matter more to their regions than those of smaller, less influential states. One of the key factors in determining whether a country will democratize is the international and regional climate, according to a study of democracies' endurance by political scientists Adam Przeworksi, Michael Alvarez, Jose Cheibub, and Fernando Limongi. So, when powerful countries fail to democratize, this diffusion effect works in reverse, hindering the cause of democratic change in their entire regions.

In many of these regionally important countries, the decline of democracy has been so sharp that it has shocked people who lived through the initial period of democratization. In the Philippines in the 1980s, crowds of nonviolent Filipinos thronging Manila's Edsa Avenue invented the "people power" movement that inspired uprisings from the "color revolutions" in Eastern Europe and Central Asia to the Iranian Green Movement of 2009, to the Arab Spring of 2011, which swept through Egypt, Yemen, Syria, and other nations. Now, as one democratically elected Philippine government after the next becomes mired in corruption and self-dealing, Filipinos are increasingly disenchanted with democratic rule.[50]

African nations that had made major progress in the previous decade also have regressed badly. Kenya, where, after the rule of longtime dictator Daniel arap Moi, many people believed that the country—the wealthiest and most globalized in east Africa—would become a vibrant democracy, has collapsed into interethnic battles and newly repressive governments. This decline is being repeated in Nigeria, the most vital nation in west Africa. In Uganda, Yoweri Museveni, who had amassed enormous popular goodwill for ending conflicts and rebuilding the economy after the disastrous regimes of Milton Obote and Idi Amin, had promised to only serve only four years when he became president in 1986. Yet he kept finding reasons to stick around, until he finally forced through a constitutional rewrite in 2005 that removed presidential term limits altogether.[51] By 2011, after he won another presidential term in a fraudulent election, his security forces had to repeatedly clear the streets of Kampala with massive shows of force.

Under Vladimir Putin and his protégé Dmitri Medvedev, Russia, which in the 1990s had developed a vibrant media and a robust if chaotic democracy that provided an example to many other former Soviet states, has discovered a nostalgia for Soviet repression. The last truly independent Russian political party, the Union, or Right Forces, merged with pro-Kremlin parties several years ago, leaving virtually no opposition in the Duma.[52] "Twenty years after the fall of the Berlin Wall, the basic idea that political opposition is a useful, legitimate political phenomenon remains remarkably weak in much of the [post-Soviet] region," noted Thomas Carothers of the Carnegie Endowment for International Peace in a study of democracy's global challenges. "Dominant political elites treat political opposition as inherently disloyal."[53]

By 2009, according to an analysis by Freedom House, the former Soviet Union was one of the least free regions of the world—-even before Putin announced that he would again be taking total control of Russia, the most important post-Soviet state.[54] Belarus, the country closest to Russia politically and culturally, flirted with reform but, by the end of the 2000s, had retreated into an authoritarian, statist regime little different from the Belarus of the early 1990s. Its long-serving leader, Alexander Lukashenko, won reelection in 2010 with a farcical 80 percent of the vote; protesters who gathered to demonstrate, sometimes simply by standing in public places and sarcastically clapping their hands, were beaten and jailed.[55] Two of the greatest hopes for the former Soviet states, Georgia and Ukraine, also are going backward, with Ukraine's president, Viktor Yanukovych, installing Putinesque policies that crushed any opposition and resulted in the arrests and jailing of many politicians, including, in the summer of 2011, the opposition leader and former presidential candidate Yulia Tymoshenko, who was given seven years in prison in a trial that was clearly predetermined. Along with Tymoshenko's trial, the Ukrainian government passed new measures giving the president nearly unlimited powers and curtailing the country's vibrant civil society, and launched investigations of eleven other opposition figures. Yanukovych simultaneously emasculated the Ukrainian parliament, made much of the country's court system subordinate to his decrees, and had the country's constitution altered to give the president domineering power.[56]

In Asia, other supposed success stories have regressed as well. The Malaysian government, which once had vowed to uphold total freedom for online media in order to promote the country as a high-tech hub, began developing new ways to censor both the print and the online media. The regime started arresting political opponents, whistleblowers, and civil society leaders, including opposition leader Anwar Ibrahim, who himself faced jail on dubious charges of sodomizing an aide.[57] (Anwar ultimately was acquitted and then hit with new charges related to organizing a political protest.) Once such people are in custody, strange things can happen. In July 2009, a man named Teoh Beng Hock visited the offices of the country's anticorruption commission in order to testify about witnessing the misuse of public funds. The next day, he was found dead on the roof of the adjacent building. Officials said he'd jumped from the anticorruption headquarters to his death. Independent forensic scientists later found evidence that Teoh had been beaten and sodomized with an object before he "leaped" to his death.[58] In Cambodia, after the collapse of the Khmer Rouge and the end of years of civil war, some 93 percent of eligible voters came to the polls in a landmark first free election in 1993, and the international community, which oversaw—and paid for—the largest reconstruction effort to that time in Cambodia, exulted in the turnout. But since then the country's political system has gone steadily downhill. Prime Minister Hun Sen, a rugged survivor of the Khmer Rouge years, has silenced nearly every opposition group, intimidated the media, and overseen beatings and outright killings of many political rivals.[59]

Meanwhile, Venezuela's Hugo Chavez, like Thaksin an elected leader with little dedication to constitutionalism or the rule of law, has pushed his "Bolivarian revolution" closer to outright authoritarianism, as has Evo Morales in Bolivia and Peruvian president Ollanta Humara.[60] And in Mexico, the security forces, working in collaboration with the president, have taken advantage of the war on drugs to basically take over many Mexican states, turning them into essentially army-run fiefdoms. Military personnel now occupy hundreds of positions traditionally held by civilian personnel, especially those in law enforcement. "The military is becoming the supreme authority—in some cases the only authority—in parts of some states," said Mexican political analyst Denise Dresser.

So many countries now remain stuck between authoritarianism and democracy, reported Marc Plattner and Larry Diamond, co-editors of the *Journal of Democracy,* that "it no longer seems plausible to regard [this condition] simply as a temporary stage in the process of democratic transition."[61]

Despite the democratic recession of recent years, and the destructive impact of the global economic crisis on democracy, even today most Western leaders more or less unthinkingly assume that democracy will eventually triumph worldwide. At the end of the Cold War, nearly all Western leaders and political scientists believed democratic values had triumphed. The notion of democratic victory was captured most famously in Francis Fukuyama's essay "The End of History," in which he claimed, "The triumph of the West, of the Western idea, is evident first of all in the total exhaustion of viable systematic alternatives to Western liberalism."[62] This view, though seldom so baldly stated, dominated most Western discourse on political change in the 1990s and early 2000s and, despite the changes in the world, still dominates today. The enormous relief triggered by the collapse of the Soviet Union and the end of five decades of tightrope diplomacy between the great powers seemed, as Robert Kagan noted, "to augur a new era of global convergence. The great adversaries of the Cold War suddenly shared many common goals, including a desire for economic and political integration."[63] Human progress, constantly marching forward, would spread democracy everywhere.

Of course, there is no consensus on the definition of democracy, but nearly all such definitions include certain components of democracy. In discussing democracy, this book uses a relatively widely accepted definition also utilized by the Economist Intelligence Unit in its analyses of the quality of democracy around the world. As the EIU notes, democracy means "government based on majority rule and the consent of the governed, the existence of free and fair elections, the protection of minorities and respect for basic human rights. Democracy presupposes equality before the law, due process and political pluralism." This book adds another component not included in this basic definition: democratic political culture, which includes respect for the concept of a loyal opposition, support for democratic political institutions, and interest in and access to political participation, among other components.

For a time, the rosy predictions of global democratization seemed warranted. Political freedom indeed blossomed in a "fourth wave" of democratization in the developing world in the 1990s and the early part of this century. The old great-power adversaries, the United States and Russia, worked together on challenges ranging from the first Gulf War to the safe decommissioning and storage of nuclear weapons. While authoritarians still ruled most of Africa, Eastern Europe, and Asia in 1990, by 2005 democracies had emerged across these continents, and some of the most powerful developing nations, including South Africa, South Korea, and Brazil, had become solid democracies. By 2005 more than half the world's people lived under democratic systems.[64] With the color revolutions in Georgia, Ukraine, and Kyrgyzstan, the fall of Saddam Hussein, the overthrow of the Taliban, the apparent end of military interventions in Turkey, the stirrings of reform in small Persian Gulf nations like Bahrain, and even a reformist presidency under Muhammad Khatami in Iran, the Middle East and Central Asia, long the exception to global democratic change, seemed ready to make the transition.

Increasingly confident Western leaders came to assume that liberal democratic capitalism would conquer every nation on earth. President George H. W. Bush promised a "new world order" in which "freedom and respect for human rights find a home among all nations."[65] George W. Bush declared in his second inaugural that the United States would promote the democratization of the world, saying, "We will persistently clarify the choice before every ruler and every nation—the moral choice between oppression, which is always wrong, and freedom, which is eternally right."[66] In a meeting with China president Jiang Zemin, Bill Clinton told Chinese leaders that they stood "on the wrong side of history" by perpetuating authoritarian rule, and later warned the Chinese leadership that trying to control the liberating effects of new technologies was like trying to "nail Jell-O to the wall."[67]

Of late, the Jell-O has been nailed. Not only has democracy experienced its longest and deepest rollback in forty years, a confluence of political, economic, and social changes could halt global democratization indefinitely. Autocracies seem to be gaining not only strength but legitimacy, with authoritarian regimes like China posting high growth rates and powerful new democracies like Brazil and South Africa unwilling to join the West in pushing for democratic change in the developing world.[68] From Thailand to Russia, middle classes and many leaders in developing nations that have regressed from real democracy appear to have little appetite for a return to democratic rule. Seeing the rise of Islamist parties, new sectarian rifts, and the flight of many religious and ethnic minorities, the middle classes in many of the countries in the Middle East and Africa where new revolts have occurred in the past two years already have begun to doubt the value of democracy, leading them to support renewed types of authoritarian rule, including continued powers for the military.

To be sure, when viewed against the entire expanse of the twentieth and twenty-first centuries, or against even longer periods of human history, the world today appears to be highly democratic. At the start of the twentieth century, as we will see in the next chapter, only a tiny fraction of the countries in the world could have been called true democracies. Nearly all of these democracies were in Western Europe, North America, and the former overseas territories of the British Empire.[69] Together they constituted no more than one-tenth of the world's population. Empires ruled much of Europe, Asia, and Africa. Even as recently as 1988, before the collapse of the Berlin Wall, a small minority of the world's people lived under democracy; Central Asia and Eastern Europe had no democracies, and sub-Saharan Africa had virtually no true democracies as well.

Compared with those bleak periods, the number of democracies in the early twenty-first century seems like a great advance. Many African nations have made the beginnings of a transition to democratic rule, and real democracy is increasingly entrenched in Eastern Europe, the Baltics, and many parts of East Asia. No one expects that democracy will backslide to its weak global position in 1900; the prospect of democracy being wiped away completely, as seemed possible in the 1930s, now appears all but impossible. Indeed, the point of this book is not to suggest that democracy is in its death throes, but that it is in decline over the past decade—a decline that should be worrying because of its vast impact on human rights, economic freedoms, and the international system. If policy makers do not recognize this decline, and understand the complex reasons, examined later on, for democracy's current weakness in many developing nations, they will fail to reverse this trend. Worse, as the economic crisis lags on, publics in many developing regions may become far more distrustful of democratic rule—a prospect that could indeed help set the world back to the situation in 1988 or before.

Choosing to look at democracy's decline over the past decade is not arbitrary. Just as 1974, and then 1989, were watershed years for democratization, so too was 2001 such a year, although not in a positive way. Over the subsequent decade certain trends, which were less apparent in the 1980s or 1990s, clearly indicated weakening democracy throughout the developing world. Those trends began to materialize in 2001, and they would grow stronger throughout the 2000s and into the early 2010s, as surveys such as those done by Freedom House and the Economist Intelligence Unit, as well as my own research, would show this distinct decline in democracy in many nations.

The global landscape that had begun to be transformed in 2001 included the weakening of American power. In the months after the September 11, 2001, attacks, American power seemed to be at its zenith, but as the United States became entangled in two long wars stemming in some ways from that day, its power would ebb, with significant consequences for America's ability and willingness to attempt democracy promotion in the developing world. In 2001, too, both Russia and China would begin to consolidate their leadership transitions, and in that year the foundations would be set for the authoritarian great powers to reassert their dominance both at home and in their near neighborhoods, where they would lead a backlash against democracy. Also in 2001, broadband Internet began to become available to a growing number of homes in developed countries, the first step toward what would become its widespread use, and would impact democratic change in many developing nations. The early 2000s also saw the height of the antiglobalization movement and the questioning of the Washington consensus regarding economic liberalization, a change that would reverberate through young democracies, as many citizens who had linked economic and political reform would come to question whether democracy was necessarily the best system to produce growth and development. Finally, in 2001 the initial signs of conservative, middle-class revolts against electoral democracy would begin to emerge in many key developing nations, including Pakistan, the Philippines, Venezuela, Russia, and others.

Though Thailand is not as unusual as many Thais seem to believe, every country certainly has its own political history and circumstances. Democracy was imposed by an occupier in Japan, midwifed by a king in Spain, and fought over for decades in Timor-Leste. Reversals of democracy in each nation likewise have unique characteristics. In Thailand the king's prolonged illness has hurt democratic consolidation, while in Russia the anarchy of the Boris Yeltsin era, in which a proud country teetered on the brink of bankruptcy while oligarchs plundered its wealth, soured many Russians on the freedoms of democracy. But the broad—and dangerous— reasons for the global democratic rollback today differ relatively little.

Democracies have faced many challenges in the past, and at other times countries that seemed to have democratized suffered serious reversals, occasionally regressing, as in the case of Germany in the 1930s, to outright totalitarianism. But those reversals tended to be relatively isolated, and eventually global democracy progressed once again. That progression can no longer be taken for granted: today a constellation of factors, from the rise of China to the lack of economic growth in new democracies to the West's financial crisis, has come together to hinder democracy throughout the developing world. Absent radical and unlikely changes in the international system, that combination of antidemocratic factors will have serious staying power.

Yet Western leaders do not seem to recognize how seriously democracy is threatened in many parts of the developing world. Though some observers, like Freedom House, have begun to recognize how democracy has become endangered, few have systematically traced how a form of government once thought to be invincible has been found lacking in so many places and consequently tossed aside, often by the very middle-class reformers who once were democracy's vanguard. Among senior American officials, few are willing to accept that the current climate is anything more than a blip in democracy's ultimate conquest of the globe, that the Arab Spring and Summer might not turn out to be like 1989's year of democratic revolution—or that a prolonged democratic rollback would have severe consequences for global security, trade, and American strategic interests, not to mention the well-being of millions of men and women across the developing world. The official national security strategy developed by the George W. Bush administration, which enshrined democracy promotion as a central value of U.S. foreign policy, carried the unstated assumption that, with U.S. backing, democracy would continue to spread around the world. Although the Obama administration's 2010 national security strategy acknowledged that this progress had met obstacles, experts within the administration seemed to assume that, given the right adjustments in American policy, the United States would soon be leading a renewed wave of global democratization.[70]

The United States is not the only entity that does not comprehend that democracy's progress may have stalled. In 2008, the Association of Southeast Asian Nations (Asean), the main regional grouping in Southeast Asia, passed a new charter that made respect for human rights a core component of membership. Even in private, senior Asean officials argue that the region is moving toward shared democratic values.[71] This despite the fact that, except in Indonesia, democratization and human rights have regressed throughout Southeast Asia in the past ten years, as well as the fact that the region is still no closer to having real shared values than it was when Asean was formed more than four decades ago.

African nations in 2001 agreed to a "New Partnership for Africa's Development," a continent-wide compact to instill norms of human rights and good governance that was greeted with much celebration by Western donors and many African leaders. Capturing this mood in 2006, the Sudanese communications entrepreneur Mo Ibrahim launched a prize for the African leader who best focused on development, governance, and education of his or her people. Ten years into the "New Partnership," African officials continue to cite the compact and claim that the continent is moving toward shared values of good governance and democracy, but this trend is hardly evident. In 2010, unable to find a leader who exemplified reform and good governance, the Ibrahim board decided not to award its annual gift.[72]

Prolonged democratic rollback will have serious implications. Evidence suggests that one of the major reasons countries democratize is that nations around them are democratizing.[73] A halt to this process—particularly if middle-class men and women lead this democratic breakdown or flee places like the Middle East and Africa rather than standing for democracy—could call into question many of the assumptions of the post–Cold War world and could lead to a new era of conflict. Though there have been exceptions, in general the theory that democracies do not go to war against other democracies has held true, while authoritarian states find it much easier to go to war, whether against democracies or against other autocracies. Even without actual war, a divergence of core political values will make it harder for nations around the world to make progress on critical international issues, from climate change to free trade. Democratic rollback could impede commerce: despite the facile assumption by some Western business leaders that authoritarian regimes provide more stable environments for investment, in reality autocracies generally fail to provide the rule of law and impartial judiciary that most Western investors require; prolonged democratic rollback could thus worsen the global business climate. Finally, a global democratic rollback will undermine perhaps the most critical foundation of American soft power—its ideology—as competing ideologies like China's model of development grow more powerful.

Perhaps most important of all, a prolonged democratic rollback could condemn the citizens of many of these countries, from Russia to Cambodia to Venezuela, to increasing repression under ever more confident autocrats. Already, over the past four years, activists not only in China but in Vietnam, Thailand, Venezuela, Russia, and many other countries whose governments once allowed greater degrees of freedom have seen a much tighter, less predictable political climate.

Grappling with this democratic decline and its potentially severe international consequences will require not only outlining the problem but also gaining a deeper understanding of why democracy has faltered. To do so, we must first look back at the previous three waves of democratic change in the twentieth century, as well as at the post–Cold War era of optimism and Western triumphalism in the 1990s and early 2000s, the time of the fourth wave of democratization in the developing world. By examining mistakes made during the high point of the global democratic revolution, we may understand how democracy has declined so rapidly and dramatically in a number of developing nations across several continents. This decline has included not only the rise of elected autocrats but also stark shifts in the views of the general public about democracy in many countries—even those in the Middle East. (We will not, however, examine the weakening of democracy in the established democracies of North America and Western Europe; even though these nations' political systems have many flaws, unlike many developing nations they do not face regression to autocratic rule, and a full study of the United States and Western Europe is well beyond the scope of this book, though we will examine Central and Eastern Europe.)

To be sure, we must recognize that, particularly in the Middle East, revolt and reform are in progress and sometimes can be hard to predict; this book was written as the Arab Spring and Summer began to curdle, but its outcomes remain very much uncertain.

Just as the democratic decline extends to nearly every part of the developing world, so too the reasons for the democratic rollback are diverse and, often, intertwined. To understand why democracy has struggled over the past decade, and to consider ways to put global democratization back on track, we have to examine not only why leaders like Putin and Chavez were able to destroy democratic institutions, but also why the middle class allowed these elected autocrats to do so, or accepted militaries reasserting their political power. The fact that the middle class, long considered the linchpin to successful democratization, actually has turned against democracy in many countries is perhaps the most striking and unsettling trend in democracy's global decline, and later on we will see in great detail how the middle class has changed from a force for reform to an obstacle. In many countries, the middle class acquiesced for a number of reasons: fear that democracy would produce chaos, corruption, and weak growth; anger at the rise of elected populists who disdain the rule of law; and worry that their own power will be diminished. And as the middle class revolts, the working class often fights back, only further damaging democratic politics.

We also have to understand the international system. We have to ask why today, even as middle- and working-class men and women in developing nations have allowed democracy to fail, many established democracies, including the United States and emerging powers like South Africa and Brazil, also have abandoned democracy promotion and human rights advocacy. Indeed, with authoritarians like China wielding more power, with established democracies in the West and the developing world reluctant to stand up for their values, or pursuing democracy promotion strategies that too often focused on rhetoric, elections, and process, the international environment has become far more complicated and challenging for democracy in the new millennium. And far too often, men and women in the developing world have paid the price for these failures of democracy promotion.

2

How We Got Here

ONLY TEN YEARS AGO, few political leaders or theorists would have predicted democracy's decline. Even as late as the early 2000s, the fourth wave of democracy, which in the 1990s and early 2000s had swept through parts of Asia, Latin America, and—most notably—Sub-Saharan Africa, still seemed to be holding up. And the fourth wave built on three earlier waves of democratization, making it seem like the natural extension of democracy's global spread.

Throughout most of the twentieth century, democracy had been confined to tiny islands of freedom in a generally repressive globe, dominated by colonies, monarchies, and warlords. At the start of the twentieth century, only twelve countries, nearly all in Western Europe and North America, could truly be called democracies, though roughly thirty nations had established minimal democratic institutions and cultures, including Italy, Argentina, Germany, Japan, and Spain. Political scientist Samuel Huntington would call this initial group of democracies, which gained freedoms in the eighteenth and nineteenth centuries and the early twentieth century, the "first wave" of democracy. These democracies—Britain, the United States, the Scandinavian nations, France, Switzerland, and British dominions like Canada and Australia—had their origins in the American and French revolutions. This small group of countries generally shared long histories of gradual democratic development, born in the theories of the Enlightenment, the European wars, and the civil strife of the early nineteenth century, and the legal systems drafted in Europe and the United States after the French and American revolutions.

Many of the first wave democracies that came of age last, in the early twentieth century, did not survive the First World War and the economic chaos of the 1930s. Spain, Italy, Austria, Germany, and many others crumpled in the face of a reverse wave of fascism and communism, and, as Huntington notes, the initial democratic institutions that were germinating in Poland, the Baltics, and in other parts of Central and Eastern Europe, as well as in Brazil and Argentina, were snuffed out. Those countries that had not already succumbed gave way to the military takeovers by fascist Japan, Italy, and Germany. Even at the end of the Second World War, democracy remained mostly limited to the same small club of countries in Scandinavia, Western Europe, North America, and former British dominions like Australia.

But the Second World War unleashed what would become known as the second wave of global democratization. The Allies' victory and occupation of nations like Germany, Austria, and Japan allowed the occupiers to foster a rebirth of democratic institutions and culture in those countries—indeed, the new constitution drafted for Japan by its American occupiers was far more liberal than Japanese society would have accepted if Japanese leaders had drafted such a document themselves at that time. The defeat of fascism, the triumph of the Anglo-American political model (at least in areas not controlled by the Soviets), and the removal of Italy and Germany as military powers provided space for Greece and Turkey to strengthen their democratic institutions. In Latin America, meanwhile, Argentina, Venezuela, Colombia, and Peru held democratic elections in the mid-1940s.

By exhausting the British, German, Dutch, and French empires, the war also triggered a wave of decolonization around the globe. A few of the newly independent states, like India, Israel, and Malaysia, already had relatively substantial traditions of opposition politics and freedom of association, and were able to build on those. Nigeria, India, Pakistan, Indonesia, and Malaysia, among other newly free states, held initial elections and seemed to be putting into place democratic institutions.

Countries like India, however, turned out to be the exception. As new states emerged in Africa, Asia, and the Middle East in the 1950s and 1960s, many Western political scientists and leaders believed that these new nations were not fertile ground for democracy, at least not anytime soon. These countries had little previous experience with elections and very few educated men and women, and they faced many challenges, from establishing education systems to simply feeding their people. "Parliamentary democracy has a dim future in Africa," predicted a typical 1961 article titled "The Prospect for Democracy in the New Africa."[1] In the late 1970s, in her famous *Commentary* article "Dictatorships and Double Standards," in which she pushed the White House to back right-wing dictatorships as a bulwark against revolutionary left-wing authoritarian regimes, Jeanne Kirkpatrick made a similar argument, writing, "In the relatively few places where they exist, democratic governments have come into being slowly, after extended prior experience with more limited forms of participation."[2] Even as late as 1980, then mayor of Paris (later president of France) Jacques Chirac told a group of African leaders, "Multi-partyism is a political error, the type of luxury that developing countries cannot afford."[3]

With a few exceptions, like India's Jawaharlal Nehru, who held a deep and intense belief in Indian democracy, leaders of the former colonies essentially echoed Kirkpatrick's theme, publicly arguing that they could not be expected to develop democracies overnight—not when they had so many other priorities. Of course, postcolonial leaders in Africa and Asia had ulterior motives for claiming that their people were not ready for democracy. But without a doubt, most of the first generation of postindependence leaders displayed little interest in democracy. Malawi's first postindependence leader, a Scottish-trained doctor named Hastings Banda who maintained an intense love for all things Scottish and an obsession with Malawians' personal grooming—his government banned long hair for men and pants for women—named himself "Life President" of the country and had his picture plastered inside every office building and movie theater, as well as in most homes.[4] Banda, one of the most controlling of the postindependence African big men, certainly believed that his people couldn't be trusted with the franchise. Malawians, he told reporters, were "children" and needed a powerful ruler to guide them.[5]

Theorists Huntington and Seymour Martin Lipset, meanwhile, argued that countries needed to attain a certain level of economic development to create the conditions for successful democracy—a level of development that virtually none of the postcolonial states had attained. The exact level of development at which democracy solidifies was difficult to pinpoint, but many proponents of this modernization theory have argued that, once a country reaches the income level, per capita, of a middle income nation, it rarely returns to authoritarian rule. (Exceptions were states totally dependent on oil wealth, in which a small elite could use oil simply to solidify its control of power.) Economic development, these theorists argued, would create such features as a sizable middle class, an educated populace, and greater integration with the rest of the world.

In particular, development theorists like Huntington placed their bets on the middle class as the primary moving force behind democratic change. As the middle class grew in size, middle class men and women would build new networks of business and society outside of the control of the state. They would gain more education, build more ties to the outside world of democratic ideas, and increasingly demand more social, political, and economic freedoms. In addition, development would promote higher levels of interpersonal trust, seen as critical to civic engagement in politics, to open debate, and to forming opposition political parties. "In virtually every country [that had democratized] the most active supporters of democratization came from the urban middle-class," Huntington wrote.

For the most part, until the early 1970s, the theory that these poor, newly independent nations could not support democracy seemed correct. Even India suffered its own dramatic democratic reversal, when in the mid-1970s Prime Minister Indira Gandhi suspended the constitution and declared a state of emergency, essentially making herself dictator. Indeed, in the 1960s and 1970s democracy suffered another reverse wave, though this reverse did not cancel out all the gains of the previous two waves. Military regimes took power again in Greece and Turkey. Nearly every postcolonial African state developed into some kind of authoritarian regime, often ruled by a domineering independence leader like Kenya's Jomo Kenyatta or Ghana's Kwame Nkrumah. Many of these nations also adopted highly centralized economic policies, which not only failed to produce high growth rates but also contributed to a general centralization of power in the hands of the ruling regime. Postcolonial states that had seemed to offer prospects for democracy, like Nigeria, Pakistan, Indonesia, and Burma, disintegrated into civil war or fell prey to military takeovers, such as the bloody civil conflict in Indonesia in 1965–66, where in the aftermath of a military takeover communal riots killed as many as one million Indonesians.

And if Asia's postcolonial leaders proved more successful economically than their counterparts in Africa, opening their countries to international trade and using the power of the state to support industrialization and primary education made them no less dictatorial than their African peers. The leaders of South Korea, Taiwan, and Singapore—Park Chung Hee, Chiang Kai-shek, and Lee Kuan Yew, respectively—established spartan, tightly controlled states. Thailand's military generals might allow American companies and American soldiers into their country, but not American-style democracy. When a group of prodemocracy opposition politicians criticized the ruling Thai junta in 1949, the security forces grabbed four men from the opposition, who never made it out of police custody. When the police finally released their bodies, the corpses were pocked with bullet holes and showed signs of torture, including swollen eyes and ears, burns over their bodies (likely from lit cigarettes), and shattered legs.[6] Overall, in the late 1960s and early 1970s, in the second reverse wave, as many as one-third of the countries that had been democracies in the early 1960s had reverted to authoritarian rule by the early 1970s. The reverse wave, Huntington noted, sparked broad pessimism that stable democracy could take hold anywhere in the developing world.

The international system enabled authoritarian rule and, generally, posed a major obstacle to democratic change during the Cold War. The Soviet Union crushed stirrings of democratic reform in Hungary, Czechoslovakia, and other Soviet satellites. Meanwhile, not only did many Western leaders tolerate anticommunist autocracies, by the 1970s—with oil shocks staggering the U.S. economy and the retreat from Vietnam denting American military confidence—they also openly wondered whether democracy could actually defeat communism around the world. In 1977 Henry Kissinger, the former secretary of state and a believer in détente with the Soviet Union, wrote, "Today, for the first time in our history, we face the stark reality that the [communist] challenge is unending."[7] Kissinger's views were widely shared among American policy makers and intellectuals, most of whom in the 1970s and early 1980s accepted that the Soviet Union would not reform, that communism and democracy would have to coexist indefinitely, and that democracy might eventually turn out to be the historical accident, restricted to a few societies of the West and perhaps doomed even there.[8]

Even when Western allies crushed potential young democracies, Cold War realities dominated. In 1975, as Portugal released its last colonial possessions, the leaders of one of those possessions, East Timor, developed plans to build an independent democracy on their tiny half-island. But that year giant Indonesia invaded Timor with the tacit consent of the United States and other powers, including the regional power, Australia. In a meeting with Indonesian dictator Suharto, President Gerald Ford and Secretary of State Kissinger made clear they would not stand in the way. "Whatever you do," Kissinger told Suharto, according to documents later released under the Freedom of Information Act, "We will try to handle it in the best way possible."[9] Indonesia launched a brutal military occupation of East Timor. According to an estimate by Geoffrey Robinson of the University of California at Los Angeles, as many as 200,000 East Timorese—close to half the population—died from the occupation in the late 1970s.[10]

In April 1974, in an event that was only later recognized as having launched the third wave of democratization, leftist military officers in Portugal, frustrated with the government's continued commitment to expensive and bloody colonial wars, deposed the authoritarian regime that had ruled the country for five decades. Thousands of Portuguese flocked into the streets of Lisbon, gathering near the flower market, where they began waving carnations and sticking them into soldiers' gun barrels to show their support for the rebels. The coup paved the way for an opening of the Portuguese political system, and within a year of the "Carnation Revolution," Portugal had held a free election.

Beginning with the Carnation Revolution, democracy spread in the third wave across southern Europe, to parts of East Asia and Latin America, and, after 1989, to much of post-Soviet Eastern Europe. Between the mid-1970s and the early 1990s, some thirty authoritarian nations would become democratic, and more would develop at least some trappings of democracy. Of course, the idea of a "democratic wave"—political science shorthand for sweeping change—could be overstated. Specific domestic factors in each nation precipitated democratization, and it would be impossible to claim that political change in one nation necessarily sparked change somewhere else. But in certain regions and at certain times, like Latin America in the late 1970s and early 1980s, or Eastern Europe in 1989, the sheer number of countries undergoing change in a short time meant that reforms in Brazil or Poland did have a demonstration effect, influencing the political situation in Argentina or Czechoslovakia. The Carnation Revolution, for instance, was watched carefully in neighboring Spain. Shortly afterward, with the death of Spanish dictator Francisco Franco, Spain embarked on its own transition, in which King Juan Carlos helped manage a democratic opening.[11] Reforms in Brazil and Argentina in the late 1970s and early 1980s encouraged the reformers in Chile, who had already begun pushing back against dictatorship. Chile restored democracy in 1990 and built what is now arguably the most stable democratic system in Latin America.[12]

Many of these third wave nations also had experienced rapid economic growth in the 1970s, seemingly adding support to Huntington's theory that growth helps build a middle class and, thus, democratic change. In the late 1960s and early 1970s, economic reforms helped usher in high growth in Spain and Greece and other southern European nations, and several of the Asian nations that would democratize in the third wave, including the Philippines, South Korea, Thailand, and Taiwan, also posted high growth rates in the 1970s and early 1980s. In the case of Korea, Thailand, and Taiwan, these growth rates were some of the highest in the world. The military regimes running these nations often played a role in sparking the growth through free market policies, but in Greece, Spain, and other nations, they proved incapable of managing some of the challenges of growth, including inflation, higher public debt, migration to urban areas and the need for greater social services, and macroeconomic instability. This lack of economic management hurt the autocrats' legitimacy, particularly with the middle class businesspeople.

In addition, these nations' middle classes seemed to respond to growth exactly as Huntington and Lipset had predicted. Demanding greater economic, social, and political freedoms, urban middle class men and women led demonstrations in the Philippines, Argentina, Chile, Taiwan, South Korea, and many other nations. In countries like Bulgaria or Burma, where the urban middle class was much smaller, democratization during the third wave faced many more challenges, and had a harder time laying foundations for democratic consolidation.

In the Philippines, it was primarily Manila's middle class, over a million men and women, who formed the bulk of the People Power movement that forced dictator Ferdinand Marcos to step down in 1986 and flee into exile. In South Korea in the late 1980s, middle class urbanites in Seoul, including many university students, led angry and sometimes violent protests against dictator Roh Tae Woo, forcing him to concede to democratic reforms and, ultimately, paving the way for the presidencies of former dissidents Kim Young Sam and Kim Dae Jung, who'd once been hunted and nearly killed by the military regime.

Looking to the Philippines example, Thailand, Malaysia, Sri Lanka, and Bangladesh also built flawed but increasingly reformist governments, while demonstrators in Burma in part modeled their massive 1988 prodemocracy protests on the People Power movements in Manila.

The middle class did not always act so forcefully, but it invariably played a major role. In Chile, Turkey, and Brazil, gradual economic development and slow pressure for reform from an emerging middle class ultimately forced leaders to negotiate transitions to democracy and to return the military to the barracks. In apartheid South Africa, middle class white liberals, tired of their country's isolation and its negative impact on commerce, subtly pressured the ruling National Party to liberalize. Many of these middle class attempts at political reform began with measures to solidify democratic institutions. In South Africa, leaders backed by the urban middle class passed one of the most progressive constitutions in the world, recognizing a vast array of human rights including the right to healthcare, housing, and education. In Thailand, idealistic young Bangkokians, sometimes working with reform-minded foreign NGOs, wrote and passed a forward-thinking constitution with broad protections for rights and clauses that created independent institutions to oversee political competition and prevent vote buying.[13]

Later in the third wave, when coups threatened nascent democracies, middle class men and women stood up for reform. As the Argentine military threatened the civilian government in 1985 and 1987, the civilian leaders called hundreds of thousands of people out into the streets of Buenos Aires to support the government's legitimacy. In the Philippines, post–People Power leader Corazon Aquino faced down multiple coup attempts, including a serious one in late 1989 by Marcos loyalists. Each time, Aquino called upon her support among middle class Manila residents, using televised speeches to rally her faithful, and staving off all of the military's attempted putsches.

The middle classes' resistance to democratic rollback was not the only sign, during the third wave, of their seemingly deep commitment to democracy. Numerous polls taken during the third wave across Latin America, Asia, Southern and Eastern Europe, and other democratizing regions showed extremely high levels of support for democracy. In one such study cited by Huntington, around 75 percent of Peruvians in 1988 believed that democracy was the most desirable political system. In another series of polls, taken in a range of former Soviet satellites, overwhelming majorities, primarily in urban middle class areas, declared that democracy was preferable to all other forms of government.

Broader public demands for democracy also challenged authoritarian leaders across the third wave at a time when many of these authoritarians no longer could count on the backing of the Soviet Union or the United States as the Cold War came to a close. The Solidarity protests at Poland's shipyards in the early 1980s did not immediately force an end to Polish communism, but they helped set the stage for the revolutions of 1989, which quickly spread from the more developed Eastern European nations to even the least developed, like Bulgaria and, eventually, Albania, which had been kept in near isolation during the Cold War by its paranoid, xenophobic ruler, Enver Hoxha. Facing its own economic challenges, the Soviet Union had less capacity to repress dissent in its satellites, while, in the United States, support for democracy and human rights was beginning to build.

The People Power movement in the Philippines indeed not only pushed Ferdinand Marcos out of power but also helped reshape American thinking about the strategic benefits of authoritarian regimes, a shift that would add fuel to global democratization in the third wave. As crowds gathered in Manila to call for Marcos's ouster, the outpouring prompted some officials within the administration of President Ronald Reagan to begin aggressively promoting the idea that democratic governments in developing nations like the Philippines ultimately would prove better partners for Washington than even the friendliest authoritarian regimes—and that the United States thus should reduce its support for even avowedly anticommunist autocrats. Paul Wolfowitz, who was assistant secretary of state for East Asian affairs during the anti-Marcos protests, wrote in 2009 following the death of People Power leader Corazon Aquino, "Some U.S. officials in the mid-1980s defended Marcos on the grounds that 'there's no real alternative' . . . but that ignored the fact that continued U.S. support for Marcos was itself discouraging opposition." In fact, Wolfowitz wrote, Washington finally made a crucial decision that would help push forward the third wave of democratization—that democratic government, not a conservative autocrat, was the best antidote to communism: "In the end, the conclusion was that it would be more dangerous if Marcos continued on his current course."[14]

Wolfowitz played a central role in pushing the Reagan administration, still wedded to a policy of backing conservative dictatorships, to abandon its support for Marcos and embrace the prodemocracy movement in Manila. Beginning with a *Wall Street Journal* article he wrote in 1985 calling for American democracy promotion to counter communism, Wolfowitz advocated, in public and in private administration interagency meetings, for the White House to embrace democratic reforms in the Philippines. Embracing the democracy movement would be a sharp change for the United States and a risk in the Philippines, which at that time was a critical American ally and home to important naval bases. Though a decade earlier Wolfowitz would have found few allies for his cause, by the mid-1980s pressure to make democracy promotion a part of American and Western European policy had begun to build among a community of academics, writers, congressional representatives, and a few policy makers, both neoconservatives like Wolfowitz and, later, liberal internationalists like Samantha Power and Michael Ignatieff, as well as many West German, British, and Nordic activists and writers. What's more, the coming end of the Cold War, a decade later, would give their arguments greater resonance, because it would become harder for American realists to use the conflict with the Soviet Union as a reason to prop up pro-Western dictators like Marcos or Mobutu, or for Western European realists to advocate their own détente with the nations of the Warsaw Pact.

Wolfowitz and his allies had argued during the Manila protests that, in the long run, the global spread of democracy would be in America's interest. Democratization, they believed, would minimize the possibility of global conflicts that might necessitate American intervention, reduce the corruption and rent-seeking that added burdens to American companies investing abroad, enlarge the sphere of countries committed to free trade and free markets, and generally enhance America's prestige abroad. It was an idea that already had begun to gain traction in the Carter administration, which had made human rights a focus. The rhetoric of democratization also appealed to Carter's successor, who usually sought broad visions rather than policy details, and it gained traction in Washington and other Western capitals. As Reagan declared in a speech to the American Conservative Union, "America's foreign policy supports freedom, democracy, and human dignity for all mankind, and we make no apologies for it. The opportunity society that we want for ourselves we also want for others, not because we're imposing our system on others but because those opportunities belong to all people."[15]

The democracy advocates had help. In 1983 the National Endowment for Democracy (NED) was founded in Washington, funded through an annual congressional grant and given a mission to support democratic institutions around the world, including free media, unions, and political parties. Partner democracy-promotion organizations like the National Democratic Institute and the International Republican Institute, also established in the early 1980s, were designed to augment NED's overseas work.[16] From the beginning, much of NED's work was popular with civil society organizations in developing nations, and extremely unpopular with rulers, though by the 2000s that would change: as American democracy-promotion efforts during the George W. Bush era became increasingly unpopular in regions like the Middle East and South Asia, NED grantees from civil society organizations would hide their affiliation with the group.[17] But earlier on, NED grants helped speed transitions to democracy in countries like Poland, where the group invested heavily in the Polish trade unions that played a major role in criticizing the communist regime.[18] Private organizations that performed similar functions, like George Soros's constellation of Open Society initiatives, also would add to the investments in democratization in the third wave nations.

With the end of the Cold War, democratization moved to the forefront of American policy making, and the third wave of democratization expanded beyond the post-Soviet states to include parts of Latin America and Asia and even some African nations. Democracy advocates on both the right and the left gained influence and power. Some, like Madeleine Albright, took high-profile positions in the administration of President Bill Clinton. The United States, now an unrivaled superpower with a soaring economy, enjoyed the luxury of making democracy promotion a central pillar of foreign policy; America could embark on armed foreign interventions to save nations trying to build new democracies, even when those countries were tangential to American strategic interests. The American public, riding the economic boom of the mid- and late 1990s, would tolerate a more internationalist foreign policy; American liberals, who since the Vietnam War had linked military intervention to overaggressive, even brutal, American power, could now support the use of force to prevent crimes against humanity and to save beleaguered potential democracies like East Timor or Kosovo. And if the United States wanted to promote democracy and help build a new class of political leaders, even close to the traditional spheres of influence of Russia or China, who was going to stop it? By the mid-1990s, Moscow was on the verge of bankruptcy and Beijing still had not fully recovered from the stain of the Tiananmen massacre.

As president, Clinton decided to make democracy promotion a core part of his foreign policy. Searching for a theme that would convey a foreign policy for the post–Cold War era and would be remembered by history, Clinton had settled on one phrase: democratic enlargement.[19] Democratic enlargement, he decided in meetings with his National Security Council, would form the center of his foreign policy and would be a successor to the containment policy of the Cold War. It would capture the optimism and hope of the post–Cold War era and would wed optimism to strategic purpose. Enlargement would mean that America's priority now would be to help expand the number of free states in the world, because, as National Security Advisor Anthony Lake told historian Douglas Brinkley, "as free states grew in number and strength the international order would become both more prosperous and more secure."[20] The Clinton administration, he said, would help consolidate young democracies, help counter the aggression of states hostile to democracy, and support the liberalization of undemocratic nations.[21] Of course, there would be exceptions, such as China and the Middle East, but from early in his first term, and even in his speeches on the campaign trail, Clinton aggressively highlighted democracy promotion as vital to American national interests. His first National Security Strategy stated that "all of America's strategic interests—from promoting prosperity at home to checking global threats abroad before they threaten our territory—are served by enlarging the community of democratic and free market nations."[22] In studying the Clinton administration's record, Thomas Carothers, of the Carnegie Endowment for International Peace, found that Clinton had for the first time institutionalized democracy promotion in the U.S. foreign policy bureaucracy—every U.S. embassy now had to submit an annual report on its democracy promotion efforts—and the White House, in its budgeting requests, clearly made democracy promotion one of its strategic priorities.[23] Between the early 1990s and 2000, U.S. government spending on democracy promotion grew from around $100 million annually to over $700 million annually.[24] Clinton attempted to support what he considered the most important nations on the verge of democratization, including Russia and Mexico; under Clinton, the United States became Russia's largest investor, American democracy-promotion organizations like NED expanded their Russia programs, and the Clinton administration pushed the International Monetary Fund, G7, and World Bank to use their resources to foster democratization in Russia.[25] The White House drastically expanded funding for democratic institution building and market reforms in the newly free nations of Eastern Europe, and, on the campaign trail in

1996, Clinton boasted, "With our help, the forces of reform in Europe's newly free nations have laid the foundations of democracy."[26]

East Timor, which in 1975 had shown the limits of what Washington would do to protect a nascent democracy during the Cold War, served as an example again in 1999. As in 1975, a brutal bloodletting exploded in Timor. After the majority of Timorese voted to separate from Indonesia, militias with links to the Indonesian armed forces began a campaign of slaughter that would not have been out of place in the Rwandan genocide. Gangs of militiamen wielding machetes and automatic weapons hacked, disemboweled, and beheaded known independence supporters, aid workers, journalists, and anyone else who happened to be in their way. Thousands died, and 70 percent of Timor's infrastructure was destroyed. But this time the world responded. Despite having minimal strategic interests in East Timor, major powers like the United States, the United Kingdom, and Australia backed an armed humanitarian intervention that, under the auspices of the United Nations, ultimately stemmed the violence, allowed relief workers to avoid a total catastrophe in East Timor, and ultimately helped Timor to finally break from Indonesia and build a fragile and independent democracy.[27]

The Timor triumph, along with successful Western intervention in Kosovo, only further emboldened Washington. With the end of the Soviet Union, Western fears that democracy would not survive and that communism would last forever suddenly vanished. Few had predicted the Soviet collapse, but in its wake a Western triumphalism quickly emerged. Francis Fukuyama later protested that he never intended his "End of History" article to express this conviction that liberal democracy had triumphed forever, but the piece captured the victorious Western mood. Democracy, Clinton administration officials now argued, had a universal appeal, and would spread, well, universally—a belief, as Robert Kagan noted, rooted in the Enlightenment concept of the inevitability of progress, of history constantly moving forward toward human improvement.[28] In aid conferences and missions to developing nations in Africa, Asia, and Latin America, officials from the World Bank, the International Monetary Fund, the United Nations, U.S. government agencies, and other Western organizations preached the new gospel of economic and political liberalization.

Kishore Mahbubani, a former senior Singaporean foreign service official, remembered meeting a top Belgian official in 1991, the year that probably marked the apex of post–Cold War triumphalism. Before a group of Asians, the official declared, "The Cold War has ended. There are only two superpowers left: The United States and Europe."[29]

Post–Cold War haughtiness even filtered into bilateral relations with powers like Russia and China. In the 1990s Western scholars like Gordon Chang predicted the coming collapse of the Chinese Communist Party and took bets on when it would fall to a democratic uprising. American officials, seeing in Yeltsin's Russia the opposite of the Soviet Union—Russia would now be a close friend, an American-style democracy—pushed to expand NATO closer to Russia's borders, ignoring warnings from experts that Russian nationalism had hardly just vanished, and that Russians—and Chinese—might resent this dramatic American intervention in their backyard.[30]

3
The Fourth Wave

THE OUTSKIRTS OF BLANTYRE, the commercial capital of Malawi, are some of the most forlorn suburbs on earth. Years of on-and-off drought and famine in the countryside have gradually destroyed Malawi's farming families, driving many people to settle in Blantyre, where the men take odd jobs as guards at stores or as part-time bus drivers. Rows of shacks made from scraps of metal and scavenged wood cover the denuded hills outside the city, and, at night, if you are brave enough to walk in these neighborhoods, you can see young men posted as guards in front of the families' tiny dwellings, since Malawi's urbanization and deep poverty—GDP per capita is roughly $800—have sparked a rise in violent crime. In wealthier parts of the city, residents employ private security companies and equip their houses with "panic rooms," which don't always work—home invasions remain common, and the thieves often seem to be in cahoots with the security guards assigned to watch the properties.

In the early morning, the sides of the rutted roads are so thick with people walking to their jobs from the shantytowns that cars can find these routes difficult to negotiate. Nearly all the land outside Blantyre has been ripped up. Wood has been stripped for houses, and edible plants taken for food on the formerly lush hills above the green valleys of Thyolo, the traditional tea-growing region north of the city. In senior housing in Thyolo, elderly planters, who settled in Malawi from Britain when it was still a colony, still take afternoon tea and tiny British-style finger cakes. But outside of the carefully tended gardens of these residences, and beyond the lush tea plantations owned by large companies, across Thyolo one can see only arid scrub, razed buildings, and fruit plants ripped apart in search of food.

Women with babies tied on their backs with brightly colored *chitenge* cloths jostle for space on the sides of the road with sickly vendors carrying battered trays of avocados and bananas.

Children are everywhere. Malawi has one of the highest birthrates in the world, and its fifteen million people are jammed into a country the size of Pennsylvania, with cities that resemble the packed metropolises of South Asia more than the archetypical open landscapes of Africa. It also has a staggeringly high rate of HIV/AIDS infection. The United Nations' AIDS program estimates that 14 percent of Malawians are infected, an epidemic that, even in the era of antiretrovirals, has orphaned many kids, leaving them to be cared for by grandparents, or by no one.[1] At intersections in Blantyre proper, packs of orphans clad in torn clothes and with matted hair often waylay stopped or slow-moving cars to beg for food or a few kwacha, the nearly worthless Malawian currency that piles up in stacks in merchants' shops.

And yet, for all its destitution Malawi was, until recently, a democratic success story. After the country's longtime dictator stepped down in the early 1990s, the country held free, multiparty elections. The first democratically elected president, Bakili Muluzi, was later accused of massive corruption—but after Malawi's top court upheld the constitution and barred him from seeking a third term in the 2009 presidential election, he complied with its ruling. His former protégé, Bingu wa Mutharika, now leading an opposition party, won the presidency.

Beginning in the late 1990s and early 2000s, Malawi also developed a culture of largely peaceful, vigorous political campaigning. The presidential election of 2009 exemplified this trend. At one point during the winter campaign a large crowd dressed in red, the color of John Tembo, was hollering wildly for their candidate in front of an overgrown soccer field next to a divided highway. Across the road a smaller group of Mutharika backers, all dressed in his party color, blue, had taken position, screaming into the sky, clapping and singing, and thrusting massive posters of their candidate's face at passing cars, nearly causing an accident. After a while some Mutharika supporters crossed the street toward the Tembo group, yet they didn't make any effort to stir up violence—a common occurrence during election campaigns in neighboring nations like Zimbabwe and Zambia. Instead, several of the younger men dropped their Mutharika posters, pulled out a ragged soccer ball, and started an impromptu dribbling exhibition with two Tembo men. Later that year, Malawi would hold a relatively peaceful presidential election, marking another seeming transition to stable democracy. The campaign was covered extensively in the local newspapers, which suffered from lack of resources—reporters were paid little, and the papers themselves often looked like they had been printed on rags—but which reported on the candidates with boldness and style, chronicling nearly every political battle that went on across the country. Despite some threats from angry politicians, reporters rarely backed down, and each day's paper usually contained a scandal sheet rapping all the major politicians' foibles.

Even as Malawi welcomed democracy, its leaders, and its citizens, also came to associate political change with promises of economic prosperity. Throughout the fourth wave of democratization, in the late 1990s and early 2000s, foreign donors and many local leaders who pushed the "Washington Consensus" prescriptions of open markets and open societies, increasingly made this association. But it was a dangerous link. No evidence had really shown that open societies were more likely to create economic growth. In fact, Kevin Hassett of the American Enterprise Institute has shown that, in recent years, many authoritarian nations have outperformed freer countries.[2] But in the late 1980s and 1990s, many developing world leaders—and their advocates in the West—linked the two.

In the late 1980s, Malawi might have seemed a remote prospect for democracy, but it was joined by many other democratizing nations from similar levels of development. The fourth wave of global democratization, which built on the gains of the third wave, began to crest in the late 1990s and continued into the early 2000s. While the third wave had swept through Southern Europe and parts of Eastern Europe, Latin America, and Asia, the fourth wave included much of sub-Saharan Africa and many other countries that were poorer, more prone to conflict, and, often, more remote, than those in the third wave: East Timor, Cambodia, Mexico, Mozambique, and Malawi, among many others.

In many ways, the uprisings in the Middle East in 2011 seemed to fit in with that fourth wave. The Middle East revolts took place in countries like Yemen or Egypt—nations that were often as poor, authoritarian, or conflict-ridden—or all three—as those in the fourth wave nations. Before the Arab Spring, just as in sub-Saharan Africa before the 1990s, many observers, and indeed many Arabs, had all but written off the prospect of real change in the Middle East for generations.

Just as in the third wave, a kind of positive diffusion effect took place in which democratic change—sometimes backed by powerful advocacy by established democracies, as in East Timor—in one fourth wave country spilled over to neighboring nations. The revolts in Tunisia in December 2010, broadcast on satellite television and social media, inspired reformers first in Egypt, and then in Bahrain, Syria, Libya, and other nations in the Middle East. The dramatic end of apartheid in South Africa in the early 1990s, as well as liberalization in neighboring nations like Mozambique and Zambia, helped create currents of change that autocratic leaders like Malawian dictator Hastings Banda ultimately could not ignore. Throwing off most of the remaining postcolonial dictators, many other poor African nations, like Benin, held multiple free and fair elections.

In the former Soviet sphere, the progress toward democracy of former communist states like Poland and Kyrgyzstan began to spill over into harder cases, like Ukraine, Central Asian nations, and Georgia. New states carved from the Soviet Central Asian republics, some of the poorest and most ethnically heterogeneous parts of the former Soviet Union, held elections. After the vicious Balkan wars of the 1990s, nearly every part of the former Yugoslavia held real, competitive elections, with several, like Slovenia, approaching Western European standards of stable democracy. Overall, by the early 2000s, nearly half of the world's population lived in countries that were either full or partial democracies, up from less than half in the mid-1970s.[3]

Sub-Saharan Africa made perhaps the greatest democratic gains in the 1990s and early 2000s, seemingly disproving arguments, sometimes made by African leaders, that the region was too poor, too ethnically divided, and too uneducated to make democracy work. From Malawi to postapartheid

South Africa, the continent disposed of so-called big men, held elections, and paid lip service to new democratic norms. Long-ruling parties in many countries finally lost elections and willingly transferred power. Western leaders, including President Bill Clinton, touted a "new generation" of African leaders, men like Uganda's Yoweri Museveni and Ethiopia's Meles Zenawi, who would commit themselves to reform and to priorities that the first postcolonial generation had often ignored.[4]

In Kenya, the era following Daniel arap Moi had begun exuberantly in 2002 with the frenzied inauguration of former longtime opposition leader Mwai Kibaki, who vowed to clean up, and open up, Kenyan politics. At Kibaki's inauguration, where the new president declared, "The era of anything goes is now gone forever: Government will no longer be run on the whims of individuals." Africa journalist Michela Wrong tried to pay a small bribe to a local driver, but he refused her money, saying that a new, cleaner era had come to Kenya.[5] Kibaki appointed John Githongo, a prominent, outspoken local journalist who had bitterly criticized Moi's autocratic and venal style, as his anticorruption czar.

Like Kibaki, Olusegun Obasanjo, a former general with a relatively clean reputation who won the Nigerian presidency in 1999 after the dictator Sani Abacha died, took office amid a wave of optimism. Obasanjo touted himself as a reformer after the predation and outright thuggery of the Abacha era; the day of his inauguration was called "Democracy Day," and a national holiday was declared.[6] In the following months U. S. Secretary of State Madeleine Albright called for greater American aid to Nigeria, praising Obasanjo for launching a democratic revolution that could rival "the Czechoslovak 'Velvet Revolution' and South Africa's long walk to freedom" in its power and influence.[7]

The fourth wave of democratization, which had seemed so improbable just a decade earlier, cemented in many Western leaders' minds the idea that democracy eventually would come to every country. If a place as poor and as conflict-ridden as Malawi or Mozambique could build a viable democratic system, what nation could not? Critical international developments, including the rapid expansion of communications technology, the end of the Cold War, and the birth of Western democracy promotion, also seemed to foster the global spread of democracy. By the beginning of the 2000s, this belief in the essential triumph of democracy had become a kind of religion among Western leaders.

The color revolutions of the early 2000s capped off the fourth wave, and only added to Western leaders' democratic triumphalism. Beginning with the Rose Revolution in Georgia in 2003 (some would add the protests in Serbia in 2000), the term "color revolutions" came to mean peaceful, popular movements for democratic change, initially in the former Soviet Union and old Eastern bloc.

To be sure, some fourth wave nations seemed, even in their best moments, to be the "illiberal democracies" that prominent intellectual and writer Fareed Zakaria has described—places like Cambodia, whose leaders never really upheld what Zakaria calls "constitutional liberalism," meaning protections of individual autonomy and dignity against coercion, including the potential tyranny of a democratic majority.[8] As Zakaria outlined in his book *The Future of Freedom: Illiberal Democracy at Home and Abroad*, many young democracies, led by popularly elected leaders who had little interest in creating democratic institutions, trampled on minority rights, religious freedoms, and economic rights. "In many developing countries, the experience of democracy over the past few decades has been one in which majorities have—often quietly, sometimes noisily—eroded separations of power, undermined human rights, and corrupted longstanding traditions of tolerance and fairness. . . . Democratization and illiberalism are directly related," he wrote.[9] In India, where Zakaria was born, the mid-1990s BJP government, popularly elected and supported by many Hindus, fostered pogroms against Muslims, a religious minority, in states like Gujarat, and apparently set back India's commitment to liberalism, which had been enshrined at the time of independence by unelected Indian elites or by leaders, like Jawaharlal Nehru, who were far more tolerant than most Indians. In Indonesia, where for thirty years relative interreligious and interethnic peace had prevailed under Suharto's iron grip (though, when he came to power in the mid-1960s, Suharto unleashed massive bloodshed), democratic change in the late 1990s led to new waves of violence between Muslims and Christians, Javanese and non-Javanese, and many other groups within Indonesian society.[10] Unlike leaders like Suharto or Singapore's Lee Kuan Yew, who could "make shrewd choices for the long term," democratic leaders also would inherently be pulled into populist economic policies focused on short-term gains at the expense of development.[11]

Zakaria argued further that the problem with these "illiberal democracies" was not that they were insufficiently democratic—that their institutions and political cultures needed to continue to mature, like those in the West that had developed for decades. This was a critique that had been made by many democratization specialists, and even by democrats in many developing nations themselves. Instead, he argued that they had too much democracy, and that the only solution was authoritarian rule, or at least a kind of oligarchic rule by the "best people"—the elites, like Nehru and other Indian founding fathers, who had attended English boarding schools and then Oxford or Cambridge. He celebrated leaders like Indonesia's Suharto and Pervez Musharraf, the military ruler of Pakistan throughout most of the 2000s who, by Zakaria's reckoning, instilled greater tolerance of religious and ethnic diversity than any civilian politician in that country could or would have done.[12] He seemed to even suggest that no Muslim-majority nation was capable of real democracy, since illiberal Islamists would always dominate an election and crush people's freedoms—thus, a "liberal" dictator like Musharraf or Tunisia's Zine Al-Abidine Ben Ali was the best alternative. He longed for earlier periods even in American history, when politics was essentially decided by a small group of men who came from the "right" background, attended the "right" universities, and then governed together at the State Department, CIA, and the White House.

Some of Zakaria's argument about illiberalism made inherent sense, such as the critical observation that democracy means more than simply elections; U.S. policy too often has focused on one relatively free election in a developing nation while ignoring other signs suggesting that democratic institutions are not being put into place. As we will see later, some "elected autocrats"—popularly elected leaders in fragile democracies like Russia or Thailand—have shown little commitment to the rule of law or to freedoms of association, press, or religion, and a democracy promotion policy focused primarily on elections, or a one-size-fits-all type of process, can hardly be successful. And in some instances, development-minded dictators like Suharto or Augusto Pinochet of Chile were able to pass economic reforms that set the stage for sustained growth.

Yet a wide range of comprehensive studies has shown that it is impossible to find a clear link between autocracy and growth. These dictators also usually did little to set the stage for any democratic transition, since the foundation of their rule was a desire to stay in power for life—when Suharto was overthrown, he was focused on concentrating more wealth and power into the hands of his family, not liberalizing the political environment or opening up Indonesia's cartelized markets. More important, these elected autocrats alone, whom Zakaria despises, did not undermine these democracies; as we will see, when this fourth wave crested these nations were neutered by a combination of poor leadership, weak institutions, a complacent middle class, slow growth, and corruption. This fourth wave also was not helped by Western democracy promotion strategies heavy on rhetoric, elections, and process, and it was light on actual funding on the ground, or an understanding of how to make democracy more attractive to both middle classes and working classes in the developing world.

But despite Zakaria's legitimate concerns about young democracies, some of which are echoed in this book, and even though many of these elected autocrats often took their countries' democracies backward, they almost never left their nations more repressive than they had been under previous true dictatorships. In Thailand, for instance, Thaksin Shinawatra did set the rule of law back during his prime ministership between 2001 and 2006: he intimidated the Thai media, bent the court system to his priorities, and essentially sacked supposedly independent bureaucrats who defied his policies. But only someone with no historical memory would argue that Thaksin's period as prime minister even began to compare to the bloodiest days of Thailand's past dictatorships, such as the late 1940s, when dictator Phibul Songkram disappeared or simply murdered political opponents, or the mid-1970s, when under a series of right-wing regimes state-backed vigilantes attacked Thammasat University, the Thai equivalent of Harvard, where they raped female students and then doused students with gasoline and immolated them, leaving their charred bodies swinging from trees.[13]

Indeed, even if they were incomplete democracies, all of the fourth wave nations that later regressed were freer in every respect during their more democratic periods than they had been earlier, during their truly authoritarian periods. Vladimir Putin, in the 2000s, did indeed set back Russian democracy, often with the consent of many Russians; its scores on Freedom House rankings fell compared to the Yeltsin era during the 1990s. But the country hardly had reverted to the terrors of the Soviet Union, in which none of Zakaria's individual liberal rights received any protections.

Zakaria's notion of illiberal democracy is inherently flawed in other ways. He chooses many examples in his book that do not even fit the definition of democracy at all, countries like Kazakhstan that, according to the international monitoring organization Freedom House and other ranking organizations, are simply autocracies. For every Pinochet or Lee Kuan Yew, there were tens of Mobutus or Malawi's Hastings Banda, who used their cults of personality to significantly restrain personal freedoms and individual liberties. In nearly every country he surveyed, many of the problems he outlined were indeed a result of not enough, rather than too much, democracy. As Harvard's Sabeel Rahman writes in an analysis of Zakaria's book, "On closer inspection, one finds that the culprits [in illiberal democracies] are not the public, who are the supposed beneficiaries of democratic empowerment, but rather special interest groups"—groups that could be minimized through greater, not lesser, democracy.[14]

Meanwhile, as they have become more autocratic, the fourth wave nations have not developed any of the supposed positive attributes of authoritarian rule that Zakaria writes about: benign dictators promoting liberal social and economic freedoms that would have been impossible in a popular democracy, or making farsighted economic decisions, since they are not accountable to the broader public. Instead, after the coup in 2006 Thailand's new military leaders badly bungled economic policy, sparking panic among investors and leading to runs on the Thai currency. In Cambodia, where the prime minister has suffocated the democratic reforms of the 1990s, the government has done little to promote sustained economic growth, instead turning into a kind of mafia state designed to enrich senior government officials and their allies.[15] Overall, a comprehensive study of fourth wave nations by Council on Foreign Relations researchers found that economic growth did not improve as they veered back toward autocracy, and that protection of these types of liberal freedoms also did not improve, even under supposedly "enlightened" autocracies like the Thai generals who deposed the elected autocrat Thaksin, or Musharraf.

In earlier democratic waves, countries had pursued a wide range of development strategies. Many third wave nations, especially those in East Asia, actually pursued highly state-directed strategies of economic growth, which some economists later would call the East Asian model. Eventually, these countries, like Taiwan and South Korea, also built vibrant democracies. While participating in global trading regimes, nations like Taiwan, Thailand, Malaysia, South Korea, and, earlier, Japan protected critical industries until they were more internationally competitive, invested heavily in primary education, and directed banks and other financial institutions, including citizens' pension plans, to support certain sectors of the economy. Some of these high-powered economies, like Malaysia (and later China), used capital controls to protect themselves from international capital markets. In Thailand, a small cadre of government bureaucrats in the Bank of Thailand and Ministry of Finance oversaw these government economic plans; in Japan, the powerful bureaucrats of the Ministry of Economy, Trade, and Industry played this role. In Thailand, import substitution and protections of critical industries would ultimately be responsible for nearly half the growth in the export manufacturing sector, while in South Korea such supports and protections nurtured a generation of companies that would become world-beaters, including automaker Hyundai and technology giant Samsung.

These state-directed measures were actually not so different from those employed by earlier, first wave democracies in North America and Western Europe when they, too, were developing economies. During the early years of its existence, the United States, for example, used high tariffs and other import restrictions to protect many of the young country's industries from competition with European firms.

Other second and third wave nations pursued different strategies of growth, with less success, yet managed at the same time to build solid democracies. After independence, India created a highly protected economy, using a wide range of tariffs and nontariff barriers to keep out foreign investment in most sectors, and to actually hinder domestic companies from growing too large. Many other postcolonial states also adhered to a socialist economic strategy, with highly mixed economic results—India grew by around 3–4 percent most years, and many African nations barely grew at all in the 1970s and early 1980s. Yet some of these nations, such as Greece and India, still managed to consolidate their democracies. Very few nations in the second or third waves adopted wholly free market policies— even countries later championed by free market advocates, like Chile, still used a sizable degree of state planning and support to buttress certain sectors. The one place often cited by free market advocates as an example of the power of economic liberalization, Hong Kong—annually ranked as the "freest" economy in the world in the Heritage Foundation think tank's Index of Economic Freedom—was neither a country nor a democracy, and its prosperity actually depended, in no small measure, on a massively inflated local property market tightly controlled by the government.

But in the fourth wave Western leaders, policy makers, and institutions like the World Bank were caught up in a kind of post–Cold War hysteria. The West's triumph over communism was proof, as Francis Fukuyama famously argued in *The End of History,* that liberal democracy, combined with market economics, represented the direction in which the world would inevitably evolve. The hard sell of democracy barely took account of the uncertainty about the actual conditions for growth in developing nations. It did not seem to matter that earlier wave nations had employed many different economic models of growth, or that many of the governments that collapsed in 1989 and in the early 1990s did so not because of economic liberalization but for a variety of reasons, ranging from international pressure (apartheid South Africa) to internal leadership dynamics that spiraled out of control (the Soviet Union under Gorbachev). At the time, this nuance was ignored: economic change was linked to political change, and a program of free markets and free politics was the only item on the menu. As candidate George W. Bush declared in 2000 on the presidential campaign trail, "Economic freedom creates habits of liberty. And habits of liberty create expectations of democracy."[16] The man he was hoping to replace, Bill Clinton, made essentially the same point many times. In one typical phrase from his book-length vision for America, *Between Hope and History,* he wrote, "Just as democracy helps make the world safe for commerce, commerce helps make the world safe for democracy."[17]

By the 1990s a large cadre of development experts, housed at the World Bank, the International Monetary Fund, ministries of Western governments, and universities and think tanks, were ready to dispense advice about the proper route to political and economic liberalization. The model advocated by many of these experts became known as the "Washington Consensus."[18] Its author, economist John Williamson, originally intended it to mean a discrete and limited set of economic initiatives particularly developed to address many of the economic problems facing Latin American nations in the late 1980s and in the 1990s, including fiscal discipline, tax reform, liberalizing exchange rates, privatization, and trade liberalization, among other changes. But the term soon took on a far broader meaning among many development experts and world leaders: it came to signify broad reforms, promoted not only for Latin America but for the entire developing world, and designed to open markets, increase financial transparency, and reduce government intervention in the economy, along with political reforms that would also foster freedom by shrinking the role of the state.[19] Proponents of the Washington Consensus made swaggering boasts about the potential results, and brooked little criticism of their proposals. In perhaps the most famous example, World Bank officials throughout the 1990s promised that these policy reforms, if implemented throughout the developing world, would slash global poverty in half.[20] Later, in an internal assessment of its policies during this decade, the Bank admitted that it still didn't know "how to improve institutional performance [i.e., how to promote economic growth]" and that the Washington Consensus had been "the dominant view, making it difficult for others to be heard," even though these proposed reforms actually had had a mixed impact on growth and political change.[21] Another retrospective comprehensive analysis of the Washington Consensus, by former World Bank chief economist Joseph Stiglitz, found that proponents of its reforms made little effort to tailor its prescriptions to individual countries and, even if it produced growth, actually paid little attention to whether that growth alleviated poverty or really addressed inequality at all. Worse, Stiglitz also concluded that the Washington

Consensus failed to even promote significant growth in most of the nations where it was applied, even as it ignored the balanced, important role that a state can play in development.

The lack of another obvious alternative model in the late 1990s and early 2000s only emboldened advocates of free markets linked with free politics. Compared with the Cold War, no major powers now dissented loudly from this new orthodoxy. After the 1989 Tiananmen crackdown, China adopted a more modest public approach to foreign policy and spent most of the 1990s and early 2000s wooing foreign investment, building its own industries (using many of the statist models pioneered by other Asian nations), and refusing to publicly offer any alternative to the Washington Consensus. Russia, decimated economically by the fall of the Soviet Union, and nearly bankrupt in the mid-1990s, also was in no position to offer any alternative.

The sheer number and diversity of countries in the fourth wave of democratization, as compared with earlier waves that took place mostly in the West, also added to pressure among many leaders and donors to develop a single model that could be applied in developing nations. After the fall of the Berlin Wall, many leaders, both in the former Soviet states and in the West, feared that if radical measures were not taken rapidly in the old Soviet bloc, these states would be unable to jettison the legacy of communist economic planning, and might wind up with hyperinflation and highly uncompetitive economies, which could lead to a stalling, or even a reversal, of political reforms and potential links to the West. These countries, many economists and donor agencies believed, needed to embark on quick transformations. Led by economists such as Jeffrey Sachs, many IMF and Bank officials promoted a kind of economic shock therapy, consisting of rapid freeing of the economies of countries like Poland.

The Bank was hardly alone in its hard sell of free markets and free politics. Sub-Saharan Africa and much of Latin America had suffered badly in the 1980s, a period of capital flight and economic policies that too often saddled Latin American and African nations with greater debts. In the worst years of the 1980s, sub-Saharan Africa's total GDP actually shrank, and even in the best years overall growth in Africa barely topped 4 percent; many Latin nations also ended the decade of the 1980s poorer than they'd begun.[22] By the early 1990s, most African and Latin leaders were looking for any solutions that would halt a death spiral of underdevelopment and isolation from the global economy. Many had failed with the socialist economic planning and import-substitution strategies of the postcolonial era, and at the time few understood the potential of the gradualist approach of the East Asian nations, which slowly weaned themselves off of many of the state subsidies and protections they had used in the 1960s and 1970s. (Later, as we will see, as China became a major world power again, and began highlighting its growth model, many other developing nations would try to copy the gradualist approach.) Compared with the weak growth and stasis of the 1960s and 1970s, and facing balance of payments problems, weak growth, and high unemployment, many developing nations assumed that the Washington Consensus could not help but improve their economies.

The savviest leaders of developing nations also realized that decent growth rates could bring stability to a young democracy. Growth, after all, would mollify members of the old regime—friends of the old dictator, the military, senior civil servants used to comfortable lifestyles, local traditional leaders—by expanding the pool of potential spoils and, possibly, convincing the most recalcitrant former regime insiders to support a democratic transition.

Malawi, like many sub-Saharan African nations, received the full measure of Washington Consensus advocacy. Stephen Carr, an economist, worked for the World Bank for years, and then retired to Malawi, where he lived on a small mountain outside of Blantyre. He had worked at the Bank during the height of the Washington Consensus era and then watched, even after he had left, as Bank specialists continued to descend upon the country. "You'd have economists come in here, never been to Malawi, knew nothing about how the country worked, and they'd make predictions, projections. . . . No follow-through, but if anyone disagreed with them, well, you just couldn't," he said. "It would be put that there was no other choice, really."[23]

In the 1990s and early 2000s, Malawi was confronted with one crisis after another: declining world prices for its staple crops of tea, coffee, and tobacco, and growing competition from new producers like Vietnam. Between 1980 and 2000, global prices for eighteen major commodities plunged by nearly one-quarter. Several times in the 1990s, droughts in the maize-planting regions, possibly caused by shifting global climate patterns, caused famines. Many Malawian families were left without enough maize even to feed themselves the staple porridge of *nsima,* much less enough maize or any other crop to sell; the ever-present deep-fried potatoes sold by street vendors throughout the country were luxuries they could not afford.

The World Bank's specialists proposed that Malawi privatize its agricultural sector, slashing state subsidies for fertilizer and feed. These policy recommendations came on the heels of Bank- and International Monetary Fund–led structural adjustment policies for Malawi, begun in the late 1980s, and they have launched a wave of privatization and macroeconomic liberalization in the country. Some Malawian government officials wanted to tell the Bank, politely, to shove off. They worried that, with even less of a government cushion of maize surplus and seeds, a drought would leave average Malawians in an even more precarious position. But Malawi relies on donors for more than half of its annual budget, and so the Bank, and other Western donors, wield enormous influence over government policy. "There was not much [of a] way they [the Malawian government] could really stand up to the donors," said Carr. In the late 1990s, the government did begin to implement many of the Bank's recommendations. As it did so, both Bank officials and many Malawians politicians who realized that strong growth was needed to maintain social stability aggressively advertised these policies.

Then, in the 2000s, disaster struck. Each season seemed to bring a drought worse than the previous one. Malawi's farms withered, and the country had to start importing food from neighboring nations. Maize production dropped by nearly half between 1998 and 2004, and in October 2005 Malawi's president declared that the famine was a "national disaster." Malnutrition soared in a country where many people already could not obtain enough food, and in the early 2000s hundreds died every year from starvation. But the government had sold off much of its grain reserves, and so it could do little to help its suffering farmers; it had to rely even more heavily on handouts from aid agencies and other African nations. Private traders who had amassed stocks of grain jacked up prices, and farmers complained bitterly. Malawi's economy contracted by nearly 5 percent in 2001, and by another 4.4 percent in 2002.

Eventually, the devastating famine forced the Malawian government to reassess its strategies. Defying the Bank's recommendation, the government instead launched a program in which roughly half of Malawi's small farmers were given coupons that allowed them to buy fertilizer and seed at a rate far below the market price. World Bank experts initially disdained the Malawian government's strategy, and the Bank may even have threatened to cut assistance if Malawi went forward with its plan.[24] Still, the Malawian government insisted on its strategy and ultimately was seemingly proven correct. The subsidized fertilizer and seeds helped Malawian farmers produce some of their best harvests in the late 2000s. Once the farmers produced, the Malawian government created funds designed to buy a percentage of the maize crop and store it for future emergencies, thereby averting the threat of empty grain silos in a future famine. Leaders from other African nations, and even from some Latin American countries like Costa Rica, began traveling to Malawi to study its turnaround. At one point, Malawi's farmers became so productive that some government officials worried whether they might be producing too much, and thereby driving down the price of their crops. Eventually, by the late 2000s the World Bank's own internal watchdog concluded that the demands by the Bank and other aid donors to privatize agriculture in countries like Malawi had actually hurt African nations. The Bank, and other Western donors, decided to cautiously back the Malawian subsidies.[25]

But by the time of the Bank's reevaluation, donors already had pursued more than a decade of ineffective and dangerous policies in Malawi, despite many warnings by local specialists that the donors were actually making the situation worse.[26] And even with the new subsidy policies, years of privatization, combined with changing climate patterns and new competitors for coffee, tea, and tobacco, weakened the country's economy and led to far greater fluctuations in unemployment than that in the 1960s, 1970s, or 1980s. As the economy stalled and hunger grew, further worsening the HIV/AIDS situation in the country, many Malawians began to wonder whether democracy, which had been promoted as part of the new economic model, was not also to blame.

4

It's the Economy, Stupid:

The Consensus Fails

B Y THE EARLY 2000s, outside donors and many fourth wave nations like Malawi had little to show for the linking of rapid economic and political liberalization. The tough reforms of democracy and the tough reforms of market capitalism supposedly went hand in hand. Together, they would bring freedom of speech and free elections but also growth, which would trickle down to working class men and women. But in reality, the correlation, or lack thereof, between democracy and economic growth has been the subject of many studies, which have yielded inconclusive results. Harvard economist Dani Rodrik has examined a wide range of case studies and concluded that democracies historically neither outperform nor underperform dictatorships in promoting economic growth.[1]

Rodrik's finding is supported by most other macroscopic literature studies, though other researchers, like the American Enterprise Institute's Kevin Hassett, have found short-term advantages for dictatorships.[2] Another recent comprehensive study analyzed countries that shifted from dictatorship to democracy, and vice versa. It found that the average rate of GDP growth for the dictatorships was 4.37 percent a year and the average rate for the democracies was 4.49 percent—virtually no difference.[3]

Authoritarian regimes can offer some advantages for growth if the leadership, such as Lee Kuan Yew in Singapore or Augusto Pinochet in Chile, pursues consistent and wise economic policies: dictatorships tend to suffer less political instability, allowing authoritarian regimes to pursue more farsighted economic policies without being captured by the political process. These policies can also impose more hardship on more people, since they do not have to survive the test of elections—think of China's willingness to implement infrastructure projects that force people to move, a far harder feat in democratic India, where every new infrastructure project requires significant political negotiation.

Democracies, meanwhile, offer other advantages: They can create more rule-based economies and can offer investors and local businesspeople more outlets to pursue grievances, including outlets that are less opaque and easier for foreign companies to navigate. Of course, some authoritarian states, such as Pinochet's Chile, or even today's China, have welcomed foreign investment and have created a relatively hospitable environment for it, but overall democracies tend to provide the rules-based environment that facilitates investment. Several studies also have suggested that democracy tends to reduce population growth, since democratic governments invest more in public education, thereby boosting women's earning potential by giving them access to a greater range of jobs, expanding the country's potential workforce, and also likely helping bring down high fertility rates since women's growing education tends to be linked with declines in population growth. Still, as Rodrik found, it can be difficult to trace economic success to any clear policies adopted by a government.[4]

Some states in the third and fourth waves of democratization did prosper after opening up their political systems, but many of these countries— including Taiwan, South Korea, and Chile—already had been succeeding under authoritarian rule, and so continued economic growth did not help much in selling the public on the merits of democracy. In other new democracies, the 1990s did become an era of decent growth—overall, Latin America grew by just over 3 percent annually during the decade, and Africa grew by 2.2 percent—but these modest gains were not enough to make up for the enormous losses suffered in the 1980s, especially with high fertility rates resulting in more and more young people entering the job market. And, in Africa and parts of Asia, increased government and private sector revenues quickly were consumed by the costs of a spiraling HIV/AIDS crisis, which had not abated well into the 2000s.[5]

By the end of the 1990s, financial crises in Russia, Argentina, and East Asia reversed many economic gains made earlier in the decade by young democracies; overall, the Washington Consensus failed to deliver on many of its promises of higher growth, or it produced growth that still did not make significant inroads into unemployment in the developing world. In fact, growth overall was lower in the developing world in the late 1990s and early 2000s than it had been in the 1950s and 1960s, the postcolonial era of import substitution and protectionism. Russia's GDP shrank in 1998, as did that of the Philippines and Malaysia; Argentina's GDP shrank in 1999 and 2000; Thailand, where the Asian financial crisis began with attacks on the Thai currency in May 1997, suffered huge economic reversals as well. Latin America and sub-Saharan Africa began to grow somewhat more strongly in the late 2000s, but again much of this growth wound up being absorbed by rising costs for pandemic disease—particularly HIV, which hit working class men and women hard—spiraling prices for essential items, and declining terms of trade for many primary commodities produced in the poorer fourth wave nations, which faced many nontariff barriers from Europe, the United States, and other wealthy nations. Sub-Saharan nations like Zambia, Mozambique, Malawi, and many others saw the economic gains they had made further diminished.

When another global economic crisis hit in the late 2000s, many of these fourth wave nations would be battered again, while the privatizations of the 1990s and early 2000s had left states with fewer resources to absorb this latest economic downturn through large-scale social welfare programs or job creation schemes. In Central and Eastern Europe, growth averaged a solid 4–5 percent between 2003 and 2007, these nations were then decimated by the global economic crisis. In the fourth quarter of 2009, the height of the crisis in Latvia, the country's economy shrunk by over 10 percent year-on-year, and unemployment rose to over 20 percent. In neighboring Estonia, the economy contracted by 9 percent year-on-year in the fourth quarter of 2009 alone. Asia's developing nations, many of which were highly dependent on exports to the West, suffered too: Singapore's economy contracted by nearly 20 percent in the first quarter of 2009, in the wake of the global economic crisis, with Malaysia, Thailand, Bangladesh, Cambodia, and the Philippines hit hard as well.

Meanwhile, in many of these fourth wave countries, radical economic restructuring in systems that still had not developed strong rules of law often resulted in old regime insiders morphing into flashy new oligarchs controlling former state companies. This was particularly true among former Soviet states, where the rapid economic liberalization frequently led to the stripping of state assets and other dubious types of privatization. In Russia, polls showed that the public had an intensely negative view of the oligarchs, the big businessmen who had taken control of state companies in the post-Soviet period, often gaining the assets at fire sale prices. In one study, by the ROMIR polling agency, only 19 percent of Russians held positive views of the oligarchs' actions in the 1990s, the height of the post-Soviet privatization.[6] In a more telling, and sad, statement, a Pew Research poll of many of the former Soviet and Eastern bloc states taken to coincide with the twentieth anniversary of the fall of the Berlin Wall found that, "in many nations, majorities or pluralities say that most people were better off under communism." Other studies by the New Europe Barometer survey group found rising levels of dissatisfaction with government in most former Eastern bloc states in the two decades after the fall of the Berlin Wall, often because of dissatisfaction with their governments' economic performance, a dissatisfaction that would, for many, reflect poorly on democracy as a political system.[7]

Even when the democratic era produced decent growth, various factors—rising inequality in a more globalized world, a decrease in state social welfare policies in most nations, disease, urbanization, environmental degradation, migration, and other changes wrought by the pace of modernization—often made working class men and women's lives harder, in some ways, than they had been during earlier years of authoritarian rule. Overall, the United Nations Human Development Program reports, the 2000s witnessed rising income inequality in nearly every developing nation. As a result, perceptions that the standard of living was declining—or, at least, that it was not keeping pace in countries that were becoming more unequal—often mattered more than the actual facts of a particular nation's economic growth or decline. "A crucial paradox—that of growth without prosperity—besets Africa's new democracies," writes Peter Lewis of Johns Hopkins University. Macroeconomic reforms instituted by governments in Africa, Latin America, and parts of Central Asia, did deliver stronger economic fundamentals and higher growth. Yet except in a few rare exceptions like Brazil, which combined macroeconomic stabilization with an innovative cash transfer antipoverty program, in most of these developing nations growth seemed to mean little to the lives of average citizens, and governments also cut social welfare programs that, in the 1970s and 1980s, had helped prevent hunger and homelessness.[8] In Ghana, Kenya, Nigeria, South Africa, and Tanzania, Lewis concluded, indicators of public well-being—such as a rising incomes, decreasing infant mortality, or home buying—lagged in the 1990s behind strong overall economic performance in all of these new democracies. And though politicians often expected that citizens would "evaluate political and economic 'goods' separately," in Lewis's words, as we have seen this did not happen—with such high expectations, many citizens of developing nations judged the two "goods" together, and increasingly concluded that if democracy could not deliver economic performance *and* public well-being, its strengths had been greatly oversold.

Expectations seemed to matter enormously in Central and Eastern Europe as well. The European Bank for Reconstruction and Development's (EBRD) survey of the region in 2011 found that the economic crisis battering Europe in the late 2000s and early 2010s led to a decrease in support for democracy among much of Central and Eastern Europe. Many households, it found, had linked markets and democracy, and blamed the two for the decrease in their living standards. But the EBRD also found that people living in countries that had experienced previous serious downturns, and that seemed to have lowered expectations for the relationship between democracy and growth, were less dissatisfied with the downturn of the late 2000s and early 2010s, and tended to remain stronger supporters of both democracy and free market systems.[9] In other words, if they had not linked the "goods" of democracy and markets together so explicitly, they were less likely to condemn democracy when the economy soured.

In Malawi, the 2000s contained several years of solid growth, at least according to year-end economic figures. In 2005, Malawi grew by over 4 percent; two years later, it grew by over 8 percent. These figures suggested that the country actually was becoming one of the stronger economic performers in Africa.

But few working class Malawians felt they had benefited much from this growth; almost to a person, they complained that their standard of living had declined, whether or not the national economic growth figures showed such a decline. And few understood that, whether Malawi liked it or not, its government could not, in a globalizing world, keep the economy closed and provide the type of social welfare it had delivered in the 1960s or 1970s. Back then, Malawi, willing to defy other black-run newly independent nations, had benefited from the largesse of apartheid South Africa, had a much smaller population, and had enjoyed high world prices for its tobacco and coffee. Now, working class men and women saw that economic liberalization had undercut the prices for their maize, tea, and tobacco, and political liberalization had allowed more freedom of movement in the 1990s and 2000s from farms to urban areas. This movement was resulting in intensive crowding in Blantyre and other cities, where all land was being torn up by squatters arriving every day, trucks choked the sky with unfiltered diesel gas, and new roads and truck routes linking Malawi to the rest of Africa contributed to the spread of HIV, which killed brothers, fathers, mothers—nearly every Malawian personally knew someone who had died from an AIDS-caused illness. The Malawian government, which had portrayed itself as a paternalistic, caring father during Banda's time, could do little for most of these suffering people. "The government has no resources to take care of people, with all the problems that are coming up," said Peter Kazembe, a well-known and outspoken Malawian doctor who worked at times for government agencies. "We are more open [in politics] but that doesn't mean we are able to deal with all these new, modern problems. . . . But people can talk more than in the past [than under the dictatorship] so maybe it also seems like there are more problems."

A country with very little economic inequality during the 1960s and 1970s now had become more unequal, and the inequality far more visible than in the past, when the country had been a primarily rural society, and foreign consumer goods had been difficult to obtain. Imported cars, cell phones, computers, and other items were coming in from South Africa and put on display to average Malawians in a way they had not been during the 1960s or 1970s—but few could afford these new luxuries. Outside one computer and electronics store on a main street in Blantyre, young boys dressed in rags peered into the windows, where inside a tiny group of wealthy Indians and Malawians pored over torn-apart keyboards, wireless mice, and motherboards. Across town, at the upscale Blantyre restaurant Greens, a favorite watering hole nestled in the hills above the city, obese businessmen and local officials, their bellies hanging over the waists of their too-tight polyester slacks, ate skewers of lamb and chicken and other grilled meats dripping with fat, and washed them down with South African wines. Later in the evening, their drivers would shuttle them, in Range Rovers, over to the South African–owned Protea Ryalls Hotel, where they could sip scotch at the long bar or lounge on pillows on the terrace outside. Meanwhile, as birthrates soared and HIV decimated families in the early 2000s, the United Nations estimated that roughly 65,000 Malawian children were malnourished, more than 10 percent of the country's children. These hungry children gathered outside the Ryalls Hotel or the upscale South African–owned Shop Rite supermarket on the outskirts of town, where the sons and daughters of wealthy Malawians stocked up on cell phone cards and low-fat yogurt imported from South Africa, as well as on other items they could now see advertised on satellite TV stations airing shows from South Africa, films from Nigeria, and other programming that never would have been available during the dictatorship. Outside the supermarket, guards wielding truncheons shooed away the children.

Perhaps, Malawians remembered, the era of authoritarian rule had been politically harsh, but at least they had enjoyed stability and a decent quality of life—regular meals, land to farm, government handouts for the very poorest. Of course, part of the past quality of life simply had to do with a smaller population, and thus more arable land—something that was hardly related to the type of government running Malawi. Part of this memory was simply a willful forgetting of the past: as years separated them further from the era of the dictatorship, many Malawians forgot its most repressive elements. They remembered instead—somewhat oversympathetically—a simpler time, in the way that people all over the world often romanticize the past. "It might have been more repressive, but at least under [former dictator Hastings] Banda we always had enough to eat, and the country was safe," one Malawian official said, a sentiment echoed by many of his peers who actually once fought the dictatorship as opposition activists.

Numbers revealed this shift in attitudes toward Banda's dictatorship, especially among the poorest Malawians, who believed they had fared the worst as the country had become more open, and also more unequal. Indeed, in the 1980s, when Malawi was still ruled by Banda, more than 80 percent of Malawians rejected the idea of authoritarian rule, though they were still living under it. By 2005, that number had fallen dramatically: only about half the population rejected the idea of authoritarian rule as the best solution for the country.

When asked why they had become willing, again, to consider the possibility of authoritarian rule, many Malawians said, like the government official, simply, that under Banda the country had enjoyed more stable and prosperous growth. This was not necessarily true: During Banda's time, GDP growth fluctuated from over 13 percent in the mid-1960s, in the early days of independence, to as little as roughly 1 percent annually in the early and mid-1980s. After independence Banda, like many other postcolonial leaders, pursued a policy of import substitution designed to make Malawi self-sufficient in many industries. Banda's policy worked, for a time, but in the 1970s and early 1980s, as it became clear that Malawi could not indefinitely protect its industries, and as the price of oil and other inputs rose, Malawi's economy weakened. Still, the smaller population at that time, and the lack of environmental degradation, meant that even the poorest Malawians usually had some family land to farm, and could raise a few chickens for eggs, or some fruit trees. In a less globalized world, without donor agencies pushing for privatization, and with significant aid flowing in from South Africa, which built the country an entire new capital in the town of Lilongwe, Banda could afford to cushion any economic downturns with job creation programs or price supports for farmers' crops.

Whatever the reality, Banda, like many leaders in the developing world in the 1960s, 1970s, and 1980s, also had not tied growth as closely to his political legitimacy as would later occur with the wave of Malawian democratic politicians who emerged in the late 1990s and early 2000s, or with the donors who funded the country's budgets. Like many other postcolonial leaders, Banda, unlike his successors, also could rely on his credentials as an independence leader to build popular support for himself. He created a kind of new Malawian nationalism, albeit one closely centered around him and a fabricated new Malawian national culture, one that might tie together the country's language groups, tribes, and regional differences. In this way, Banda's efforts echoed those of many other postcolonial leaders, from Ghana's Kwame Nkrumah to India's Jawaharlal Nehru, who could use their history as independence campaigners, as well as their political ideologies, to shore up their government's legitimacy. Some postindependence leaders, such as Zimbabwe's Robert Mugabe, were able to utilize the legitimacy they obtained from fighting the colonists to remain in power even as they ran their nations' economies into the ground.

In the 1990s and 2000s, Banda's democratic successors could not call upon their credentials as independence heroes, and in a far less ideological era than the 1960s, they could hardly fashion grand political ideologies designed to remake the country. So, they did make the explicit link between growth and their political system, over and over again, and thus rested much of their legitimacy on the ability to deliver that growth. "Malawians thought that these types of changes would raise their standard of living, so it was these higher expectations that couldn't be lived up to," said Stephen Carr, the longtime World Bank economist who lives in Malawi. Even if, in reality, the democratic era had produced decent growth, high expectations had gone unmet. And so, many working class Malawians wondered whether political openness really was best for their country, a question that would be repeated increasingly among people in other fourth wave nations.

In the early 2010s, Malawi's leaders seemed to draw on this authoritarian nostalgia. President Mutharika, who had been elected as a reformer, turned increasingly authoritarian, sometimes justifying his more autocratic rule by claiming he needed more power to right the economy. When demonstrators gathered in July 2011 to protest in the streets of the capital, Lilongwe, and in other cities about the rising cost of staple foods and fuel, Mutharika had hundreds of them arrested, with many badly beaten and reportedly shot by security forces. At least eighteen people were killed in the crackdown. The government banned broadcasters from showing the protests, and after the crackdown Mutharika toured the affected cities and vowed that any future opponents would feel the "wrath of government." Although many Malawians protested this crackdown, particularly in urban areas, Mutharika seemed to believe—with some reason—that if he could get the country's economy under control, while amassing more power for himself, many people would forgive his abuses. Though ultimately Mutharika died in the spring of 2012, the autocratic culture he had instilled survived, as his supporters at first refused to acknowledge his death publicly, apparently hoping to launch a coup or some other intervention that would prevent the vice president, not known as a Mutharika loyalist, from succeeding him in office as president.

Across the developing world, when economies did not take off, the sales pitch of the Washington Consensus worked in reverse, actually subverting democratic progress. The failure of growth fell hardest on working class men and women, who often were barely getting by under the old authoritarian regime, and who did not have the skills, education, and capital to take advantage of international trade and economic liberalization. Often, as in Malawi, the working classes were employed almost solely in agriculture, and so were also hurt badly by declining terms of global trade for developing nations' textiles, commodities, and other products, as Western nations used tariffs and subsidies to support their own farmers, and to keep out cheaper agricultural goods from places like Africa, Vietnam, or Thailand.

These working class men and women began associating economic failures with democracy, even though economic globalization, changing terms of international trade, or many other factors also could explain weak growth in the developing world. To be sure, middle classes and elites also were unhappy with weak growth, but they could more easily take advantage of economic liberalization and freer trade, and they tended to reap whatever economic gains were made in developing nations. Over the past decade they would turn against democracy for other reasons.

For working classes, though, the failure of growth, or at least the failure to live up to the kind of expectations created in Malawi, was critical. In Latin America, for example, the Latin Barometer surveys showed that, in the early 2000s, support for democracy across the region closely tracked per capita growth; when regionwide growth went up, support for democracy rose, and when it declined, support for democracy did as well, particularly among lower-income men and women.[10] In Ukraine, one of the most notable examples of this working class alienation, the country's economy shrank by a staggering 15 percent in 2009, the victim of the global economic crisis as well as the poor national leadership by Viktor Yushchenko, the hero of the country's 2004 and 2005 Orange Revolution. By the end of his term, in 2010, Yushchenko was, according to polls, the most unpopular leader in the world, in large part because Ukrainians were immensely dissatisfied with how poorly he—and Ukraine's democracy—had done in fostering growth.[11] The urban middle classes of Kiev still generally supported Yushchenko and other Orange Revolution leaders, despite the tepid growth; they were still faring relatively well economically. But among lower-income Ukrainians Yushchenko had essentially become a pariah. In 2010, Ukraine would elect a new president, Viktor Yanukovych, who would roll back many of the nation's freedoms. But he seemed, to many Ukrainians, a better bet for promoting lasting growth, a figure modeled on Vladimir Putin, who had slowly whittled away Russians' political and social freedoms in the 2000s while presiding over a period of strong growth. On the campaign trail, Yanukovych promised that he would bring Ukraine stability and sustained growth, the kind of growth that the previous, more democratic government had failed to provide. He did not exactly hide his political intentions. Kremlin aides advised Yanukovych's campaign. Many Ukrainians understood that, if Yanukovych were elected, their country would both move closer to Russia and also probably see its political freedoms curtailed—a tradeoff that, by voting Yanukovych into office, many accepted in exchange for what they believed would be stronger economic growth. Indeed, after Yanukovych won he was able to negotiate more favorable terms on energy imports from Russia.

In fact, by analyzing a range of surveys from the Barometer series, results of local polling organizations in developing nations, and the Pew Research organization's regular results, Council on Foreign Relations researchers, including myself, found that nearly every study of developing nations reported that, by the end of the 2000s, satisfaction with democracy had dropped, even in countries where citizens still preferred democracy to other alternatives; they also found that in most of these countries the majority of survey respondents, and particularly those from lower-income households, thought that transitions to democracy had brought no improvement to their lives.

In Africa, where foreign donors probably exert the most influence, and the link of growth and political liberalization was pushed the hardest, satisfaction with democracy also dropped in large part because of perceptions that democracy had not brought promised material gains. In a broad study of African nations taken between 2000 and 2006, satisfaction with democracy fell from 58 percent of the population to 45 percent; over roughly the same period, the percentage of Africans saying the economy in their nation was fairly good or very good fell to only 28 percent.[12] Overall, my analysis of the 2009 data from the Afrobarometer surveys, the most recent data, reveals that satisfaction with democracy is negatively correlated with "present living conditions." In these surveys, people who thought their living conditions had become "very bad" were most likely to say that their nation was not becoming a democracy and that they were unsatisfied, while those people who said that their living conditions had become "very good" were much more likely than anyone else to say that they were "very satisfied" with democracy.[13] As we will see, just as in Ukraine, this dissatisfaction would provide an opportunity, in many of these developing nations, for a more authoritarian leader who could promise better, more equal growth, to make inroads.

5
The Middle Class Revolts

IN THE LATE 1990S AND EARLY 2000S, the lack of economic growth began to sour working class men and women on democratization. But in many developing nations the middle classes turned against democracy too. The Washington Consensus prescriptions had been, in many ways, predicated on the modernization theory of experts like Huntington and Lipset; for economic liberalization to be linked with political liberalization, an economic opening had to produce a middle class that then would help push for political change. Yet over the past decade, the middle class has, in many developing nations, subverted those predictions, just as the growth–political change linkage has, more broadly, subverted democratic progress.

Perhaps nowhere has the middle class turned so clearly, and disastrously, against the modernization theory's predictions as in the Philippines. To a traveler arriving from more orderly cities in East Asia, dropping into Manila feels like descending into some combination of *Blade Runner* and a Broadway musical. Rutted roads lead into the city, many lined with twisted pieces of discarded metal that could be confused with modernist sculptures. "Jeepneys"—converted jeeps overstuffed with paying passengers and decorated with garish murals of Christ—crowd each other in the traffic, which stretches for miles in the polluted and soupy air. The jeepneys meander past mountainous garbage dumps and hastily erected slums of tin shacks and tiny wood homes that look like they were made from packing crates. Occasionally, amid the slums sits a heavily guarded gated community where Manila's elites can live as if they were in suburban Los Angeles or Houston, ignoring the squalor as they head off to shop at nearby air-conditioned malls.

With turbocharged economies surrounding it, the Philippines has in recent years grown at only 3 or 4 percent per year, a rate not high enough to provide jobs for all the new workers in a country with one of the highest birthrates in Asia.[1] In a country naturally blessed with abundant fish and produce, nearly 15 percent of Filipinos do not have enough to eat. Virtually every other nation in the region has made strides in eradicating poverty and hunger, but the Philippines has made none.[2]

Most Filipinos would not have anticipated this failure back in 1986, when they thronged the streets of Manila not only to force out the dictator Ferdinand Marcos but to demand a better life for themselves and their countrymen—a protest led, as we have seen, by the city's urban middle classes. Benigno Aquino, the opposition leader whose assassination by Marcos security forces set off the People Power movement that carried Aquino's wife to power, had made "The Filipino is worth dying for" his motto.[3] Amid the jubilation of that era, many Filipinos, and particularly the urban middle classes who possessed skills and college educations, thought that with Marcos gone, all aspects of their lives would improve. "The optimism of that time, it's hard to imagine now," remembered Roel Landingin, a Filipino journalist who has worked for years in Manila. "It wasn't just getting rid of Marcos, we really thought those things that seemed unchangeable in the country would change now."[4]

After Marcos fled, and after his successor, Corazon Aquino, survived numerous coups as president, the country did enjoy solid growth and relatively stable government under her successor, President Fidel Ramos—growth that generally boosted the incomes of middle class professionals and small businesspeople. But in the decade and a half since Ramos left office, the economy has stagnated badly. Though the Philippines always had been a stratified society—a legacy of Latin America–Spanish colonialism—in the post-Ramos era the inequality has become far worse, with a tiny elite garnering an ever-larger share of the wealth, and both the poor and the middle class falling further and further behind. Homelessness and violent crime have skyrocketed, turning Manila into one of the most dangerous cities in Asia—a condition made worse by a corrupt and incompetent police force.[5] This crime falls harder on middle class businesspeople, who cannot afford to live in the gated communities of the rich, with their armed guards and high walls topped with barbed wire. One politician after another has succumbed to corruption scandals, and an annual study conducted by the Asia Foundation found that fewer than 20 percent of businesses in the country reported paying their taxes honestly.[6] The speaker of the Philippine House of Representatives undertook a charity drive for the national treasury, asking people to donate to the state budget like it was a Salvation Army fund drive. The Philippine ombudsman's office reports that the country lost $48 billion in revenue in graft over the past twenty years, and companies needing contracts roam the halls of Congress there with envelopes full of cash to stuff into congresspeople's desks. In such a climate, vote rigging becomes the norm: a survey before the 2007 Philippines elections found that nearly 70 percent of voters expected vote buying in the election, and more than half anticipated that the vote counting would involve cheating.[7]

Though Aquino's son, Benigno, was elected in 2010 partly on a mandate to clean up corruption, in office he could do little to halt such entrenched practices. His government filed several high-profile corruption cases, and he made numerous speeches about addressing graft, but payoffs and handouts remained the norm throughout the political system. After only one year in office, Aquino's popularity ratings had fallen, partly because of his failure to fight corruption. The head of one of the country's biggest business groups dedicated to good governance admitted, "[The Aquino] administration has failed in its fight against corruption."[8]

For years, leaders of the Philippines' neighbor Singapore, essentially a one-party state, have publicly contrasted Manila's chaos and stagnant growth with their gleaming, high-tech city, where every roadside shrub seems to have been manicured by a gardening master, and you can whiz from the airport to the central business district in minutes. The difference is more than superficial. Though the two countries had relatively equal standards of living in 1965, today Singapore boasts a GDP per capita more than ten times that of the Philippines.[9] In a speech in the Philippines in 1992, Lee Kuan Yew, modern Singapore's founding father, delivered a direct insult to the host country. "I do not believe that democracy necessarily leads to development. . . . The exuberance of democracy leads to undisciplined and disorderly conditions."

Lee did offer a backhanded compliment: "The Philippines is immensely better off compared to Afghanistan or Lebanon or Sri Lanka"—three states
decimated by bloody civil wars.[10]

For years, many middle class Filipinos, proud of their hard-won democracy and their free—if wild—media, shrugged off Lee Kuan Yew's
barbs. But as the divide between the two states has turned into a chasm,
and as more and more Filipinos head overseas just to find jobs—more than
10 percent of the population lived abroad in 2009, and their remittances
keep the country's economy afloat—they can't ignore the criticism so easily.[11] In surveys taken by the Asia Barometer project, which primarily interviews urban middle class men and women, nearly half of the respondents
in the Philippines now agree with the statement "The nation is run by a
powerful few and ordinary citizens cannot do much about it." Most Filipinos, the survey showed, distrust virtually every institution of the state and
have little hope that it will improve.[12] "Middle-class Filipinos who've been
outside the country, who see what's happening in other nations in Asia,
they come back here, and it's just disappointment, hopelessness," says Landingin. "We have too much democracy here," agreed Jose Romero Jr., a former Philippine diplomat who, along with other educated Filipinos, had led
the revolt against Marcos.

Some middle class Filipinos even yearn for the return of the dictator,
seemingly having forgotten the thuggery and personality cult of the dictator's later years and instead remembering the order and growth of his early
period in office. According to the Asia Barometer study, the Filipino public
had a high degree of "authoritarian nostalgia" for the Marcos era.[13] The old
dictator is still around, but he doesn't get out much: His waxy body is displayed in a refrigerated mausoleum, like a Southeast Asian Lenin, in the
family compound in Ilocos Norte, the Marcos's home province. Still, even
though Ferdinand cannot serve anymore, in 2010 Filipinos elected his son,
Ferdinand Jr., to the Philippines Senate, and his daughter, Imee, as governor of Ilocos Norte.[14] Ferdinand Jr. might well seek a higher office in the
next election, completing the Marcos restoration.[15]

The Philippines middle class has, in another important way, demonstrated its growing disillusionment with the lack of growth and the inequality, graft, and poor governance of the country's young democracy. In 1998,

after the end of Fidel Ramos's presidency (Philippine presidents are allowed only one six-year term), the presidential election was won by Joseph Estrada, an actor-turned-politician famous for his many roles playing action heroes. Estrada was beloved by the poor in the Philippines for his rugged charm, his easy, down-to-earth manner, and his promises of populist policies, but he was hardly a deep thinker, and in office he soon proved both incompetent and corrupt. His administration squandered many of the economic and management reforms made under Ramos, foreign investors fled to other countries, and graft allegations soon swirled around his administration and around Estrada himself, who was known to be personally friendly with several organized crime leaders. By 2001, three years into his presidency, the Philippine deficit had nearly doubled since 1998, and Estrada stood accused of taking payoffs from illegal gambling syndicates while serving as president. (After leaving office, he would later be convicted of plunder and sentenced to a maximum of forty years in jail, though he was ultimately pardoned after serving six years in detention because of his age and infirmities.)

Urban middle class Filipinos, many of whom had not voted for Estrada, instead supporting other candidates, could have stuck to democratic means to try to remove the president for his many alleged crimes. Indeed, the Philippines legislature did begin impeachment proceedings against Estrada. But middle class Filipinos had little patience for them. They had watched, during Estrada's term, as the country's democracy produced an incompetent and corrupt president. They had seen how Estrada could maintain support from the poor masses who constitute the majority of voters, and they worried he might whittle away both the rule of law and the economic, social, and political privileges long enjoyed by the middle class. True to his macho film image, Estrada had pursued increasingly tough policies, toward both dissent in urban areas and separatist movements in the country's Muslim southern provinces, launching a massive offensive against one of the Muslim rebel groups, the Moro Islamic Liberation Front, that ultimately resulted in a bloody stalemate.

So, in late 2000 and early 2001, middle class Filipinos took to the streets of Manila, launching large scale street protests designed to push Estrada out. In some ways, these protests mimicked the 1986 People Power movement that ultimately overthrew the Marcos regime. Many Filipinos took to calling the 2001 protests "People Power Two," except that now the demonstrators were trying to remove an elected president, by resorting to the street, a practice that ultimately would only weaken the country's democratic institutions like the legislature and the judiciary, which had been designed to address just such serious breaches by the president.

As protests swelled in the streets of Manila, hundreds of thousands of people, mainly middle class, university-educated Filipinos, joined in. Many demonstrators, who once had battled Marcos's armed forces for years, and who had stood up for Corazon Aquino in the face of coups, now called for the military to resolve the situation. And indeed, behind the scenes the armed forces made clear to Estrada that they were withdrawing their support for him, implicitly threatening that, if he did not leave, the army would make a move. Estrada's supporters, later learning of the army's decision, called it a kind of silent coup, but at the time the president realized that he could not hang on to power. He agreed to vacate the presidency. His vice president, Gloria Macapagal-Arroyo, a U.S.-trained economist and technocrat preferred (at the time) by the middle classes, quickly was sworn into office, before Estrada's large base of poor supporters around the country could mobilize in response.

Though the anti-Estrada protests did force the president to flee, sparking a short period of jubilation in Manila, they hardly quieted the Filipino middle class's anger over incompetent and corrupt government, or its fear of losing its rights and privileges to a populist president. Three years later, middle class men and women camped in the streets of Manila once more, trying again to use protests—rather than democratic institutions like the ballot box or legislative maneuvering or impeachment—to force the president to leave office. Though Macapagal-Arroyo once had seemed a competent technocrat, she too had earned the ire of the urban middle class after she allegedly had overseen highly corrupt national elections and increasingly had cracked down on any opposition, proposing tougher legislation akin to martial law and arresting many civil society activists. After Iraq the Philippines became, under Arroyo, the second most dangerous place in the world for journalists; in some years more than thirty were killed, in murky circumstances in which the murders seemed to be linked to the journalists' critical reporting.[16]

Unlike Estrada, the savvier and smarter Macapagal-Arroyo survived, partly through maintaining the support of the army, but she was not yet safe. Filipino middle classes returned to the streets again and again in the following years in attempts to make her resign or even possibly provoke a coup. Even Corazon Aquino herself, the old symbol of Filipino democracy, joined the protesters trying to oust Macapagal-Arroyo, marching in the streets to push out the president.

In some areas of the city these protesters became a kind of permanent encampment, though the president would manage to serve out her term. "The people in Manila are just giving up on democracy, that's why they take to the streets to try to force out an elected leader," said Landingin, the longtime Filipino journalist who had covered People Power One as well. "It seems like a democratic protest, but it's actually hurting."[17] And as we will see, in many other developing nations, middle class men and women are turning against democracy in similar ways, striking perhaps the biggest blow to democracy's survival.

In the Philippines, it took fifteen years for the urban middle class to move from leading the country's battle *for* democracy to leading the battle *against* democracy. In other developing nations, across Asia, Latin America, and Africa, the shift has taken place even faster, as Huntington's theory has been turned on its head. Now it appears that once that political transition began, a sizable middle class actually became a primary impediment to democratic consolidation.[18]

If the middle class can no longer be taken for granted as a force for democratic change, it will mark an enormous shift that will challenge the accepted wisdom about democratization. This new understanding of the middle class calls into question predictions that powerful authoritarian states like China will eventually democratize, and forces policy makers and democracy activists to question who their real allies are.

The middle class in emerging markets is still growing rapidly. The World Bank estimates that, between 1990 and 2005, the middle class tripled in size in developing countries in Asia, and nearly doubled in Africa. Today, according to an estimate by Goldman Sachs, roughly seventy million people worldwide begin to earn enough to join the middle class (defined as making between $6,000 and $30,000 annually) in emerging markets each year. By 2030, Goldman estimates, the global middle class will have added another two billion people, with particularly strong growth in Brazil and other large emerging democracies. While $6,000 a year may be a poverty-level income in a wealthy democracy like the United States or Japan, in developing nations like Thailand it puts a family in the middle class. And unlike, say, the United States, where more than 50 percent of adults classify themselves as middle class, the middle class in most developing nations remains a minority—usually no more than 30 percent of the population.[19] Yet in these nations the middle class does not mean the wealthiest elites, either—the top 1 or 2 percent of the population that actually controls the largest companies and enjoys lifestyles that would be considered rich by any standard. Instead, these middle classes normally comprise professionals, small businesspeople, and other educated men and women.

The fact that the middle class does not actually constitute a majority of the population in these nations matters greatly, since it means democratization often empowers the poor more than it empowers the middle class. At the same time, though, the middle class is not so small that democratization threatens to foster intense hatred against it, in the way that analysts like Yale's Amy Chua believe political change can boomerang against wealthy ethnic minorities.[20] Chua argues that entrepreneurial but demographically tiny minorities—the ethnic Chinese in Southeast Asia, or the Lebanese in West Africa—face physical danger, and even massacres, in countries that democratize rapidly. There are examples of this trend, such as the killings of Lebanese in West Africa or of Chinese in Indonesia after the fall of longtime dictator Suharto—but these mass killings have targeted small groups of elite minorities, and not the broader middle classes. Still, in many emerging democracies, the middle classes have valued growth over freedom and stability over change, giving little reason to believe these middle class men and women have any real commitment to democracy.[21]

In theory, educated middle class people in most developing nations possess strong commitments to democracy: recent polling by the Pew Research Center found theoretical support for democracy especially strong among the global middle class.[22] But that theoretical commitment to democracy has meant little in practice.[23] In many developing nations, middle class reformers have been badly let down by the first generations of democratic leaders. Some, like Viktor Yushchenko of Ukraine, have demonstrated woefully poor economic management, alienating not only working classes but also middle class businesspeople who need economic stability to thrive. But besides managing the economy poorly, the first generation of elected leaders has not demonstrated much real commitment to democracy—a lack of commitment that has resonated among urban middle classes. Urban middle class men and women who had spent years fighting an authoritarian regime simply assumed, perhaps naively, that when opposition leaders finally gained power, they would govern more inclusively than the deposed autocrats. The Democratic Progressive Party (DPP) in Taiwan, made up of many former political prisoners from during the Nationalist dictatorship of Chiang Kai-shek and his son Chiang Ching-kuo, had fought for two decades to challenge the power of the ruling Kuomintang. The party also had stood up for Taiwan's separation from, and even formal independence from, the People's Republic of China, in part because it believed that only real separation could guarantee Taiwan's democratic freedoms. Many DPP politicians had deep ties to labor unions, environmental groups, and other progressive causes, and in opposition had suffered badly for their beliefs. DPP leader Chen Shui-bian himself had served time in prison for his beliefs, and in 1985 his wife became paralyzed after being hit by a truck in what Chen and his supporters believed was an attack by progovernment forces.

As Chen rose up the political ladder in an increasingly open and democratic Taiwan, from local councillor to mayor of Taipei to, eventually, president, he brought with him a bright young circle of advisers who had also suffered as opposition activists. These DPP politicians, many educated in America's Ivy League schools, promised, if they were elected, to usher in Taiwan's most open era. They vowed to work for equal rights in a country with a highly patriarchal traditional culture, to reduce inequality after Taiwan's long economic boom, and to guarantee women a certain number of cabinet seats, putting them at the policy-making table in Taiwan for the first time. "The DPP is for progress—on women's issues, on labor rights—it can be slow, but it's far better than it was a decade ago," said Hsiao Bi-khim, one of the DPP's leading minds and, in the early 2000s, one of the youngest members of Taiwan's legislature.

When the DPP finally won the 2000 election, opposition politicians, activists, labor union leaders, and journalists rejoiced. Taiwan's political system seemed to have morphed into a stable two-party democracy, contested between the Kuomintang, no longer a dictatorial regime but a normal political party, and the DPP, which now held the presidency for the first time. Many also believed that having come from political exile, and suffering themselves at the hands of an oppressive government, the DPP would strengthen Taiwan's young democracy. Thousands gathered after the election results were in to hear Chen speak. In the country's first legislative elections after Chen was elected president, a record number of women won seats. The party quickly passed a series of progressive environmental and labor laws.

Several weeks after Chen's victory he was sworn in as president on May 20, 2000. During his inaugural speech he shouted "Long live freedom and democracy!" as if he were still leading a street rally rather than giving a formal address. During the inauguration, DPP activists danced at parties in strongholds in Taipei and the south, its base in the country, while foreign observers, from the *New York Times* editorial board to American diplomats stationed in the country, praised Taiwan's transition as a model of democracy. When Chen traveled to America in spring 2001, he was greeted in New York City and Houston by an outpouring of support from Bush administration officials, and he held meetings with senior American congressmen—even though nearly every previous Taiwanese leader since the U.S. had cut diplomatic ties with the island in 1979 had been treated like pariahs even if they stopped in the United States only to refuel their plane.

In some cases—though not, unfortunately, in Taiwan—longtime opposition leaders who finally gained the presidency or the prime ministership did remember past struggles and made real attempts to foster compromise and tolerance, even toward their old enemies. Nelson Mandela famously reached out to South Africa's white minority as president, not only publicly supporting their beloved rugby team but also retaining senior officials who could reassure white businesspeople and investors. More often, however, the first generation of elected leaders only fueled middle class rage. From Venezuela to Bolivia to Kenya to Thailand to Taiwan, these leaders too often have turned into elected autocrats, dominating young democracies whose institutions are not strong enough to restrain a powerful leader uninterested in compromise, negotiation, and tolerance of opposition. To this first generation, many of whom came of age politically under authoritarian regimes, votes are referendums on their rule; having triumphed, they can then use all the powers of the state to crush opposition and favor their personal, political, and ethnic allies.

In other words, these elected autocrats, though fulfilling one function of democracy—winning the most votes—do not uphold constitutional liberalism, or ensure that the rule of law is maintained and that individual liberties and minority rights are protected. They follow the form of democracy but are weakening its practice.

It is not hard to see why this first generation of elected leaders so often regressed in this way. Holding an opposition movement together in the face of a repressive regime requires a high degree of cohesion, even autocracy, within that movement; serving in opposition for so long also can make a leader intensely fearful. In South Africa during apartheid rule, the African National Congress viciously attacked, and sometimes even killed, members of its own movement whom it perceived as too conciliatory toward the government, or as simply working against the ANC's aims. (Nelson Mandela was in jail on Robben Island during much of this internal bloodletting, but his wife, Winnie, was accused of promoting the beating and murder of ANC members accused of being government informers.)[24] Chen Shui-bian, the Taiwanese DPP leader, exhibited many of the same traits while the DPP was in opposition—tight control of his party and paranoia regarding outsiders. These were survival skills in opposition during the Kuomintang dictatorship, when Chen could never trust whether anyone beyond his intimate circle had been coopted by government agents, but later this course would doom his administration once he gained the presidency and the country had transitioned to democracy.

Like Chen, many former opposition leaders can find it especially difficult to jettison these survival traits when the transition to democracy is extremely rapid, as happened in many African nations in the 1990s. These
circumstances leave little opportunity for former opponents to forgive the
crimes and mistakes of the past. Instead, having finally attained power, leaders who'd seen authoritarian rulers enrich their own tribes, ethnic groups,
families, and supporters would then often use their new power simply to
reward their own—who can justly claim that they were shortchanged under
the previous regime. By comparison, in a more gradual transition, such as in
Spain after the death of Francisco Franco in 1975, conservative and liberal
political opponents had more time to build trust and jointly agree on the
norms and rules that would govern Spanish democracy.

Taking office in 2000, Taiwan's DPP movement soon dashed hopes
that it would usher in an era of greater democracy and freedom on the
island. True to its election promises, the DPP did take a harder line against
China, defending Taiwan's right to govern itself, and to protect its freedoms. (China initially responded harshly but eventually came to a kind of
frosty détente with the DPP leaders.) But on the island itself, Chen Shui-
bian, and a circle of party leaders around him who had developed a siege
mentality in exile, brought their almost authoritarian style to governing in
Taipei. Two years into Chen's term as president, party activists who opposed anything Chen did soon found themselves ostracized, cut off from
circles of power. Some DPP insiders began to murmur that Chen and his
wife were increasingly using the power of his office, which is one of the
strongest presidencies in the world, to direct favors, jobs, and cash to family
members and friends.[25]

Later, Chen's wife would admit to laundering over $2 million from a
government contractor. Chen himself would go to jail on corruption charges,
after allegations that he had personally stolen millions in campaign money
and other government funds. And as we will see later on, Chen and his
wife's corruption were hardly unusual—in Taiwan and in new democracies, graft seems actually to worsen as the political system opens up, at least
at first, further alienating average men and women, and besmirching the
concept of democratic reform.[26]

In the early 2000s, stories of Chen's corruption were only whispers; DPP supporters were far more shocked to witness his insular, domineering style. Many believed that, once in office, Chen would naturally give up some of the secrecy and paranoia that had served him during his time in opposition, but they were wrong. Chen angrily fired aides who refused to carry out his wishes, and he brought family members into his inner political circle— at least eleven family members would face corruption charges similar to those made against the president, and his son would face charges of insider trading. Several senior ministers, including the foreign minister, would resign after charging that Chen's high-handed, self-dealing style had seriously impaired Taiwan's ability to hold on to its few remaining formal allies, and had allowed Taiwan's government to be taken advantage of by unscrupulous middlemen with ties to Chen. "People feel humiliated by the government's incompetence," George Tsai, a political analyst at Chinese Culture University in Taipei, told the *New York Times,* referring to a scandal in which one of the middlemen apparently had taken $30 million in government money. "It's a joke to the outside world—how could the government be cheated like this?"[27] By the mid-2000s, the once-supportive Bush administration, furious with Chen's incompetence and arrogance, simply refused to let him stay overnight in the United States.[28]

In other cases, the first leaders of young democracies come not from long-time opposition movements but from within the former regime, where they also received little education in democratic norms. Nearly every former Soviet republic, for example, transitioned to a government run by former Soviet bureaucrats; few of these leaders, save for a handful from the Baltics and Georgia who'd lived for years in the West, had experience with democracy. For them, politics had always been a zero-sum endeavor. Losers within the Soviet hierarchy lost everything—their power, their prestige, sometimes their lives. Had the transitions been more gradual, this lack of democratic experience might have mattered less; newer, younger leaders with fewer ties to the Soviet era might have emerged, and even old Soviet bureaucrats might have learned that a defeat in the new political system did not send one to the gulags. But in such a rapid transition, the former Soviet bureaucrats simply brought with them the political mindsets and strategies that had served them well in the Soviet Union.

Throughout the former Soviet Union, nearly everywhere except the Baltics, the first generation of elected leaders has revealed itself to be autocrats at heart. Kurmanbek Bakiyev, who was one of the leaders of Kyrgyzstan's 2005 Tulip Revolution against the autocratic regime of President Askar Akayev, proved himself in office to be nearly as authoritarian as his predecessor, and his tough policies ultimately sparked another bloody revolution in 2010. In Georgia, Mikheil Saakashvili was also a leader of a color revolution. But as president in 2007, faced with demonstrations against him, Saakashvili unleashed overwhelming force against the protesters and later declared a state of emergency, allowing him to close down media outlets, detain opposition journalists, and silence much of the protest.[29] Today he appears likely, after ending his term-limited presidency in 2012, to try to run for the prime ministership, and make parliament the center of his power, much as Vladimir Putin shifted from president to prime minister but remained the most important actor in Russian politics. And now, in the Middle East, a similar pattern is emerging, with many leaders of transitional governments and, possibly, future parliaments, coming from within systems that for decades allowed no dissent, and where winner-take-all internal politics were the norm.

Beyond the shock and anger that elected politicians are undermining reforms and ignoring the rule of law, many members of the middle class have begun to grasp democracy's downside: If the franchise is extended to everyone, and if the poor, who make up the majority of the population in most developing nations, band together behind one candidate, they could elect someone determined to reduce the economic, political, and social privileges enjoyed by the middle class.

Hugo Chavez, the charismatic Venezuelan military officer, certainly grasped the notion that, with the support of the poor, a politician could gain immense power in a developing nation. Born to a working class family himself, Chavez seems from an early age to have developed a deep distaste for Venezuela's traditional capitalists, the large landowning families and businessmen of Caracas. Chavez went into the army partly, it seems, as a means of rising up into politics. As a young soldier, he traveled through Caracas and witnessed the severe poverty of the city's slums—the country was, at that time, one of the most unequal in the world. It made a profound impact on Chavez. Early in his career, he founded a group called the Revolutionary Bolivarian Movement-200, which aimed to topple the country's traditional politics, which were nominally democratic but also dominated by powerful business interests and traditionally rich families.

In 1992, as Venezuela's ruling party implemented painful neoliberal reforms pushed by donors, including cuts in social welfare spending, Chavez tried to seize power in a coup. His putsch failed and he was sentenced to jail, but he had gained nationwide fame as a man willing to stand up to neoliberal reforms. Following his jail term, Chavez launched his own political party, and in 1998, riding massive support from the poor, who had fared poorly as Venezuela had pursued the Washington Consensus reforms, he was elected president.

Though Venezuela, like many Latin countries, had long been dominated by politicians from a few powerful families, in 1998 the country did boast strong democratic institutions and culture, including an independent judiciary, a vibrant print and broadcast media, and a healthy tradition of political debate.[30]

Chavez would change that. He soon set about advocating for the interests of the poor and the lower middle classes against the interests of the urban middle classes and the elite, while also amassing more and more power to himself and a close circle of allies. Chavez nationalized many key industries, with private businesspeople often getting what they perceived as unfair compensation for their assets. He launched a program called "Plan Bolivar," in which the state would help upgrade the physical infrastructure of poor areas, while also providing highly subsidized health care and food, and cheap credit to the poor to start up community projects around the country. He launched communal councils, an experiment in direct democracy that, in many poor neighborhoods of the country, gave the poor a greater voice in policy making, though these council also undermined legislators in parliament.[31] While announcing these policies, he clearly positioned them as tools for the poor and as attacks on the middle and upper classes, often during rambling addresses on his popular weekly radio show, *Alo Presidente* (*Hello, President*). Using his powerful, mercurial speaking style to its fullest extent, on his show Chavez repeatedly fulminated against his favorite targets—local businesspeople, whom he claimed were trying to take over the country, as well as the United States and other Western powers.

The longer Chavez remained in office, the more populist his economic policies became. In 1998 he still retained some more moderate economic advisers, and he traveled to the United States and other countries to advertise that Venezuela was still open for investment, particularly in the oil and gas sector. But by the mid-2000s Chavez had jettisoned most of the advisers who had links to middle class urban businesspeople, and he had thrown out many foreign investors, particularly in the oil sector. Government spending continued to increase, boosting Venezuela's debt, and Chavez handed control of many important companies to a small circle of close friends, making them rich, even as his government's laws, price controls, and economic mismanagement made it tougher and tougher for average small businesspeople to earn a living.

Chavez's policies had a mixed effect. At first, they did help slash poverty significantly, which only further bonded the poor to him, and they also did initially bring more of the poor into the political process, clearly reducing the political power of the middle and upper classes. But they also hurt the overall macroeconomic environment. Foreign investors bailed out of the country, and the national oil company could not meet its production quotas and saw its aging infrastructure deteriorate. Whenever the price of oil, the major export, dropped, Venezuela had trouble providing even basic services to its people. By 2011, even as the price of oil had recovered and its Latin neighbors, including Brazil and Colombia, were growing strongly, Venezuela was limping, posting some of the worst growth rates in South America and relying on loans from China to survive. Electricity blackouts hindered business in the cities, inflation soared, and in many parts of the country staple goods became harder and harder to find. As the economy worsened, violent crime rose, and by 2011 Caracas had the highest murder rate per capita of any city in the world—a staggering 233 per 100,000 inhabitants—higher than the killings per capita in war zones like Kabul and Baghdad.

Many human rights organizations believed that the official figures actually were understated.[32]

Still, Venezuela's poor repaid Chavez with their loyalty, even as he slowly strangled the country's relatively strong democratic institutions. When Chavez toured slums in Caracas and other cities, tens of thousands turned out to greet him like he was a god. He won election after election—united and engaged in politics, the poor by far constitute the majority of Venezuelan voters. Chavez kept offering job creation programs and other populist measures to keep them happy, along with new nationalizations, price controls, and other measures hated by many businesspeople and other professionals.

Toward the middle classes and upper classes, Chavez practiced a harsher style of politics. He used his domination of broadcasting licenses to replace private television stations, which tended to favor the urban middle class opposition candidates, with state TV. Eventually he forced the most critical private channel off the air.[33] He introduced legislation making it a crime for critics to offer "false" information that "harms the interests of the state"; he locked up judges who issued rulings he did not like and packed the courts with his supporters. Chavez and his backers in the National Assembly passed laws that essentially allow Chavez to rule the country by decree, making the Assembly meaningless.[34] By the end of the 2000s, the international monitoring organization Freedom House ranked Venezuela, one of the oldest democracies in Latin America, as only "partly free." In 2010, the Organization of American States (OAS), a regional grouping that included several Latin states with left-leaning governments favorably inclined toward Chavez, issued a report condemning Venezuela for widespread abuses of media freedom, human rights, freedom of association, and other freedoms. "The state's punitive power is being used to intimidate or punish people on account of their political opinions," declared the OAS's human rights watchdog.[35]

Chavez had not totally destroyed the country's freedoms. In the early 2000s, some newspapers and television stations remained in private hands, critical of the president's policies, and if opposition politicians had been able to unite around one platform and one anti-Chavez figure, they might have been able to dislodge Chavez. But instead, many middle class Caracas residents, and middle class politicians, took the easy way out. They launched street demonstrations, general strikes, and marches on the presidential palace starting in 2001 and 2002. Many protesters openly called for the military to intervene and push Chavez, authoritarian but also elected, out of office. During the protests, and the run-up to the military intervention, at least eighteen people were killed.

In April 2002, the armed forces responded, launching a coup and threatening to bomb the presidential palace if Chavez did not step down. When he did, they took Chavez hostage on a Caribbean island. While Chavez was jailed, the coup makers installed a prominent businessman as interim president. The George W. Bush administration seemed to tacitly condone the coup, with press spokesperson Ari Fleischer essentially blaming Chavez for the situation; later the Central Intelligence Agency was discovered to have known that the military was planning a coup against Chavez but did not provide a serious warning about the plot.[36]

Rallying his support among the poor, who massed in the streets of the capital, and within lower ranks of the armed forces, Chavez would prevail. Unable to win much support outside the capital, the coup government collapsed. With the president's backers thronging the streets, he emerged from incarceration some forty-eight hours later at the presidential palace.

From that point on, the Venezuelan leader would only sharpen his attacks on the middle class and elites, further dragging down the country's democracy. But by backing the coup—and then stepping up the number of street protests designed to force Chavez out—his middle class opponents had showed that they cared little for the institutions of democracy, either.

Despite the early euphoria of the Arab uprisings, middle classes in the Middle East appeared to be just as conservative as their peers in East Asia and Latin America. Though many of the groups that helped overthrow Hosni Mubarak's government fear the continuing power of the military, some Egyptian middle class men and women actually have welcomed the army's continued political power. Increasingly they view the armed forces as a check against Islamists and against growing instability, crime, and urban violence, and wonder whether the country might not be better off under another authoritarian regime, at least one less corrupt than the Mubarak regime. Though Cairo historically had been a relatively safe city, after the downfall of Mubarak, and with much of the Egyptian police on strike or simply at home because they are not getting paid, armed robbery, gang warfare, and more petty crime has become common in the city, deterring investment and scaring many businesspeople.[37] Consequently, some liberals have come to support continued military rule even after security forces killed Coptic Christians during the October protests, provoking a wave of anger among Egypt's Christians. Other liberals and some minorities simply have fled the country during the Arab Spring: the *New York Times* reported that the number of Egyptians who successfully obtained passports doubled in the first five months of 2011, compared to the previous year.[38]

Indeed, by the autumn of 2011 many in the Egyptian middle classes seemed to be scared of the prospect of free elections, which, they were convinced, would make the chaos worse, or lead to a victory by the Muslim Brotherhood, as Islamists had triumphed in the first postuprising election in neighboring Tunisia. Some Egyptian middle class men and women even expressed concern that the country's military actually was moving too *quickly* in turning over power and organizing elections before secular, liberal parties could build their strength and seriously compete with the Muslim Brotherhood and other Islamist parties that had built strong organizations underground during the Mubarak era.[39]

Given the wariness of the middle class in Egypt and in other Middle Eastern nations, the Arab uprisings easily could stall before countries even organize regular elections. "There seems little doubt—as protesters tire and as the general public tires of them—in what direction the balance will tilt" in the Arab world, write analysts Robert Malley and Hussein Agha in the *New York Review of Books*.[40] The militaries in these nations have the organization, political experience, and power to dominate any postdictator era, and they will be at the forefront of the Arab experiment, they write. Meanwhile, they note, crowds that once fervently backed the anti-Mubarak, anti-Qadaffi, and anti–Ben Ali protesters have become more equivocal, as Islamists, who have built their parties for decades, have shown themselves to be the most capable organizations in the new political climate as law and order has broken down in places, and as ethnic and tribal divisions flourish. So, to many

Arab middle classes, a military-backed counterrevolution, an antidote to the revolutions of the Arab Spring, does not look like such a bad idea.[41]

As they did in Venezuela, once the middle classes turn against elected leaders, convinced they are actually protecting democracy, they seem willing to use virtually any means to topple presidents and prime ministers. As we saw in the first chapter, nearly half of the military coups launched in the past twenty years either enjoyed middle class support or were openly called for by middle class protesters. This trend shows no sign of waning: as recently as the middle of 2011, Thai urbanites, furious that Thaksin's party had won yet another national election, again were calling on the military to step in and annul the poll. When this did not happen, the middle class anti-Thaksin groups in Thai society relentlessly attacked Thaksin's sister, the prime minister. Even when massive flooding swamped the country in the fall of 2011, submerging many parts of Bangkok and killing hundreds, the Thai military seemed unwilling to cooperate with Thaksin's sister, the new prime minister.[42]

This promilitary sentiment was repeated in 2011 in places as diverse as Mexico, Pakistan, and Syria. In the case of Syria, urban middle classes and religious minorities, like Christians, have continued to back the armed forces and Bashar al-Assad even as the security forces have unleashed a brutal campaign of violence against peaceful protesters in many parts of the country. As we have seen, middle classes and elites in many other Middle Eastern nations also have become more conflicted about whether to continue supporting democratic reform, with many putting their trust once again in the armed forces.[43]

Many of these elected autocrats, from Putin to Chavez to Thaksin, also tend to be savvy politicians, retaining sizable popularity with the majority of their country even as they undermine the rule of law, usually by embarking upon populist policies that help reduce poverty, stirring up nationalism, or some combination of the two. The endurance and survival of these leaders have made urban middle class men and women only angrier, more desperate, and more willing to use extreme tactics, from violent protests to coups, to remove an elected autocrat.

To take one example, in late 2006 and early 2007 Bangladesh's military essentially staged a coup, maneuvering into power an unelected "caretaker" government that then declared a state of emergency and assumed significant powers. During the state of emergency, the government arrested Sheikh Hasina, one of the two powerful women who for years had dominated Bangladeshi electoral politics but who allegedly had been implicated in massive graft and extortion. But eventually the government just dropped its charges against the political leader, who clearly retained enormous popularity among poor Bangladeshis. In the next free election, following the demise of the caretaker government, Sheikh Hasina's party dominated the poll, delighting Bangladesh's poor but infuriating Dhaka's urbanites, many of whom had supported the military intervention.

Even in Taiwan, which, during Chen's rule, was still considered one of the strongest democracies in Asia, middle class activists, many of them veterans of the long struggle against the authoritarian Nationalist regime, began to turn. Increasingly furious at Chen's incompetence, alleged corruption, and crushing of protest, thousands of demonstrators, and then hundreds of thousands, gathered in front of the presidential palace in Taipei in September 2006. They were led by a man named Shih Ming-teh, himself a longtime democracy activist who once had greatly admired Chen, and who had been beaten badly in jail during prison stints under Taiwan's authoritarian rulers. In the mid-1990s, Shih actually had served as chairman of the DPP, Chen's political party. Shih had fought so long against the dictatorship that ruled Taiwan until the 1990s that he enjoyed enormous moral authority among average Taiwanese. As many reporters noted, Shih often was locally referred to as the "Nelson Mandela of Taiwan."[44]

Still, there Shih was, in September 2006, at the front of the crowd, made up primarily of middle class and upper middle class Taipei men and women. Shih led the crowd in chants and catcalls at the mention of the president's name, and in choruses of "Chen Step Down!" before they marched from the palace through the business district. Later, the protesters fanned out into other parts of the city, holding red sparklers—red being their color of anger. In Chen strongholds, they started fighting with his supporters, and eventually crashed several meetings Chen held with foreign officials.

Although Chen had twice won elections, the demonstrators hoped to recall him from his post, a strategy of dubious legality—but one that some protesters had tried earlier, in 2004, holding violent demonstrations in the capital in a previous effort to get Chen to leave. At that time they had faced off against armored troop carriers in front of the palace and taunted the police, daring the officers to attack them. The president was not in residence—he had traveled to his heartland in southern Taiwan to ask his supporters to pray for him and to vow never to step down—but the demonstrators did not relent. Some openly hoped for a repeat of the silent coup that had, in the Philippines, removed Joseph Estrada, though Shih later insisted that he had no desire to provoke a military intervention. Still, during the demonstrations in 2004, and ones held earlier, some 300,000 people calling for Chen's ouster had skirmished with police, leading to battles in front of the presidential palace. Some of those demonstrators carried clubs, steel pipes, bats, and other weapons to the protest, clearly looking to start violence.[45]

This time, in 2006, the protesters promised to turn out a million people in front of the palace, in a rally called "Million People Depose A-Bian" (A-Bian was Chen's nickname). Ultimately, for all their rallies and attacks the demonstrators did not force Chen out despite his popularity ratings, which had fallen below 20 percent. Chen could still call on his support in working class southern Taiwan, and he was savvy enough to evade, prevent, or stop any larger demonstrations. He eventually was indicted and convicted of corruption, in a decision his supporters saw as politically motivated—but the protests only added to the vitriol and distrust in Taiwanese democracy.[46]

To be sure, middle classes have not uniformly turned against democracy. Within many countries still struggling for democracy, middle classes remain the locus of reform movements. To take just two examples among many, in Iran, middle class urbanites form the core of the opposition Green protest against President Mahmoud Ahmadinejad and the authoritarian/clerical regime, while in Burma middle class men and women, including students from Rangoon and Mandalay, have continued to push for democracy as the country begins to change.

But when they do turn against democracy, the middle classes' intervention can prove utterly destructive. By inviting the military back into politics, the middle class potentially undermines civil/military relations for generations and sets the stage for the army to undermine civilian leaders repeatedly, a recurring cycle from Pakistan to Thailand to Venezuela. By legitimizing the use of street demonstrations to oust elected leaders, the middle class delegitimizes elections and other legitimate democratic institutions. This is particularly dangerous when the middle class uses protest to oust an elected leader popular with the majority poor of a country, who themselves now have become more politically engaged and convinced that only street demonstrations, rather than democratic institutions, can work to fight back against the middle classes. In Thailand or Taiwan, Venezuela or Bolivia, the revolt of the middle class has left a bitter divide that is unlikely to be healed anytime soon—the poor, feeling disenfranchised, store up their rage for a future showdown.

Indeed, while working class men and women in many developing nations already have grown disillusioned with democracy because of the lack of growth, the middle classes' willingness to abrogate democracy in order to protect their privileges only further alienates working classes. "Why do they have the right to just outlaw our party whenever they want?" said Noppadon Pattama, a minister in the populist Thai governments run by Thaksin Shinawatra, who was forced to flee into exile after his party was banned.[47]

Empowered by populists like Thaksin, Joseph Estrada, or Hugo Chavez, and no longer willing to simply hand over political power to middle classes and elites, as they might have done ten or twenty years ago, the voting poor in country after country have fought back after their mandates have been overruled. In Thailand, for example, poor supporters of Thaksin formed the United Front for Democracy Against Dictatorship, a mass organization whose members, wearing their trademark red shirts, targeted middle class and elite institutions with demonstrations and violent protests in 2009 and 2010. They held massive rallies drawing tens of thousands of people, but they also attacked government meetings, pelted the motorcade of then prime minister Abhisit Vejjajiva, and launched rallies in the center of Bangkok that deteriorated into brawls with middle class shopkeepers in certain neighborhoods. Ultimately, it seemed, the red shirts had decided that, if Thailand's middle classes could ruin the country's democracy, so could they.

6
Graft, Graft, and More Graft

FOR MANY FIRST-TIME VISITORS to Jakarta, capital of Indonesia and the largest city on the intensely crowded island of Java, the metropolis seems to be in constant motion, its incessant activity and brutal equatorial heat wearing down travelers. Alongside the wide boulevards of the central financial district, where glass-and-steel skyscrapers jostle for space with five-star hotels, vendors peddling sticks of satay and clove cigarettes and copies of the Indonesian tabloids push their carts past mobs of local office workers dressed in Western suits. Away from the grandiose financial areas, in the cramped side streets of newer districts that have sprung up to accommodate migrants from other parts of the sprawling archipelago of 17,000 islands, motorcyclists weave through gridlocked traffic, their exhaust stinging the throat and mixing with soupy air already polluted by cars, buses, and haze from forest fires burning out of control across other parts of Indonesia.

Yet compared with the late 1990s, Jakarta today has become so placid it could resemble Oslo. At that time, the collapse of longtime dictator Suharto and the Asian financial crisis had battered Indonesia's economy and simultaneously released the cork that had repressed religious, ethnic, class, and other divides in the staggeringly diverse archipelago. The result was a political and social meltdown. At the time, many frequent visitors to Indonesia wondered whether the country was going to disintegrate into a Southeast Asian version of Pakistan or Nigeria, a giant failing state poisoning its neighbors and, potentially, the international community. The Indonesian economy shrank by 13 percent in 1998, tens of millions of Indonesians fell below the poverty line, and rioters ransacked and burned large areas of the capital.

Long lines formed for handouts of staple goods like rice and cooking oil, and the value of the rupiah, Indonesia's currency, plummeted by about 75 percent in the end of 1997 and the beginning of 1998.[1]

Outside Jakarta, the violence could actually be worse. Besides violent anti-Chinese sentiment, other ethnic and religious fault lines exploded in the late 1990s and early 2000s. In the Malukus, the famous "Spice Islands" where Western colonists once had competed for access to valuable nutmeg and cloves, Christians and Muslims attacked each others' villages, burning them to the ground and beheading survivors, whose heads were left on skewers like a tropical Vlad the Impaler. Outlying regions like Aceh, East Timor, and West Papua threatened to secede, potentially breaking up the country.

To people who lived through the late 1990s and early 2000s in Indonesia, the turnaround to the situation today seems, on the surface, to be remarkable. The sprawling country, with the fourth-largest population in the world, appears to have achieved stability and defused the violence that had threatened to tear the archipelago asunder. Rather than disintegrating into Nigeria or Pakistan, Indonesia, to some observers, has become the democratic success story of the decade. Indonesia has devolved much of the central budget and empowered local officials, increasing nationwide participation in politics. It has fostered a broader and more inclusive civil society, and has increasingly tolerated public protest, political opposition, and legislative horse-trading. Local areas have gained greater control over their natural resources and their social welfare systems, and have introduced new forms of local-level elections and other types of voter feedback. Jakarta's Indonesian and English-language newspapers now give a daily roundup— right next to the weather pages—of planned (peaceful) protests that will be held on the capital's streets, a sign of how normal and routine such public participation has become.

Unlike political leaders in other countries such as Pakistan, who are reticent to confront militancy for fear of seeming like tools of the United States, Indonesia's recent leaders have utilized the bully pulpit to condemn militants, while also integrating Muslim parties into the mainstream political sphere. "I would like to emphasize that the country must not, and will not, be defeated by terrorism. . . . To the whole of the Indonesian people, let us collectively unite in the fight against the acts of terrorism," Indonesian President Susilo Bambang Yudhoyono declared in one speech.[2] Indeed, by combining this public outreach with effective police work, Indonesia has shattered Jemaah Islamiah, once the most powerful terror network in Southeast Asia, responsible for the bloody 2002 Bali bombings, which killed over 200 people, as well as for numerous attacks on Western hotels and embassies in Jakarta. According to the International Crisis Group, the most authoritative analyst of Jemaah Islamiah, the group is now splintered, weakened, and largely ineffective.[3]

Stability, engendered by public participation and devolution, has allowed for investment and stronger growth; except for India and China, Indonesia has posted some of the highest growth rates in the world in recent years. Yudhoyono also has presided over truly free and contested elections. After its violent birth, the independent country of East Timor did emerge. Another secessionist conflict, in Aceh, was resolved following the devastating tsunami in December 2004; Yudhoyono had the wisdom to try to help negotiate an end to the decades-long conflict in Aceh, rather than attempt to overwhelm insurgents by force. Attacks against Indonesian Chinese have decreased sharply as calm has been restored. Today, far from sheltering themselves in heavily guarded enclaves across Jakarta, behind razor wire and security checks, many ethnic Chinese businesspeople are beginning to participate openly in politics.

In recognition of Indonesia's supposed turnaround, the United States, which all but ignored the country for a decade after Suharto's fall in 1998, is once again courting it. The Obama administration has launched what it calls "comprehensive partnership" with Indonesia.[4] As countries in the Middle East throw off their own dictators, the White House commissioned an internal study to examine Indonesia's transition, and to see whether the archipelago now could be an example to the Arab world.[5] Returning in November 2010 to the country where he spent four years of his childhood, President Barack Obama heaped praise on Indonesia, declaring, "Indonesia has charted its own course through an extraordinary democratic transformation."[6] Secretary of State Hillary Clinton, meeting with Indonesian officials the following year, urged them to promote democracy in the Middle East and in Burma, saying that Indonesia "provides an example for a transition to civilian rule and building strong democratic institutions."[7]

And yet, even as it supposedly goes from success to success, Indonesia has developed what could be a fatal flaw. As in many other young democracies, the opening of politics also has opened the tap for corruption. In this liberalization of corruption, the breakdown of a centralized system of graft, common under authoritarian rule, leads to more bureaucrats, officials, and average policemen with their hands out—so many more people for citizens to pay in order to start a business, get their kids into school, drive on the highway, mail a letter, or fulfill any number of other tasks taken for granted by citizens of wealthy democracies. Corruption has become so commonplace that, when politicians accused the national anticorruption commission of being penetrated by corruption and other crimes itself, few Indonesians were surprised—though it turned out that the accusations were mostly an attempt to undermine the commission.[8] Still, in 2010 one former head of the anticorruption commission was found guilty of masterminding the murder of a rival.[9]

In theory, more open politics should reduce corruption, by throwing sunlight onto the actions of politicians. This may be true in the long run, but in the short run the opposite often seems to happen. During an era of tight authoritarian rule, graft often remains relatively centralized and predictable, allowing citizens to understand and manage established networks of corruption. The regime siphons off a certain percentage of money from local businesses, but the number of actors involved in the corruption remains relatively small. (To be sure, there are exceptions, like Mobutu Sese Seko's Zaire, in which the venality of this small number of actors was so great that it became utterly unmanageable.) Yet as countries democratize, the old channels of graft and monopolies over important information tend to vanish, and more actors have access to important government information that could be sold, and so these new and different actors—local political bosses, broader segments of the bureaucracy, staff of members of parliament—put out their hands. This liberalization of corruption can add to business costs for everyone, from the largest local corporations to the smallest street vendors, who now, in cities like Jakarta, have to pay a litany of small "fines" to everyone from beat cops to traffic police to small-time local officials.

Indeed, Indonesia provides a clear illustration of how political opening leads to the liberalization of corruption. At the beginning of the transition from longtime dictator Suharto, whose regime collapsed in 1998, graft became decentralized, following decades of tightly controlled networks of corruption run by the military and Suharto's extended family.[10] The central government handed over more power to local leaders, and, in addition to empowering local politicians, the new situation also provided many more opportunities for corruption. "Actors in the bureaucracy, judiciary, political parties, and in the army have reemerged as central players in a corruption free for all in democratic Indonesia," wrote economist Michael Rock in a comprehensive study of corruption in Indonesia and several other developing countries.[11]

A truly competitive legislature, a sharp change from Suharto's compliant parliament, also has added to an increase in corruption. Again, in the long run a competitive legislature could bring transparency to politics, and studies by multiple economists have found that corruption eventually decreases as a democracy ages. But for now, it significantly increases the amount of money in the political system. Although Indonesian legislators no longer can count on winning office just by joining Suharto's party, Golkar, the young democracy has developed few rules governing how politicians should raise money to campaign. "With the emergence of a confrontational relationship between newly empowered legislatures and embattled presidents, members of parliament, who needed ample war chests to win re-election, used their new political powers to extort funds. . . . Local officials also participated in extorting and taxing private firms," Rock wrote.[12] Democracy has provided rent seekers with many more opportunities to make money off the state, or from elections, but Indonesia has not yet developed the checks and balances to restrain them, he concluded.

Simply the fact that Indonesia now has more elections—for local political positions, for party leadership, for legislative seats—provides more opportunity for graft in the absence of strong traditions of clean elections or effective monitoring. During the 2006–7 race for the governor of Jakarta, a position similar to that of an American mayor, the U.S. embassy reported that some parties were trying to sell their nominations for the post to the highest bidder.[13] Two years earlier, in the run-up to the national presidential election ultimately won by Yudhoyono, a similar problem had emerged: powerful politician Jusuf Kalla, who would serve as Yudhoyono's first vice president, allegedly won the chairmanship of the Golkar party by "[paying] enormous bribes to secure votes from party branches," according to another U.S. embassy analysis. Since there were now so many more party branches than during the dictatorship, and each one could exercise the kind of influence that local party offices never had during Suharto's time, the amount of money needed to pay them off was far higher than in the past.[14]

Even Yudhoyono, who tried to build a reputation as a clean politician, rhetorically supporting the nation's anticorruption watchdog even as it went after some of his closest associates, could not escape the country's growing graft problem. The treasurer of Yudhoyono's Democratic Party, a man named Muhammad Nazaruddin, fled the country in May 2011 after being accused of massive corruption in the tender of buildings in Jakarta. Once abroad, Nazaruddin claimed that many members of Yudhoyono's party had been involved in his state contracts scheme, an allegation widely believed among Indonesian political, media, and business leaders.[15]

Not surprisingly, despite its increasingly open politics, Indonesia has made little headway in recent years in Transparency International's annual rankings of perceptions of corruption. The Political Economy and Risk Consulting, a leading Asian survey, ranked Indonesia as the most corrupt country in Asia, behind such paragons of clean politics as Cambodia and the Philippines.[16]

This decline in Transparency International rankings is echoed in other emerging democracies, where the enlargement of the franchise and the decentralization of political power, at least at first, seems to make graft easier. As Thailand became more democratic in the 2000s, in terms of a broader franchise, freer voting, and a decentralization of power to provinces from Bangkok, its Transparency International ranking fell from sixty-first in the world in 2001 to seventy-eighth in 2010. The Philippines's ranking in Transparency International's survey of corruption perceptions declined from fifty-fifth in the world in 1998 to one hundred thirty-fourth in 2010. In fact, in analyzing over thirty developing countries that emerged from authoritarian rule and shifted to democracy in the late 1990s and early 2000s, Council on Foreign Relations researchers have found that the Transparency International score for corruption perceptions actually declined in most of the countries in the first five years of democratic rule.

In a number of cities and provinces across Indonesia, newly empowered local officials—or party leaders like Nazaruddin—have built megaprojects, like a $600-million, 50,000-seat outdoor stadium in East Kalimintan on the island of Borneo, that allegedly have provided innumerable opportunities for contractors, in collusion with local officials, to skim money from projects. Today nearly a quarter of the Indonesian leaders charged with corruption come from district and provincial-level jobs, compared with almost none a decade ago, when graft was controlled by Jakarta.[17]

This corruption is hard to miss, even for outsiders. Even as Obama pushes for the "comprehensive partnership" with Indonesia, American investors, who have looked closely at the country, understand how graft is spiraling out of control. Despite Indonesia's size, it remains only the twenty-eighth-largest trading partner of America, behind such global minnows as Belgium. When quizzed about their interest in investing in Indonesia, most American companies—other than large natural resources firms that already have huge investments in the country—reply that they are still deferring any investments, largely because of the country's problem with graft.[18] When, in 2011, Google decided to launch new investments in Southeast Asia, it initially passed over Indonesia, by far the largest country in the region, and then essentially asked the Indonesian government for waivers that would allow it to avoid all the red tape (and potential graft) clogging Indonesian business today.[19]

Indonesia's story is repeated in many young democracies. In Russia and other post-Soviet states, people watched, after 1989, as the old *nomenklatura,* the former communist officials, benefited from an orgy of self-dealing of state assets. Yet, at the same time, the chaotic freeing of the economy often allowed these former bureaucrats, who now "owned" many former state

assets, to extort bribes from the general public to get access to certain foreign goods, licenses to launch a business, or entrée into companies created
from old state firms. In a study of several post-Communist states by the New
Democracies Barometer at the University of Strathclyde in Scotland, over 70
percent of respondents said that corruption had increased in comparison
with that under their former communist regimes, and that this had significantly impacted their views of the quality of democracy.[20]

Indeed, several multicountry studies of corruption suggest that graft
increases in the early years of democratization. In one analysis of democracy and rent seeking, economists Hamid Mohtadi and Terry Roe of the
University of Minnesota found that in nearly every one of the sixty-one
countries they studied, rent seeking and corruption rose in the early stages
of democratization.[21] Other studies, focusing on specific regions or countries, have found similar results. Political scientists Chris Baker and Pasuk
Phonpaichit concluded that corruption rose as Thailand democratized; other
economists discovered that corruption has increased in most democratizing
Latin American nations as centralized networks give way to more decentralized politics.[22]

Even when graft might not actually be getting worse, the openness of new
democracies often leads to the *perception* among the general public that it is.
In large part, this is simply because a freer media, and more independent
anticorruption agencies, investigate the government and publish reports on
graft. In the long run, again, this is a positive development: Exposés of graft
eventually could encourage politicians and civil servants to think twice about
their actions. But in the short run, the freer media and anticorruption agencies' reports tend to increase public perceptions of government corruption.
Under authoritarian governments, rumors of graft within political circles
may spread, but they are easier to keep out of the local press. In China, for
example, Prime Minster Wen Jiabao has successfully maintained an image
of a caring, earthy, and incorruptible grandfather type. Because of this image, Wen is always the first top Chinese official on the scene at any major
tragedy, like the deadly 2008 earthquake in Sichuan province, where he
comforted the grieving and vowed an honest government investigation of

any malfeasance that might have made the disaster worse. Wen has maintained this image despite the fact that political insiders—and foreign journalists—know that his wife, Zhang Peili, wears staggeringly expensive jewelry, which makes one wonder how she can afford such items given his modest official salary.[23] But because the tightly controlled Chinese press never reports on the business interests of Wen's wife, and China's state anticorruption agencies do not touch such senior officials, most average Chinese have no idea about her wealth. When, in 2007, the Taiwanese media reported that Zhang owned jade jewelry worth hundreds of thousands of dollars, Chinese censors quickly blocked the stories from the Chinese Internet. "The Propaganda Ministry issued blanket orders to the news media not to cover Zhang's jewelry activities, according to a senior Chinese editor who asked not to be identified. Filtering software was updated to block all queries about "Wen's wife" and "jewelry," reported the *Los Angeles Times*.[24]

Similarly, during the time of the dictator Suharto, whose family stole as much as $35 billion in government wealth, according to several estimates, to publish an exposé of the Suharto empire would have meant guaranteed arrest for any local reporter who attempted to do so. By contrast, the free, and scandal-driven, press in Indonesia now produces endless exposés of corruption in high political circles. In addition, democratic Indonesia has developed a Supreme Audit Agency and other anticorruption watchdogs, which generally produce independent, fair investigations of graft allegations. Yudhoyono, though certainly far less corrupt than Suharto by any standard, has been battered by a long string of media reports about corruption linked to his administration, including the Nazaruddin allegations and allegations that the president ordered the bailout of a leading bank, Bank Century, that made major campaign contributions to his vice president. These allegations were given more fuel by a report, released in late 2009, by the Supreme Audit Agency, which suggested that the vice president, who had formerly governed Indonesia's central bank, had used his powers as central banker to help rescue Bank Century. The allegations became so numerous that Yudhoyono was forced to go on national television to address his role in them, and to promise a tougher fight against graft. During Suharto's time, such allegations simply would have been completely quashed, and the president would not even have had to respond to them in public.[25]

These perceptions of corruption heighten economic uncertainty, since average people simply hear more about graft than they used to under an authoritarian regime, and they also add to civic disengagement from a political elite perceived as cynical and uninterested in the public welfare. As economist Rock notes, under Suharto the private sector was, in a way, protected from excessive graft—Suharto granted a "franchise" to a certain number of senior regime cronies to extort money from companies, but he prevented any other officials who did not have this "franchise" from doing so. Now, "democratization witnessed the collapse of the franchise system," making private companies in Indonesia even more uncertain about whether their investments would be protected, or whether they would have to pay a continual, unending string of bribes.[26]

In earlier global democratic waves, freedom of the press may have had a similar impact, exposing corruption to the public. But the reach and scope of media outlets were much smaller in the second and third waves of democracy, and so even if the press did print more stories on corruption, its ability to quickly influence large sections of the public was limited. With the Internet and social media, the media's reach is far greater and faster. Even in a developing nation like Indonesia, widespread Internet penetration and use of social media provide even the poorest men and women with access to the latest news coverage—including numerous stories about corruption. Indonesia, in fact, now has the largest number of Facebook users of any country other than the United States.[27]

Rising corruption, or even perceptions of rising corruption, can add to popular alienation with democracy. A meta-analysis of over thirty emerging democracies around the world conducted by several of my research associates at the Council on Foreign Relations and myself used survey data between 2002 and 2007, the most recent years with comprehensive survey information, to examine the correlation between support for democracy and corruption. We conducted our analysis by using Barometer surveys from various regions to examine support for democracy, and also utilized data from the Pew Global Attitudes Survey, in which people in several regions were questioned to assess whether they considered corruption a "very big problem" in their country. We found that, in roughly one-quarter of the countries, support for democracy decreased when perceptions of corruption increased. Conversely, in several of the case studies, such as Bangladesh, Argentina, and India, significant decreases in perceptions of corruption were correlated with increases in popular support for democracy. These results suggest that, if governments in emerging democracies can quickly get graft under control, they can more easily consolidate democratic transitions.[28]

In countries in this meta-analysis that showed a clear link, the relationship between corruption and diminishing support for democracy was substantial—a finding supported by the work of other researchers such as Yun-han Chu of National Taiwan University, who has found that corruption perceptions have eroded trust in government in many young Asian democracies.[29] In Pakistan, where even many middle class liberals privately admit that graft has increased in recent years of civilian governments as compared with past military regimes, the survey data shows that perceptions of corruption have been bad for democracy. Between 2002 and 2007, the number of Pakistanis who perceived that the country had a serious corruption problem grew by 6 percent; over the same period, support for democracy among the Pakistani population fell by nearly 9 percent. Similarly, in Ukraine, where many middle class men and women grew frustrated in the late 2000s with the government of Orange Revolution leader Viktor Yushchenko because they saw graft rising despite the country's greater political openness, the survey data also shows that this frustration has led to disillusionment with democracy. Between 2002 and 2007, the percentage of Ukrainians who believed that the country had a serious problem with corruption grew by 9 percent; over that same period, support among the population for democracy fell by a sizable 11 percent.[30]

Other studies show similar results. Examining perceptions of corruption in Africa between 2002 and 2005, several researchers found that "corruption is a major, perhaps the major, obstacle to building popular trust in state institutions and electoral processes in Africa." Corruption was the strongest factor hurting Africans' trust in democratic institutions—institutions whose functioning was critical to these young democracies.[31]

In other cases, corruption fosters public dissatisfaction with elected officials. This dissatisfaction can then lead to citizens looking to other, unelected actors to resolve political problems. This might not be such a problem: one comprehensive survey, taken in the mid-2000s, and covering all of South Asia, found that less than 50 percent of Indians trusted political parties, but that Indians had instead placed high degrees of trust in their country's judiciary and nonpartisan Election Commission, two important institutions in a democracy. Even so, the rallies against corruption by Indian hunger strikers in the summer of 2011, who openly disdained the political system and elected politicians, drew large middle class crowds, suggesting that even those low levels of trust in Indian politicians had fallen precipitously.[32]

But at least in India, the public has placed trust in some democratic institutions. In places like Pakistan, Thailand, or Egypt, where the public today has low levels of trust in political parties, middle class citizens instead often have put their trust in the army, which, though it has played a central role in those nations' histories, can hardly be called guarantors of democracy.

As we have seen in the case of the Jakarta polls, this growth in corruption also extends to election campaigns in young democracies, which, at first, become more corrupt and, potentially, divisive. As economist Paul Collier shows in his analysis of democratic systems in Africa, initial democratic elections in developing countries often create what he calls a "Darwinian struggle for political survival in which the winner is the one who adopts the most cost-effective means of attracting votes."[33] Lacking the strong institutions capable of rewarding good governance and punishing cheating—such as anticorruption watchdogs, a strong election monitoring commission, and impartial courts—the most cost-effective means of winning votes in a young and poor democracy, Collier found, is not delivering good governance but bribery, voter intimidation, and ballot fraud. And without an established tradition of tolerance for opposition parties, these first free elections turn into zero-sum battles, in which no party can afford to lose, and so all parties are willing to use the most dramatic—and even violent—tactics to triumph. And in each subsequent democratic election, as the stakes of winning or losing become clearer—each party understands that, unless it wins, it will be cut out of all patronage—the amount of vote buying and intimidation tends to increase. In Nigeria, for instance, vote buying apparently has increased in each democratic presidential election, with the median price paid for a vote rising with each election as well.

So, during the first truly competitive elections in Kenya, for example, in the early 2000s, it made sense, from a perspective of survival, for all the parties contesting the poll to use bribery, voter and candidate intimidation, and even outright killings to try to dominate polling districts during the election campaign. All of the parties knew, after all, that if they lost an election, their party, and all their political, business, and ethnic allies, would be frozen out of power.[34]

Even in wealthier emerging democracies such as those in East Asia, where one might think there would be more room for politicians to share spoils—and thus less incentive to view elections simply as survival of the fittest—democracy has actually led to spikes in election violence and vote buying. A 2011 analysis of several emerging democracies in Asia, produced by the United Nations Development Program (UNDP), found that while elections can allow for public participation, in many emerging democracies they are exacerbating violence and graft. Elections "can trigger violence. . . . Elections are not in themselves sufficient mechanisms for managing political change when the players have not bought into the rules of the game"—in other words, contesting polls cleanly and peacefully, it noted. Electoral democracy, it concluded, "has come at a high price [in emerging Asian democracies.] Each year hundreds of people lose their lives in connection with competitive election."[35] In Thailand, Nepal, Bangladesh, the Philippines, and Pakistan, among other emerging Asian democracies, elections have, as in Africa, turned into winner-take-all contests in which any losing party gets completely shut out, UNDP concluded. As a result, just as in Kenya or Nigeria, Asian political parties are willing to go to any extent to win elections, since they know a loss means their power will be eviscerated. For example, one estimate suggests that vote buying in Thailand has become so entrenched, despite laws that punish it with prison terms, that this activity puts some $1 billion into the economy during election time.[36]

In Indonesia, money politics now has become the norm during campaign seasons—in Jakarta and nearly everywhere else in the archipelago. During Suharto's time, there were really no parties other than Golkar, the dictator's political vehicle. Golkar representatives might hand out small amounts of Indonesian rupiah during the elections, which were held every five years and which resulted in Suharto and his party getting Saddam Hussein–like vote tallies. But those disbursements of money were necessarily limited by the fact that Suharto had no real opposition, and the dictator's party, together with the army, always could use the threat of force to get people to vote for them as well.

Today, Indonesian political parties are far more competitive: in parliamentary elections, at least five sizable national parties now contest each election. None really can rely on force to intimidate voters into supporting them, so handing out money during campaigns, or on Election Day, has become far more important. One prominent Indonesian academic, Effenda Ghazali, looked at voter attitudes in several parts of the country, and found that the amount people were paid for their votes had more than doubled between the early 2000s and the late 2000s.[37]

Even a quick tour of campaign stops by Indonesian political parties reveals hyperinflation in the price of votes. At rallies in one Jakarta suburb, where migrants from around the country have built small, two-room houses of concrete and wood, candidates from one leading Indonesian party canvass for support. While a candidate speaks on the suburb's makeshift stage, his aides hand out small baskets of rice, cooking oil, and peanuts to people in the audience, and then the candidate leads the crowd in chants and flag-waving in the party's colors. Few in the crowd seem to even bother listening to the speech; many are waiting for an appearance onstage of a popular local pop singer known for dancing while shaking her rump toward the crowd.

But the men and women in the audience, mostly working class people who came to the capital to work in construction or other manual labor, start to pay more attention as the candidate's aides wander through the audience with other presents. Inside new baskets being handed out are small hand-fuls of rupiah, along with cards instructing people how to find the party's symbol and colors on ballots. Men and women who a minute ago had been relaxing on the ground, chewing sticks of spicy chicken, jump to their feet and press forward—many grab one, two, three baskets with the cash inside in a scene that is reminiscent of an American radio station promotion. But several of the people who grabbed baskets turn to the party's aides in disap-pointment after looking inside. "This is half what we got from the other parties," says one.[38]

The ongoing vote buying, the perceptions of growing corruption among elected politicians, the little bribes demanded over and over, have begun to wear down many Indonesians. When asked, many Indonesian business-people reflexively express pride in their young democracy, and in how their country has grown since the chaos and economic crises of the late 1990s. But when pushed a bit harder, they allow their frustration to surface quickly—street vendors, taxi drivers, and even wealthy tycoons will promptly complain about all the bribes they must pay to keep their businesses running. So per-haps it should not have been surprising when the former dictator's son, known as "Tommy" Suharto, decided in mid-2011 that he would enter politics—even though his father had overseen numerous brutal campaigns of repression and he himself had served a long jail sentence for allegedly mas-terminding the murder of a Supreme Court judge. Tommy launched a new political party and became chairman of its board, and laid plans for Indone-sia's national elections in 2014. "The people don't believe in the [Yudhoyono] government," one of Tommy's top political aides told reporters. "Thirteen years of 'reform' hasn't made people's lives better."[39]

Tommy seemed to have understood the zeitgeist. In a study by the In-donesian research organization Survey Circle, released in late 2011, only 12 percent of respondents believed that the current group of politicians in the democratic era were doing a better job than leaders during the era of Suharto.[40] An overwhelming number of respondents cited graft as one of the biggest complaints about the democratic era; commentaries on the survey noted that a sizable percentage of Indonesia's elected members of parlia-ment were targeted by corruption investigations within a year after taking their seats. "This underscores the fact that for a majority of Indonesians, democracy has not delivered a better life," noted the *Jakarta Globe,* commenting on the results of the survey.[41] In another poll released in May 2011, residents of Indonesia, the supposed democratic success story of the 2000s, said, by a margin of two to one, that conditions in the country were better during Suharto's time than under the government of democratically elected Yudhoyono.[42]

7

The China Model

THE ATTENDEES OF THE ANNUAL World Economic Forum in Davos are not exactly used to being told what to do. The Swiss resort draws the global elite: the highest-powered investment bankers, the top government officials and leaders, the biggest philanthropists, and the most famous celebrities, who gather each year to attempt to solve the world's most pressing problems and still have time for evening cocktails.

But in January 2009, the Davos crowd had to listen to a blistering lecture from a most unlikely source. Some thought that the first senior Chinese leader to attend the World Economic Forum, premier Wen Jiabao, might take a low-key approach to his speech to the Forum.[1] But at Davos, that genial grandpa was not in evidence. Months after Lehman Brothers collapsed, triggering the global economic crisis, Wen told the Davos attendees that the West was squarely to blame for the meltdown roiling the entire world. An "excessive expansion of financial institutions in blind pursuit of profit," a failure of government supervision of the financial sector, and an "unsustainable model of development, characterized by prolonged low savings and high consumption" caused the crisis, said an angry Wen.[2]

Five years earlier, such a broadside from a Chinese leader would have been unthinkable. Though in the 1990s and early 2000s China had used its soft power to reassure its Asian neighbors and to expand its influence in regions like Africa and Latin America, until the end of 2008 nearly every top Chinese official still lived by Deng Xiaoping's old advice to build China's strength while maintaining a low profile in international affairs.[3] As Deng told one visiting African leader in 1985, "Please don't copy our model. If there is any experience on our part, it is to formulate policies in light of one's own national conditions."[4] In the mid-2000s, American journalist Joshua Cooper Ramo already had coined the term "Beijing Consensus" to describe China's brand of authoritarian capitalism, and in private some Chinese academics had begun discussing whether Beijing might have lessons to teach other countries in Asia, Africa, or Latin America.[5] Still, no Chinese officials, academics, or other opinion leaders were willing to say, on the record, that they believed China had a model of political and economic development that other developing nations could follow.[6] Many top leaders publicly stuck to the line that China was a developing nation that still had much to learn from the world.[7]

But in 2008 and 2009 the global economic crisis decimated the economies of nearly every leading democracy, while China surfed through the downturn virtually unscathed, though Beijing did implement its own large stimulus package, worth roughly $600 billion.[8] China's economy grew by nearly 9 percent in 2009, while Japan's shrunk by over 5 percent, and the American economy contracted by 2.6 percent.[9] By August 2010, China (not including Hong Kong) held over $860 billion in U.S. treasuries; when Chinese leaders returned to Davos the year after Wen's scolding of the West, they came not to chat but to hunt for distressed Western assets they could buy up on the cheap.[10] In the downturn's wake, the crisis made many Western leaders tentative, questioning whether not only their own economies but also their political systems actually contained deep, possibly unfixable flaws. The economic crisis, said former U.S. Deputy Treasury Secretary Roger Altman, has left "the American model . . . under a cloud."[11] "This relatively unscathed position gives China the opportunity to solidify its strategic advantages as the United States and Europe struggle to recover," Altman writes.

These flaws appeared especially notable when compared with what seemed like the streamlined, rapid decision making of the Chinese leadership, which did not have to deal with such "obstacles" as a legislature, judiciary, or free media that actually could question or block its actions. "One-party autocracy certainly has its drawbacks. But when it is led by a reasonably enlightened group of people, as in China today, it can also have great advantages," writes the influential *New York Times* foreign affairs columnist Thomas Friedman. "One party can just impose the politically difficult but critically important policies needed to move a society forward."[12] Even John Williamson, the economist who originally coined the term "Washington Consensus," admitted, in an essay in 2012, that the Beijing Consensus appeared to be gaining ground rapidly, at the expense of the Washington Consensus.

As Western leaders, policy makers, and journalists questioned whether their own systems had failed, Chinese leaders began to promote their authoritarian capitalist model of development more explicitly. After all, in the wake of the crisis many Western governments, including France and the United States, bailed out their financial sectors and many of their leading companies. These bailouts made it harder for Western leaders to criticize Beijing's economic interventions, and led some Chinese officials to question whether Western democracies now were copying the China model. In Beijing, a raft of new books came out promoting the China model of development and blasting the failures of Western liberal capitalism. "It is very possible that the Beijing Consensus can replace the Washington Consensus," Cui Zhiyuan, a professor at Tsinghua University in Beijing, told the *International Herald Tribune* in early 2010.[13] Suddenly, too, the same Chinese leaders who in the early and mid-2000s still had played the role of the meek learner became, in speeches and public appearances and writings, very much the triumphalist teacher. In an article in the *China Daily* one think-tank expert from China's Commerce Ministry writes, "The US' top financial officials need to shift their people's attention from the country's struggling economy to cover up their incompetence and blame China for everything that is going wrong in their country."[14]

In previous reverse waves, eras when global democratic gains stalled and went backward, there was no alternate example of development remotely as successful as China today; the Soviet Union claimed to be an alternate example, but it never produced anywhere near the sustained growth rates and successful, globally competitive companies of China today. In the early 1960s, another time of a reverse wave following the post-WWII democratization in Europe and parts of Asia, the only real challenger to liberal, capitalist democracy was the communist bloc. At the time, many developing nations did attempt to follow the Soviet economic model, partly because it offered an alternative to the West, which was attractive to former colonies, partly because the Soviet model came with significant Soviet aid, and partly because many leaders of newly independent nations, such as Tanzania's Julius Nyerere, had studied in socialist systems, or in universities in the West that had favorable views of socialism and believed a Soviet-style system could work.

But even among many true believers, who remained convinced that the Soviet Union and Mao's China offered viable alternatives of development, the massive disaster of Mao's Great Leap Forward in 1958–61, which led to a famine that killed tens of millions, and the stagnation of the Eastern bloc economies, revealed by émigrés, showed that, given time, the communist system probably would collapse. After the first generation of postcolonial leaders, many newly independent states that had once embraced socialist models began to slowly dismantle them. By the 1980s, when many newly independent states were struggling with serious economic crises, and neo-liberal reforms promoted by the West began to take hold, communist-style economics were nearly dead.

Today, China—and to a lesser extent other successful authoritarian capitalists—offer a viable alternative to the leading democracies. In many ways, their systems, which we will see in more detail, pose the most serious challenge to democratic capitalism since the rise of communism and fascism in the 1920s and early 1930s. And in the wake of the global economic crisis, and the dissatisfaction with democracy in many developing nations, leaders in Asia, Africa, and Latin America are studying the Chinese model far more closely—a model that, eventually, will help undermine democracy in these leaders' countries.

In recent years, the "China model" has become shorthand for economic liberalization without political liberalization. But China's model of development is actually more complex. It builds on earlier, state-centered Asian models of development such as in South Korea and Taiwan, while taking uniquely Chinese steps designed to ensure that the Communist Party remains central to economic and political policy making.[15] Like previous Asian modernizers, China in its reform era has devoted significant resources to primary education, resulting in youth literacy rates of nearly 98 percent; in many other developing nations, the youth literacy rate is less than 70 percent.[16] Like other high-growth Asian economies, and the most reformist of the Persian Gulf modernizers, China also has created highly favorable environments for foreign investment, particularly in the special economic zones along the country's coast; in many years over the past two decades China has been the world's top recipient of foreign direct investment.[17] Yet in the China model, the Beijing government maintains a high degree of control over the economy, but it is hardly returning to socialism. Instead, Beijing has developed a hybrid form of capitalism in which it has opened its economy to some extent, but it also ensures that the government controls strategic industries, picks corporate winners, determines investments by state funds, and pushes the banking sector to support national champion firms. Indeed, though in the 1980s and 1990s China privatized many state firms, the central government today still controls roughly 120 companies. Among these are the biggest and most powerful corporations in China: of the forty-two biggest companies in China, only three are privately owned. In the thirty-nine economic sectors considered most important by the government, state firms control roughly 85 percent of all assets, according to a study by China economist Carl Walter. In China the party appoints senior directors of many of the largest companies, who are expected to become party members, if they are not already. Working through these networks, the Beijing leadership sets state priorities, gives signals to companies, and determines corporate agendas, but does so without the direct hand of the state appearing in public. And even when the state does not directly control the most important companies, Beijing increasingly has used nontariff barriers to encourage what it calls "indigenous innovation" in industries it considers strategic, like energy, computing, and others—barriers that favor certain local firms for procurement and research and development.

What's more, in this type of authoritarian capitalism, government intervention in business is utilized in a way not possible in a free market democracy: to strengthen the power of the ruling regime and China's position internationally. When Beijing wants to increase investments in strategically important nations, such as Thailand or South Africa, it can put pressure on China's major banks, all of which are linked to the state, to boost lending to Chinese companies operating in those nations. For example, Chinese tele-communications giant Huawei, which is attempting to compete with multi-nationals like Siemens, received some $30 billion in credit from state-controlled China Development Bank, on terms its foreign competitors would have sali-vated over. By contrast, though the Obama administration wanted to dras-tically upgrade the United States' relationship with Indonesia, an important strategic partner, it could not convince many American companies to invest there, and, unlike the Chinese leadership, it could not force them to do so.[18]

In short, the China model sees commerce as a means to promote na-tional interests, and not just to empower (and potentially to make wealthy) individuals. And for over three decades, China's model of development has delivered staggering successes. Since the beginning of China's reform and opening in the late 1970s, the country has gone from a poor, mostly agrar-ian nation to, in 2010, the second-largest economy in the world.[19] Some coastal Chinese cities, like Shenzhen and Shanghai, now boast gross do-mestic products per capita equivalent to those of cities in Southern Europe or Southeast Asia.[20] In the process, this growth has lifted hundreds of mil-lions of Chinese out of poverty.[21] With the economies of leading industrial-ized democracies still suffering, today China, and to a lesser extent India, are providing virtually the only growth in the whole global economy.[22]

Since 2008, not only top Chinese leaders but also people across the coun-try clearly have become more confident about Beijing's place in the world. Some of this confidence is only natural, part of China reclaiming its posi-tion as a major world power, a role it occupied for centuries until it fell be-hind the West's modernization in the nineteenth century. But some of the confidence comes from China's more recent rise during the global economic crisis, which put Beijing in an international leadership role far before its leaders expected. And, some of the confidence comes from Chinese leaders, diplomats, and scholars traveling more widely, and realizing that their demo-cratic neighbors—Indonesia, the Philippines, Thailand, and many others that used to lecture China about human rights and freedoms—actually are falling behind China's breakneck growth. "Chinese leaders used to come here and want to learn from us," one senior Thai official said. "Now it's like they don't have anything left to learn. . . . They have no interest in listening to us."[23]

China's newfound confidence has manifested itself in many forms. When the Nobel committee awarded the 2010 Peace Prize to Chinese dissident Liu Xiaobo, jailed in China for organizing an online petition calling for the rule of law, Beijing condemned Norway and other European nations, and applied intense pressure on European officials, and on many from Asian nations as well, not to attend the award ceremony.[24] Ultimately, several of the nations China pressured the hardest, like the Philippines, declined to send representatives to the Nobel ceremony.

A few months earlier, Beijing had applied similar pressure on European nations, this time to join with it in an unprecedented public call to replace the dollar as the global reserve currency. Previously, Beijing had been relatively willing to abide by the dollar as the major global currency, but China, owning a massive amount of U.S. Treasuries, had become more and more worried about America's unsustainable debt and reckless fiscal policies. China followed up on its call by helping Chinese firms, and foreign companies, to begin using the renminbi more readily in international transactions, as well as in funds based in Hong Kong.[25] When, in the fall of 2011, European nations looked for saviors to solve their growing economic crisis, China stepped in. Chinese officials signaled their willingness to contribute as much as €100 billion to the European Financial Stability Fund, or possibly to a new bailout mechanism set up by the International Monetary Fund. In Greece, China launched plans to invest billions in infrastructure, including its ports, while also repeatedly offering to buy up Greek debt.[26] But China did so only while at the same time demanding that Europe nations drop any claims against China for unfair trade policies. Eventually, when these conditions could not be met, China withdrew the idea of trying to bolster Europe's ailing banks.

Beijing has become more forceful in dealing with Washington, too, an assertiveness that can add to its appeal with developing countries who've often looked for another major power, and particularly a power hailing from Asia, to balance their relations with the United States. When the Obama

White House informed Chinese officials in the summer of 2009 that it, like every other recent American administration, planned to host the Dalai Lama for a private meeting, Beijing aggressively lobbied the White House not to meet the Tibetan leader. The White House acquiesced, and for the first time since the administration of George H. W. Bush the Dalai Lama came to America without meeting the president, a huge victory for China.[27] A few weeks later, Chinese officials used a global conference on climate change to furiously admonish their American counterparts for their position on global warming, one of the first times the Chinese had taken such a public approach to the issue. "There has been a change in China's attitude," Kenneth G. Lieberthal, a former senior National Security Council official focusing on China, told the *Washington Post*. "The Chinese find with startling speed that people have come to view them as a major global player. And that has fed a sense of confidence."[28] Or as one current senior American official who deals with China said, "They are powerful, and now they're finally acting like it."[29]

In 2010 and 2011, China also surprised its neighbors by stepping up its demands for large swaths of the South China Sea, other contested waters, and regions along its disputed land borders.[30] In the summer and fall of 2010, China reacted so furiously to Japan's decision to impound a Chinese fishing boat in disputed waters that it cut off shipments to Tokyo of rare earth materials critical to the manufacture of modern electronics like cellular phones and fiber optics.[31] Beijing also warned its neighbor Vietnam not to work with Western oil companies like ExxonMobil on joint explorations of potential oil and gas in the South China Sea, detained Philippine and Vietnamese boats, and claimed nearly the entire sea—Beijing's claims extended nearly to the shores of the Philippines, hundreds of miles from China's territory.[32] When Southeast Asian nations, attending a regional summit in the summer of 2010, protested Beijing's stance on the South China Sea and asked Washington to mediate their disputes with Beijing, Chinese foreign minister Yang Jiechi lost his composure. He suddenly got up and exited the meeting, leaving the room in an uncomfortable silence. One hour later, he stormed back in and launched into a thirty-minute monologue, practically screaming at the other participants. At one point Yang mocked his hosts, the Vietnamese; at another he declared, "China is a big country and other countries are small countries, and that's just a fact." In other words, he was implying that China could outmuscle these smaller nations.[33]

This increasingly assertive Chinese diplomacy has alienated some countries, particularly in Asia. Yet along with more forceful diplomacy, Beijing has started to proactively promote its model of development, and in some ways its newfound confidence, expressed in its more forceful relations with the United States and other powers, only adds to its global appeal, since other, smaller countries want to join forces with a clearly rising power. But even as China has become more confident, its leadership still recognizes that it cannot challenge American military power, at least not anytime soon. As China analyst Stephen Halper writes, "In reality, Chinese leaders want neither the strain on finances nor the negative and potentially costly atmospherics that would accompany a genuine arms race with the United States."[34] Despite boosting its defense budget by over 10 percent annually, China remains a long way from developing a global blue water navy, or expeditionary forces capable of fighting far from China's borders.[35] Most years, the Pentagon's budget surpasses the defense budgets of all other major military powers combined, and because of this disparity in spending Beijing increasingly has focused on "asymmetric warfare"—ways for weaker military powers to damage stronger ones, such as cyber attacks and ballistic missiles.[36] "We need to think more on how to preserve national integrity. We have no intention of challenging the US [militarily,]" admitted Major General Luo Yan, a senior member of the People's Liberation Army.[37]

Recognizing that China remains decades from challenging the Pentagon, Beijing's leaders realize they can compete in other ways, such as by promoting their development model, and as other countries learn and adopt aspects of the China model, they will become more likely to align with China, to share China's values, and to connect with China's leaders. Over the past two years, prominent Chinese academics have released a raft of new books on the China model and its applicability to other countries, and several Chinese media outlets called the 2010 World Expo in Shanghai, for which China reportedly spent some $60 billion, a platform to advertise its development successes to other countries.[38] On another occasion, according to China scholar Randall Peerenboom, China and the World Bank jointly hosted a forum called the Shanghai Global Learning Process, where some 1,200 participants from 117 nations attended sessions designed partly to explain how they could learn from China's development experience.[39] The economic crisis, Chinese economist Cheng Enfu told reporters, "displays the advantages of the Chinese model. . . . Some mainstream [Chinese] economists are saying that India should learn from China; Latin American countries are trying to learn from China. When foreign countries send delegations to China, they show interest in the Chinese way of developing."[40]

By the early 2000s, China already had developed training programs for foreign officials, usually from developing nations in Africa, Southeast Asia, and Central Asia. These officials came to China for courses in economic management, policing, and judicial practice, among other areas. At the time, Chinese officials would not necessarily suggest that China had an economic model to impart. But by the late 2000s, many of these courses explicitly focused on elements of the China model, from the way Beijing uses its power to allocate loans and grants to certain companies, to China's strategies for co-opting entrepreneurs into the Communist Party, to China's use of special economic zones to attract foreign investment over the past thirty years.[41] Attendees at these sessions described how, unlike in the past, their Chinese counterparts explicitly contrasted the Chinese system and its ability to rapidly handle crises and successfully pursue long-term goals—though they did not explicitly say that China is an authoritarian country, of course—with the gridlock of Western governments. One Vietnamese official who repeatedly has traveled to China for such programs noted how the style of the programs has changed over time. Now, he said, Chinese officials, far more confident than even ten years ago, would introduce the example of one or another Chinese city that had successfully attracted sizable investments, talking through how the city government coordinates all permits and other needs, and moves favored projects swiftly through any approval process. Some of the officials would compare this with investments in India or even wealthy democracies, noting how hard it was to get approvals for even the smallest investments in many parts of these countries. Other Central Asian attendees at Chinese training sessions noted how they increasingly learned about the Chinese judicial system, in which the party has almost complete control, and then returned to their home countries, where their governments used similar types of control measures over their judiciaries.

Beijing also has built close political-party-to-political-party ties with several other developing nations. Increasingly, it has utilized these ties to promote its model of political and economic development. For at least two decades, Vietnamese officials have traveled to China and then consequently have based many of their development policies on China's strategies.[42] More recently, Chinese officials have worked on development planning with leading politicians in neighboring Mongolia, which democratized after 1989 but where the public has become increasingly disenchanted with corruption and weak growth. Chinese officials also have cooperated with United Russia, the main pro-Kremlin party, whose leaders want to study how China has opened its economy without giving up political control. In 2009, United Russia held a special meeting with top Chinese leaders to learn Beijing's strategy of development and political power.[43] China also has held training sessions for many leaders from the Cambodian People's Party, the party of Prime Minister Hun Sen.[44] Combined with the massive Chinese aid and investment flowing into Cambodia, where Beijing is now the largest donor and biggest investor, these introductions to the China model have had a significant impact on Cambodia's shaky democracy.[45] "You already don't have a lot of strong democratic values here," said one longtime senior Cambodian official. "You have [government] people seeing how well China has done, going to China all the time, what they come back [to Cambodia] with is how much faster and easier China has had it without having to deal with an opposition."[46]

These efforts to promote a China model of undemocratic development build on a decade-long effort by Beijing to amass soft power in the developing world—soft power that would then add to the appeal of China's ideas and China itself. Among other efforts, this strategy has included expanding the international reach of Chinese media, such as by launching new

China-funded supplements in newspapers in many different countries, and by vastly expanding the reach and professionalism of the Chinese newswire Xinhua, which recently bought a flashy new American bureau in the heart of Times Square in New York.[47] Today, according to its own figures, China's state-backed international television channel reaches over sixty-five million viewers outside the country.[48] This strategy also includes broadening the appeal of Chinese culture by opening Confucius Institutes—programs on Chinese language and culture, at universities from Uzbekistan to Tanzania.[49] It has involved a rapid and substantial expansion of China's foreign aid programs, so that Beijing is now the largest donor to many neighboring nations like Cambodia, Burma, and Laos. A study by the Wagner School of New York University found that Chinese aid to Africa grew from $838 million in 2003 to nearly $18 billion in 2007, the most recent year for which data was available.[50] Another analysis of China's overseas lending, compiled by the *Financial Times* in 2010, found that China lent more money to developing nations in 2009 and 2010 than the World Bank had, a stark display of Beijing's growing foreign assistance.[51] And the soft power initiative has also included outreach to foreign students, providing scholarships, work-study programs, and other incentives to young men and women from developing countries. The number of foreign students studying in China grew from roughly 52,000 in 2000 to 240,000 in 2009.[52]

Over the past decade, too, China has set up networks of formal and informal summits with other developing nations. With meetings held either in China or in the developing world, these summits are designed to bring together officials and opinion leaders.[53] At first, the summits offered China the opportunity to emphasize its role as a potential strategic partner and source of investment and trade. But over the past five years some summits, like those with Southeast Asian and African leaders, also subtly advertised China's model of development, according to numerous participants. Several Thai politicians who attended the Boao Forum for Asia, a kind of China-centered version of the World Economic Forum in Davos, noted that, in recent years, some of the discussions at the meeting had shifted from a kind of general talk of globalization and its impact in Asia to more specific conversations about some of the failings of Western economic models exposed by the global economic crisis, and whether China's type of development might be less prone to such risks. "Many of the African leaders coming here [to Beijing] for the Chinese-African summit are attracted not only by opportunities for aid and trade, but also by the China model of development," argues Zhang Weiwei, a prominent Chinese scholar and former aide to Deng Xiaoping, after leaders from nearly every African nation traveled to Beijing in 2006 for a summit. These African leaders realize, he writes, that for them the Chinese model of development will work better than a Western model dependent on a liberal democratic government.[54]

The soft power initiative also has involved a coordinated effort to upgrade the quality of China's diplomatic corps, replacing an older generation of media-shy, stiff bureaucrats with a younger group of Chinese men and women, many of whom are fluent in English and comfortable bantering with local journalists. On one occasion Chinese reporters working in Thailand watched as the then U.S. ambassador Ralph Boyce appeared on a prominent Thai talk show. Boyce was known in the diplomatic community for his knowledge of Thailand and command of Thai; on the show he spoke fluently and elegantly. Not to be outdone, alongside him the Chinese ambassador to Thailand also appeared, speaking fluent Thai and appearing right at home in the freewheeling television talk show format. In one cable released by Wikileaks, even American diplomats stationed in Thailand admitted that Thai officials had become increasingly admiring of China and its model of development, and less interested in the American model.

Until the past two or three years, the China model appealed mostly to the world's most repressive autocrats, eager to learn how China has modernized its authoritarianism: Mahmoud Ahmadinejad of Iran, Bashar al-Assad of Syria, and Islam Karimov of Uzbekistan. In Iran, senior regime officials reportedly have engaged in intense debate about how to import China's strategy of nondemocratic development to the Islamic Republic.[55] In Syria, a similar kind of debate reportedly has taken place among senior officials surrounding Assad, while in Ethiopia, where strongman Meles Zenawi has ruled for nearly two decades, the foreign minister and other top officials have publicly encouraged the country to follow China's model of development.[56]

In the past, these repressive regimes attracted most of the media coverage of the China model. But in recent years it is not just autocrats who have been learning from Beijing. China's soft power offensive has given it increasing leverage over democracies in the developing world, and has made Beijing's model of development more attractive to leaders even in freer nations, places where there has already been some degree of democratic transition. Increasingly, leaders and even average citizens of young democracies like Indonesia, Thailand, Senegal, Venezuela, Nicaragua, or Bolivia—countries where popular support for democracy has weakened—have taken an interest in China's model, and as China's model becomes more influential, it can weaken democracy in these countries, since it brings with it growing state control over both economics and politics.

Because China's advocacy of its model of development is still relatively new, it will take years to see the full effect of its challenge to Western liberal orthodoxy. Still, one can see some initial effects in developing democracies. In Venezuela and Nicaragua, Beijing has ingratiated itself with the leadership, offering $20 billion in loans to Caracas in the spring of 2010, a time of economic downturn in Venezuela; China's loans have helped Hugo Chavez perpetuate his government, even in the face of significant opposition, and even as he has used increasingly antidemocratic methods to crack down.[57]

As China has gained a larger presence in nations like Venezuela, Chavez increasingly has sent top diplomats and bureaucrats to Beijing to specifically examine China's strategies of development, and how they might be applied in Central or South America.[58]

Similar shifts have taken place in Southeast Asia, where China's soft power and its economic strength have broadened its appeal, even as its military aggressiveness simultaneously has sometimes hurt it. In acknowledging China as becoming the predominant influence in Cambodia, as well as the loss of leverage of Western donors over the government of Hun Sen, several Cambodian officials said that the Cambodian prime minister increasingly has based his political and economic strategies on China, from his use of his political party to control big business to his use of the court system to dominate the opposition. In particular, according to a number of Cambodian activists and human rights specialists, advisers from China's Communist

Party have given suggestions to Hun Sen's party about how to utilize laws for libel and defamation to scare the independent media, how to create a network of senior officials who can move in and out of major companies, and how to train special police forces, including Hun Sen's personal body-guard, who will always be loyal to him, even in the face of street protests. What's more, China has pushed Hun Sen's government to crack down on various protesters and refugees who might be an embarrassment to Beijing. When a group of Uighurs, who live in the western Chinese province that is home to about ten million Muslim and ethnic Turkic Uighurs, fled to Cambodia in the winter of 2009, Chinese officials applied significant behind-the-scenes pressure on Hun Sen's government to expel the Uighurs, even though they were classified as refugees. In December 2009, the Cambodian government deported the Uighurs back to China, where many of them vanished. Beijing praised Cambodia as "a model of friendly cooperation"; shortly after the deportation, China signed new aid deals with Cambodia worth roughly $1 billion, the biggest single disbursement of aid to the country ever.

China allegedly has made similar efforts to push Laos, Vietnam, and Thailand to deport Uighurs, Falun Gong practitioners, and other political migrants fleeing China, as it has used its growing power in Nepal to push the Nepalese government to return Tibetans fleeing China, even though Nepal has for years provided shelter to many Tibetans. And in Central Asia, where China increasingly conducts training seminars for local police, judges, and other justice officials, officials there say that Beijing has pushed them to use their judicial systems to arrest and deport Uighurs as well. In fact, even Kyrgyzstan, which once was the freest nation in Central Asia, and a home for regional prodemocracy activists, including Uighurs, has tightened the noose, searching for and deporting Uighurs back to China, where they are often arrested, jailed, and tortured.

Across Southeast Asia, in fact, China's model has gained considerable acclaim. "There are, of course, no official statements from [Southeast Asian] countries about their decisions to follow the Beijing Consensus or not," writes prominent Indonesian scholar Ignatius Wibowo. "The attraction to the Chinese model is unconscious." Still, it is possible to quantify this "unconscious" appeal. Having analyzed surveys of political values in Southeast Asia going back a decade, Wibowo concludes that people in many Southeast Asian countries share a willingness to abandon some of their democratic values for higher growth and the kind of increasingly state-directed economic system that many of these countries in fact had in their authoritarian days, and that China still has today. Southeast Asian nations "have shifted their development strategy from one based on free markets and democracy to one based on semi-free markets and an illiberal political system," Wibowo writes. "The 'Beijing Consensus' clearly has gained ground in Southeast Asia."[59] Indeed, by examining the political trajectory of the ten states that belong to the Association of Southeast Asian Nations, Wibowo found that with only a few exceptions, each country's political model, examined through a series of political indicators, has moved in the direction of China and away from liberal democracy over the past decade, largely because these nations had watched China's successes and contrasted them with the West's failures. Many Southeast Asian leaders and top officials were implementing strategies of development modeled on China's, including taking back state control of strategic industries, recentralizing political decision making, using the judicial system increasingly as a tool of state power, and reestablishing one-party rule—all changes that undermine democratic development. Supporting his claims, the most recent Economist Intelligence Unit survey of global democracy, which analyzes nearly every nation in the world, found that the global financial and economic crisis "has increased the attractiveness of the Chinese model of authoritarian capitalism for some emerging markets"—which has added to democracy's setbacks.

In Thailand, for example, growing numbers of politicians, bureaucrats, and even journalists favorably contrast China's undemocratic model of government decision making with Thailand's messy and sometimes violent pseudodemocracy.[60] In the past five years, as Thailand's urban-based middle class, and its favored political parties, have taken back dominance of politics, they have increasingly adopted tools of control similar to China. These have included creating an Internet monitoring and blocking system like China's and skewing the judiciary, through judicial appointments and "instructions" to judges from the royal palace, so that judicial rulings weaken potential opposition parties and ensure the dominance of the ruling party.[61] Although not every element of Thailand's political change was explicitly modeled on China, of course, many Thai officials, in the period after the coup of 2006, noted how the use of the judiciary, the control of the Internet, and other political tools did have some inspiration from China. Thailand's judiciary became so influential, and so obviously skewed against any opposition movements, that some opposition politicians and writers began to complain that the country was turning into a "judiocracy"—an autocracy of judges.[62]

Even outside Southeast Asia, in other parts of Asia, China's gravitational pull and its soft power have had an influence on democracies. Overall, concludes political scientist Yun-han Chu, who studied Asian Barometer surveys about East Asians' commitment to democracy, "Authoritarianism remains a fierce competitor of democracy in East Asia," in no small part because of the influence of China's ability to foster economic success without real political change, providing an alternative model that is clearly visible to other East Asians who travel to China, work with Chinese companies, buy Chinese products, or host Chinese officials.[63] As he notes, China will, in the coming years, become the center of East Asian trade and economic integration, giving it even more power. "Newly democratized [Asian] countries [will] increasingly become economically integrated with and dependent on non-democratic countries," Chu writes. Perhaps unsurprisingly, given China's growing power and influence in its region, in a poll of global public opinion, in which people in twenty countries were asked which world leaders they had the most confidence in, Chinese President Hu Jintao topped the list.[64]

To be sure, China's model of development, just like democratic capitalism, suffers from numerous flaws. These potentially include an inability to hold corrupt or foolish leaders to account, a lack of checks on state power, and a reliance on benign and wise autocrats for the China model to work, which is hardly a given—for every Deng Xiaoping, the politically savvy and foresighted architect of China's economic reforms, one could find ten Mobutu Sese Sekos or Kim Jong Ils, dictators who used their power solely for venal purposes. And as we will see later, those flaws, though obscured by China's recent successes, may in the long run spark a global backlash against Beijing, a backlash that would empower democrats in many developing nations. Rising inequality within China, between the favored urban areas and the less-well-off interior rural provinces, also threatens to unhinge China's economic miracle, through either growing waves of protests by rural dwellers or massive popular migrations that unleash instability. Already, China has shifted from one of the most equal—if poor—nations in Asia in the late 1970s to one of the most unequal societies today in East Asia. But for now, China has seen relative success in its attempt to quietly impart its model of development to other nations.

8

The Autocrats Strike Back

OFFERING AN ALTERNATIVE MODEL of successful but undemocratic development to other nations, China and other authoritarian states may implicitly be fostering today's powerful antidemocratic wave. But China, Russia, and, to a lesser extent, Venezuela and Iran have at times gone further. Worried by how the fourth wave of democratization, including the color revolutions in places like Ukraine and Kyrgyzstan, has crept up to their borders, Beijing and Moscow have developed a range of explicit strategies to undermine democracy among their neighbors.[1] And in a number of neighboring states, including Ukraine, Kyrgyzstan, and Cambodia, these authoritarian powers have enjoyed some striking successes in undermining young democracies.

Between the late 1980s and the early 2000s, neither Moscow nor Beijing made it a priority to forestall democracy in their neighborhoods. Weakened by economic crises and, in the case of China, international pariah status following the 1989 Tiananmen crackdown, both Russia and China spent much of the 1990s trying to put their economies on solid footing again, reassure investors, and foster political stability at home. Still, both countries clearly chafed at the West's willingness to wield power right up to their borders. NATO expanded to include Poland and other former Warsaw Pact nations, putting it on Russia's doorstep, and also talked of including Ukraine. Meanwhile, the United States not only fostered rapprochement with old enemies in Asia like Vietnam but also consistently declared its right to patrol the South China Sea and other waters near China and to adjudicate disputes in these seas.[2] And though many Russian liberals wanted their country to join the leading Western organizations like the International Monetary Fund and the Global Agreement on Tariffs and Trade, Washington refused on numerous occasions, further alienating Moscow and weakening liberals in the Kremlin.[3]

Quite a few Russians, including many opinion leaders, saw the NATO expansion as one of many Western strategies to weaken and take advantage of post-Soviet Russia. "Even pro-Western liberals worried that exclusion of Russia from the emerging all-European security system based on NATO would lead to its [Russia's] marginalization," wrote Russian analyst Dmitri Trenin.[4] "We do not think NATO expansion is necessary, and believe the policy is a relapse into the Cold War," warned Russian Foreign Minister Sergei Lavrov.[5] By the 2000s, Russians already angry at NATO expansion often would argue that the color revolutions in Central Asia and the Caucasus, which often involved some assistance from American and European democracy promotion groups, were the latest Western plots to weaken Russia.

Both China and Russia, once Vladimir Putin assumed the presidency, also clearly feared that democracy in East or Central Asia would foster regional instability and, potentially, dangerous anti-Russia and anti-China sentiment. This was not a wholly irrational fear. In some Southeast Asian nations, like Malaysia or Indonesia, and in some Central Asian and Caucasian states, like Georgia, majorities had long seethed at wealthier or more politically advantaged Chinese and Russian minorities living in their midst. Given the freedom of a newly democratic system, these majorities could use their numerical dominance to repress ethnic Chinese or Russians. During a previous era of freer politics in Indonesia, in the mid-1960s, mobs massacred thousands of Indonesian Chinese (ultimately, some 500,000 people were killed, though they were not all Indonesian Chinese; China gave safe haven to some fleeing Indonesian Chinese) after accusing them of communist leanings. The Suharto dictatorship, which came to power after the 1965–66 massacres, suppressed much of this interethnic tension. But after Suharto fell in 1998, in the chaos of Indonesia's early democratic reforms, mobs again attacked Indonesian Chinese communities in Jakarta and other cities, burning Chinese homes and businesses and allegedly raping and murdering ethnic Chinese women.[6]

Of course, in many democratizing nations freer politics did not result in stigmatizing minorities. In Thailand, where, under military dictators in the 1950s, 1960s, and 1970s, Chinese were targeted and the teaching of Chinese language was banned, the democratic era ushered in a new celebration of Chinese heritage.[7] Politicians who once would have hid their ethnic Chinese backgrounds now openly celebrated: visiting China in 2005, Thai Prime Minister Thaksin Shinawatra made a high-profile visit to his family's ancestral home in southern China, which would have been unthinkable for an earlier generation of Thai leaders.[8]

More often, Beijing and Moscow simply seemed more comfortable dealing with autocratic leaders—similar to those of the Putin-era Russian system or the top ranks of the Chinese Communist Party—who could operate like powerful executives. Until recently, most Chinese officials in Washington still had a difficult time understanding the American system of checks and balances, or comprehending that the American president could not simply do whatever he liked. For example, until recently Beijing invested little in training its officials to lobby the U.S. Congress or other legislatures in democratic nations. By ignoring Congress, it allowed its rival Taiwan, a far smaller player, to dominate the congressional influence game, and consequently lost important battles on Capitol Hill, such as the attempt by Chinese oil giant CNOOC to take over the American petroleum firm Unocal in 2005.[9] With weak lobbying efforts in Congress, Chinese officials were unable to convince Capitol Hill that the CNOOC takeover would not pose a national security risk to the United States, and Unocal wound up being sold to the American firm ChevronTexaco.[10]

The two authoritarian powers also obviously worried that regional democratization might spill over into China or Russia, ultimately creating a national movement for reform like the protests that led up to the 1989 Tiananmen crackdown. Again, this was not an irrational fear. In 1989, waves of change in Eastern Europe had moved from one country to the next, with citizens in some states modeling their reform efforts on what they had seen next door. And China and Russia already contained large populations of ethnic minorities who might be swayed by watching neighboring states democratize and offer greater freedoms and autonomy to ethnic groups. Were these outlying areas to revolt against Beijing or Moscow, as Chechnya did in the mid-1990s, they could threaten the very integrity of the state. The democratization of other ethnic Turkic nations like Turkey had a profound impact on many Uighurs in Xinjiang, the vast western Chinese province home to about ten million Muslim and ethnic Turkic Uighurs. Long repressed by China, the Uighurs, who briefly had a de facto state of their own in the early twentieth century, often traveled to Central Asia and Turkey to trade or to attend schools. Outside China these Uighurs saw how some of their ethnic peers had built states with far greater freedom of expression and religion and cultural identity than in China, where Muslim worship in restive Xinjiang remained tightly controlled, with the government dominating selections of imams, approving who could travel on pilgrimage, and dictating religious curricula.[11] "When I left East Turkestan [the Uighurs' name for Xinjiang] then I realized that you didn't have to have the government control religion, there was no danger to having a state where we could worship on our own, and it could still be a democracy," one Uighur activist said.[12] The democratization of Mongolia, after the collapse of the Soviet Union, had a similar galvanizing effect on Inner Mongolia, a province of China home to many ethnic Mongolians. And Beijing and Moscow also feared that demands for greater democracy among ethnic minorities could spread into ethnic Russian or Han Chinese regions. In the 1980s, an era of widespread discontent in China, major antigovernment riots in Tibet in 1987 and 1988 were followed closely by Han Chinese activists and certainly added to the national climate of protest that culminated in the Tiananmen uprising.[13]

By the mid-2000s, several changes in Chinese and Russian politics, and in the international environment, coalesced, giving Moscow and Beijing the rationale (in their officials' minds) and the means to fight democracy in their backyards. For one, both giants regained their stability. The first peaceful and orderly political transitions in the history of the People's Republic of China, from Deng Xiaoping to Jiang Zemin, and then from Jiang to Hu Jintao, made the Communist Party leadership more confident and stable—

and also more able to focus on events outside China's borders.[14] A renewed flow of investment into China after the stain of Tiananmen faded also helped booster the party's power and legitimacy.[15] By the late 1990s and early 2000s, as the rest of Asia tumbled into financial crisis, and the United States and Western institutions like the International Monetary Fund reacted slowly to the Asian crisis, China assumed a larger regional role, publicly refusing to devalue its currency, which might have triggered a worse crisis, and increasing its aid disbursements to some of the hardest-hit Asian countries.[16] Following the Asian financial crisis, many other states in the region never forgot China's symbolically important pledge to help other countries, even if, ultimately, that pledge was not critical to resolving the crisis.

In Russia, Putin's consolidation of political power, though disastrous for Russian democracy, did create a kind of stability and confidence in the Kremlin, confidence that also provided an impetus to reassert power throughout the former Soviet Union. A spike in the price of oil meanwhile helped restore petroleum-rich Russia's economic stability. By the latter half of the 2000s, Russia under Putin had used its oil wealth to amass nearly $500 billion in currency reserves, and increasingly utilized the state-controlled gas giant Gazprom to menace neighboring nations that did not go along with Moscow's foreign policy objectives.[17]

But even as Chinese and Russian leaders became more confident in the early and mid-2000s, the color revolutions worried the two authoritarian giants, leading them to take more proactive action to stifle democracy on their borders. Beginning with the Rose Revolution in Georgia in 2003 (some would add the protests in Serbia in 2000), the term "color revolutions" came to mean peaceful, popular movements for democratic change, primarily in the former Soviet Union and old Eastern bloc, though the concept eventually expanded to include Lebanon and Burma and, in 2010, the Jasmine Revolution in Tunisia. The 2003 Georgia uprising, which toppled president (and former Soviet foreign minister) Eduard Shevardnadze, led to elections won by pro-Western leader Mikheil Saakashvili. Several Georgian nongovernmental organizations (NGOs) that received funding from American philanthropist George Soros, a prominent advocate of democratic change in the former Eastern bloc, played a role in the Rose Revolution, as

Soros-funded NGOs helped train reformist politicians and organized other meetings for civil society activists. Though these NGOs' role in the Rose Revolution was overstated by many Russian commentators, their mere presence, combined with the dramatic reversal in political fortunes in Georgia, both infuriated and scared Moscow. The state-dominated Russian press demonized Saakashvili, and Putin displayed an obvious contempt for the Georgian leader (he later reportedly told French president Nicolas Sarkozy that he had wanted to "hang Saakashvili by the balls").[18]

The Rose Revolution was followed a year later by an Orange one in Ukraine that pushed out President Leonid Kuchma, a leader who governed autocratically and who had presided over a degeneration of freedoms in Ukraine. As in Georgia, the Western-leaning opposition leader and favorite of the protesters triumphed in the election following the revolution—in Ukraine the winner was Viktor Yushchenko—leading many Russians to suspect the revolt was an American undertaking.[19] (Other than rhetorically praising the Orange demonstrators and funding the National Endowment for Democracy, which had some grantees in Ukraine, Congress and the White House had played no role in Ukraine.) Yushchenko's views of Moscow certainly weren't helped by an incident during his election campaign in which someone apparently poisoned him with dioxin, nearly killing him and permanently disfiguring his face—his youthful, robust visage became a landscape of pockmarks and cysts that resembled a Slavic Manuel Noriega.[20] Toxicologists told the BBC that the sophisticated dioxin poison used on Yushchenko could have been produced in only a handful of laboratories in the world, nearly all of which are located in Russia or the United States.[21]

By 2005, when a Tulip Revolution in Kyrgyzstan followed the Orange one and drove out Kyrgyz autocrat Askar Akayev, who had maintained close ties with the Kremlin, both Moscow and Beijing clearly were rattled. "The Russian leadership viewed the outbreak of the color revolutions across the former Soviet republics from 2003 to 2005 with deep apprehension," concluded Jeanne Wilson, a Russian specialist at Harvard. "In the Russian view the Rose Revolution in Georgia, the Orange Revolution in Ukraine and the Tulip Revolution in Kyrgyzstan indicated the efforts of Western actors, foremost the United States, to initiate regime change in the post-Soviet states, an ambitious undertaking that potentially extended to Russia itself."[22]

And according to Hong Kong–based publications, after the Kyrgyz revolution Chinese president Hu Jintao commissioned an internal party report, titled "Fighting the People's War Without Gunsmoke," that outlined how the color revolutions had toppled other regimes and proposed ways the Chinese Communist Party could prevent such a possibility from occurring in China.[23] The Chinese leadership, too, saw the hand of the United States and its intelligence agencies rather than local political factors as the main reason for the color revolutions. "The ability of the color revolutions to succeed cannot be separated from the behind the scenes manipulation by the United States," argued one commentator in the *People's Daily,* the party's best-known mouthpiece.[24] Reflecting this viewpoint, the Chinese leadership reportedly sent intelligence agents to Georgia, Ukraine, and Kyrgyzstan to analyze why the revolts occurred, and to look for the hand of the United States.[25] Beijing later reportedly commissioned several state-linked think tanks to produce analyses on the color revolutions. At a symposium on the color revolutions, Chinese think-tank experts and intelligence officials presented recommendations for how China could forestall its own similar popular revolt.[26]

The revolts in the Middle East in late 2010 and early 2011 also clearly rattled both Beijing and Moscow. Almost immediately after the initial demonstrations in Tunisia and Egypt, the Chinese authorities intensified their Web filtering, so that Internet users in China who tried to search for the word "Egypt" got few or no results.[27] According to Chinese officials and press accounts, the senior leadership in Beijing also held emergency meetings to consider how the Middle East protests might impact China. When an unknown group in China posted an online call for a "Jasmine Revolution," echoing the Middle East protests, Beijing cracked down hard. It stepped up arrests of human rights activists and imposed new restrictions on foreign journalists, limits on their reporting that had not been used in China in years. Some foreign journalists who tried to evade the restrictions and venture out to cover potential protests in Beijing were beaten by the Chinese security forces.[28] Chinese reporters said that the climate had become the most repressive for local journalists in at least two decades, while even foreign scholars who previously had never had trouble with the authorities found themselves suddenly blocked when they attempted to do work in China.

The Chinese security forces employed such tough measures even though, in most recent surveys, the majority of urban middle class Chinese, who have prospered enormously since China's reform period began in the late 1970s, did not seem to want to change their government. In a 2009 poll conducted by the Program on International Policy Attitudes, China was the only country in which a majority of citizens supported their government's response to the global economic crisis—63 percent of respondents said their government's efforts to address the economic crisis were "about right."[29] Of all the countries surveyed in the poll. Another comprehensive analysis of Chinese citizens by the U.S.-based East-West Center found that "as China's economic reform and growth have progressed, public interest in promoting liberal democracy seems to have diminished,"[30] since the public believes reform might threaten economic and social gains.

China's state-controlled press cast the Middle East protests in the most negative light possible. It accused protesters in Arab-Muslim countries of creating chaos that would detract from growth and potentially hurt living standards, partly by sparking a wave of rural, poorer people—currently kept out of richer cities by many formal and informal barriers—who would flood into urban areas, competing for jobs with the urban middle classes. "The vast majority of the people [in the Middle East] are strongly dissatisfied [with the protests], so the performance by the minority becomes a self-delusional ruckus," the *Beijing Daily* said in one typical editorial.[31]

Compared with the 1990s, by the late 2000s Russia and China also had the means to act on their desire to limit democracy's spread along their borders. China's soft power offensive had spread beyond Southeast Asia into Central Asia and even the Caucasus, and, by training thousands of officials annually from countries like Kyrgyzstan and Cambodia, Beijing now was in a position to exert sizable influence over foreign governments' decision making. From virtually nothing, China also had become a major aid donor in Central Asia. Many Central Asian states, like Kyrgyzstan, also had become dependent on Chinese investment to develop their infrastructure, or simply to keep their economy afloat.[32] Chinese construction firms laid the new roads in Kyrgyzstan and built the new pipelines. A new Chinese Peace Corps–like program to boost people-to-people contacts with neighboring nations, called the China Association of Youth Volunteers, added to China's soft power reach.[33]

Russia, too, had assumed a far greater influence over Central Asia and other former Soviet states than it enjoyed in the immediate aftermath of the collapse of the Soviet Union. Through Gazprom, the Kremlin controlled gas deliveries for its neighbors, and in many Caucasian and Central Asian states, where senior leaders had begun their political careers in the Soviet Union, Moscow's rhetorical and cultural influence still mattered as well. The continuing high price of oil, which fattened the Kremlin's treasury, also made Moscow's antidemocratic regional initiatives a rounding error in the national budget. In fact, as Charlie Szrom and Thomas Brugato of the American Enterprise Institute found, from 2000 to 2007 there was an empirical correlation between the price of oil and the Kremlin's foreign policy aggressiveness, with Moscow becoming more forceful when the price of oil rose.[34]

Worried by the color revolutions, Moscow and Beijing first shored up their own control. While in the 1980s and early 1990s Beijing had allowed vibrant debate at the highest levels of government about transition to more open and democratic politics, after Hu Jintao became president in 2003, this debate largely died, and the Communist Party consolidated its control of leading companies, top officials and policy makers, journalists, and other opinion leaders. The senior leadership under Hu, in fact, contained few leaders anywhere near as liberal as Zhao Ziyang, the premier who served under Deng Xiaoping in the 1980s and who was purged after the 1989 Tiananmen crackdown.[35] China cracked down on foreign NGOs to make sure they couldn't serve as instigators of unrest. Chinese security forces raided the offices of several local NGOs backed by American democracy promotion organizations, and after 2005 Beijing imposed much tougher restrictions on local NGOs, resulting in the closure of thousands of them.[36] According to a report by the Shanghai Academy of Social Sciences, the government started spending a sum of 514 billion yuan (over $60 billion) annually on what it calls "stability maintenance," the largest allocation of the national budget after military expenditures.[37] And, following the July 2009 protests by ethnic Uighurs in Urumqi, the largest city in Xinjiang, Beijing turned the vast western province, larger than Western Europe, into a communications black hole, shutting off Internet and international mobile phone access to the province for nearly ten months.[38] Beijing imposed similar restrictions after a new wave of protests by ethnic Mongolians in Inner Mongolia province in early 2011.

While China essentially has no elections, after the color revolutions the Kremlin made it even harder for Russia's tiny and besieged political opposition to win any votes, building up the vicious pro-Kremlin and pro-Putin Nashi youth movement and calling on members to prevent a color revolution in Russia led by Western-backed instigators—the Russian opposition parties.[39] These youth activists targeted the few remaining opposition leaders, who were harassed and frequently attacked. Meanwhile, after leveling much of the Chechen capital, Grozny, during several wars, the Kremlin under Putin essentially installed a Moscow loyalist, Ramzan Kadyrov, as president of the Chechen republic. In Chechnya, Kadyrov did create a semblance of stability and growth, but did so largely by brutally repressing any anti-Kremlin or pro-autonomy sentiment.[40]

But these actions were hardly surprising or, really, new—as authoritarian regimes, Moscow and Beijing long had come up with ever-more-inventive ways to maintain their hold on power at home. But after 2005, what was different was that the two authoritarian powers tried to extend their anti-democracy battle abroad. First, they tried to delegitimize the color revolutions, by arguing that the color revolutions were not genuine popular movements but actually Western attempts at regime change that violated the sovereignty of independent countries. This argument, though not really supported by facts on the ground in Georgia, Ukraine, or Kyrgyzstan, did resonate with many people around the world, since the Bush administration had of course touted democracy promotion as a reason for the invasion of Iraq. In the wake of the Iraq war, the defense of national sovereignty, long a foundation of Beijing's foreign policy, since it did not want foreign nations involving themselves with Tibet or Taiwan, made the Chinese leadership an anti-Bush champion to many other nations. In so linking Iraq and democracy promotion, the White House had tarred the name of American democracy promotion, but it also had given Russia and China ammunition for their defense of sovereignty and provided the opportunity for the two countries to question the color revolutions.

In May 2005, Russian Foreign Minister Igor Ivanov previewed this strategy of linking support for autocrats to a defense of sovereignty, arguing in an interview that the color revolutions were "unconstitutional" overthrows of legitimate leaders, and actually would result in greater political oppression and instability in the international system.[41] Another senior Kremlin official, Vladislav Surkov, later would tell the German magazine *Der Spiegel* that the color revolutions were simply coups by another name.[42] The Russian Duma soon picked up this claim, holding sessions to discuss the illegitimacy of the Orange Revolution and then using its representatives at the Council of Europe to raise the issue.[43] The state-dominated Russian press, too, piled on, calling the Orange protest the "orange virus" or "orange plague," according to Russia-watcher Thomas Ambrosio.[44] The Russian leaders, of course, did not differentiate between a revolution to topple an authoritarian leader who had not been elected legitimately, and one to overthrow a fairly elected leader, as would happen in Thailand, for instance, in 2006. To the Kremlin, a government in power was automatically legitimate, and so any overthrow was necessarily wrong. Still, Ivanov's claims carried weight internationally. "The great issue that divides the U.N. is no longer Communism versus capitalism, as it once was; it is sovereignty," wrote James Traub, one of the most astute observers of the United Nations. By standing up for "sovereignty," even in farcical cases like autocrats trying to prevent color revolutions, Russia and China gained supporters at the UN, including many developing countries—and not only authoritarian ones—with histories of intervention by foreign powers.[45] To be sure, the UN in the late 2000s did adopt the principle of Responsibility to Protect, or R2P, in which the international community could intervene in a country, violating its sovereignty, in the case of war crimes, genocide, and crimes against humanity.[46] But many developing nations only halfheartedly backed the concept of Responsibility to Protect, and both they and the authoritarian powers watered down the concept between its introduction and final adoption.

Indonesia offers an example of a nation that, despite its democratization, supported many of China and Russia's ideas on sovereignty. Indonesia had been a Cold War battleground, with tensions between rightists, Muslim organizations, and communists resulting in a bloodletting in 1965 and 1966 that resulted in between a half-million and one million deaths, according to reliable estimates.[47] Even today, a democratic government in Jakarta still over-sees massive human rights abuses in outlying provinces like Papua, where the security forces are accused of torture, disappearances, and killings.[48] So, Indonesian leaders even today see much to support in China and Russia's concept of sovereignty. During a state visit to China in 2005 by Indonesian President Susilo Bambang Yudhoyono, he and China's leaders together affirmed their aversion to "meddling" by foreign actors in their internal affairs—whether that meant human rights organizations criticizing abuses by the Indonesian security forces, or foreign governments calling for some real reforms in Tibet or Xinjiang.[49]

Together, Russia and China also used the Shanghai Cooperation Orga-nization (SCO), a regional group linking the two powers with several Central Asian nations, to make the argument that color revolutions, and democratic change in general, were violations of national sovereignty. At an SCO sum-mit in 2005, the organization announced that "the right of every people to its own path of development must be fully guaranteed," a coded critique of the color revolutions.[50] It would then condemn the color revolutions as akin to "terrorism," attempting to link the autocrats' fight against the color demon-strators to the United States' global war on terror. By issuing these statements in an internationally recognized organization, the authoritarian powers obtained greater global credibility for this position as defenders of absolute sovereignty. The SCO, wrote Ambrosio, was attempting to be not another intergovernmental talk shop but "the embodiment of a new set of values and norms governing the future development of Central Asia. . . . Those seeking to promote democracy [in Eurasia] will meet another, less expected layer of resistance. Not only will the autocratic regimes themselves oppose demo-cratization, but the opposition [to democracy] will find resonance at the intergovernmental level as well."[51]

The organization also clearly portrayed electoral democracy as a kind of Western—foreign—idea, one that was not necessarily suited for Cen-tral Asia. Thus, when color revolutions broke out in Central Asia, SCO officials could claim that the protests were somehow unsuited to Central Asia's traditions.

In other cases, China has worked to shore up autocrats facing popular pressure, or has even helped authoritarian rulers track down and arrest their own dissidents and critics. In one notable example, after large-scale demonstrations in Uzbekistan in 2005, the authoritarian Uzbek regime cracked down on protesters, killing at least several hundred in the city of Andijon when government forces fired indiscriminately into crowds. In response, Uzbek activists called for foreign governments to pressure their government to own up to the massacre and to reform. Many governments complied, including not only the United States but also other Asian nations. China took the opposite approach: Not long after the massacre, Beijing praised the crackdown as necessary and then welcomed Uzbek leader Islam Karimov in Beijing with a state visit and a gun salute, showing that China would stand firmly behind him. More dangerously, China then worked with other nations in the region to deny asylum to any refugees fleeing Uzbekistan.

Meanwhile, Russia and other Central Asian autocracies like Kazakhstan used their positions in the Organization for Security and Cooperation in Europe (OSCE) to change the focus of that group from human rights and democratization to other issues like counterterrorism and security cooperation, according to numerous participants in OSCE forums.[52] Such a shift would be critical, since in the past the OSCE had been one of the leading organizations monitoring elections—and potentially criticizing whether they were free and fair. At several OSCE meetings, Russia threatened that it would cut its funding for the organization if election monitoring remained a primary focus of the group.[53] Similarly, the Kremlin allegedly used its delegation to the Parliamentary Assembly of the Council of Europe, an organization of parliamentarians, to tamp down criticism of pro-Russian Ukrainian leaders and to critique pro–Orange Revolution Ukrainian politicians.[54] And Russia, along with several other former Soviet states, created their own election monitoring system to observe polls in the old Soviet Union. But unlike most internationally accepted election monitoring systems, the one created by Russia relied on a small circle of trusted Kremlin allies, rather than on groups of monitors selected at random from a range of NGOs like the Carter Center. As Ambrosio found, in nearly every election in the former Soviet Union, these Kremlin-allied monitors approved votes as free and fair, often in sharp contrast to the reporting of those same polls by Western European monitoring organizations.[55] When European monitoring groups criticized these polls, the Kremlin, and other autocrats in the former Soviet Union, could hold up their own monitors as evidence of free polling and then accuse the Europeans of applying inaccurate standards. "The differing conclusions allowed Russia to discredit the external observers' findings by fostering a seemingly unwinnable 'he said-she said' debate," Ambrosio found.[56]

The two authoritarian powers also took more specific actions to undermine regional democracy. If Beijing and the Kremlin could undermine democrats, and show that their governments were less effective, more corrupt, and worse for development than the authoritarian regimes that previously had run countries like Ukraine, they might be able to convince the public in those countries to accept a return to autocratic rule—a return that would forestall any regional democratic wave that might touch the two powers.

In Ukraine, the Kremlin's party, United Russia, signed an agreement to cooperate with the party of pro-Russian Ukrainian leader Viktor Yanukovych, who was hardly sympathetic to the Orange revolt.[57] This deal included plans by the Kremlin to help Yanukovych's party in the next election. Moscow later provided Kremlin-backed political consultants to advise Yanukovych's presidential campaign, and proved willing to sanction Ukrainian elections marred by serious vote rigging, elections in which pro-Russia candidates triumphed.[58] In the winter of 2005–06, the Kremlin went further. Facing a government run by the Orange favorite Yushchenko, Moscow cut off Ukraine's discounts on natural gas. Western European nations forced the Kremlin to back off its gas threat, but the new price it negotiated with Ukraine still was twice the old one. Later, the Kremlin would further threaten the Orange government by questioning Ukraine's borders and highlighting the rights of Russian speakers in the Ukraine, widely believed to be a means of further inserting the Kremlin into Ukrainian politics. The Kremlin's assistance, combined with the poor governing performance of the post–Orange Revolution government in Kiev, did allow Yanukovych to regain his power, and in 2010 he won the presidency. As Yanukovych consolidated his power, arresting many of the top officials from the Orange government including the former prime minister, Yulia Tymoshenko, investigating domestic and foreign NGOs working in Ukraine, and apparently pressuring the media to portray him only positively, Moscow backed him staunchly. While Moscow had tried to hike gas prices for Ukraine under his predecessor, with Yanukovych the Kremlin negotiated a new deal to sell gas to Ukraine at subsidized low rates again, a deal that could help boost Ukraine's economy, and thus suggest that a more authoritarian leader could deliver stronger growth than the fractious democrats who came into office following the Orange Revolution.[59]

Similarly, in Georgia, Kyrgyzstan, and other former Soviet nations like Moldova, the Kremlin intervened directly in attempts to reverse color revolutions or to prevent new ones from occurring. In so doing, Russia actually violated these nations' sovereignty far more than any actions by American democracy promotion organizations or funders like Soros. The Kremlin's youth group, Nashi, known for its aggressive tactics against democracy activists, launched branches in other Central Asian nations, and another pro-Kremlin youth organization signed an agreement to help youth groups in Kiev.[60] In Moldova, the poorest country in Europe but an increasingly open democracy, the Kremlin has used its Ukrainian allies to pressure the Moldovan government, intermittently barred Moldovan exports from entering Russia, and taken other steps to promote parties skeptical about democratization. In Kyrgyzstan, Russian advisers helped a series of leaders emulate the Kremlin's model of political control. In part because of this Russian influence, the respected International Crisis Group found, "Parliamentary democracy in Kyrgyzstan has been hobbled. . . . A good example of how the Vladimir Putin model of governance is being copied in Central Asia." By 2010, the top politicians in four Kyrgyz parties were traveling regularly to Moscow, where they could compete for the Kremlin's financial support and rhetorical backing.[61]

In Georgia, which under Saakashvili became a favorite of the Bush administration, the Kremlin denounced the color revolution as a violation of sovereignty and a rollback of democracy.[62] Then, weeks after Moscow cut off Ukraine's subsidized gas in the winter of 2005–06, an explosion disrupted natural gas pipelines from Russia to Georgia, plunging Georgia into a state of fear during an exceptionally cold winter.[63] Still, having failed to force a change in the government of Georgia, including the imposition of economic sanctions in 2006, Putin ratcheted up tensions, abetted by Saakashvili, who himself seemed to delight in angering the Kremlin. In August 2008, Russian forces took advantage of skirmishes between Georgian troops and separatist insurgents to attack Georgia, advancing to within a few miles of the Georgian capital. The Russian assault, which included the blocking of Georgia's harbor and the deployment of tanks out of proportion to the initial skirmishing, had far more to do with teaching Georgia a lesson—and possibly showing other democratizing neighbors how Moscow would treat them—than with the ostensible dispute over Georgian-Russian border regions. Although Russia portrayed its actions as a move to protect ethnic Russians in the South Ossetia region of Georgia, years earlier Russian intelligence services and military forces had clearly tried to foster separatist sentiment among ethnic Russians in South Ossetia, distributing Russian passports to South Ossetians and taking many other steps to prod the region to break away, according to several reports by European human rights groups.

Perhaps even more dangerous than the direct intervention in neighboring nations, both China and Russia began to redefine the very meaning of democracy so that, in true Orwellian fashion, the word started to lose its meaning, which was exactly what the authoritarian powers wanted. "Rarely has democracy been so acclaimed yet so breached," noted Human Rights Watch in its 2008 survey of global freedoms. "Today, democracy has become the sine qua non of legitimacy . . . yet the credentials of the claimants have not kept pace with democracy's growing popularity. . . . Determined not to let mere facts stand in the way [autocratic] rulers have mastered the art of democratic rhetoric that bears little relationship to the principle of governing."[64]

Under Putin, the Kremlin, working with many Russian academics, developed the idea of "sovereign democracy," a concept that would provide the Kremlin with the ideological underpinnings for Putin's autocracy. As one of Putin's closest advisers defined it, sovereign democracy meant a "democracy" run by a highly centralized state and in which civil society is used by the state to monitor government officials, yet society is not independent of the government.[65] Sovereign democracy also meant, according to Kremlin strategists, that each nation was free to choose its own form of "democracy," even if that meant holding essentially fake elections designed to buttress an autocrat—a leader's "sovereignty" inoculated him against foreign criticism of the fairness of his or her "democracy." To maintain the facade of democracy, in 2006 the Kremlin even created a fake opposition party, called A Just Russia, designed to simulate the appearance of competition with the Kremlin-backed United Russia, which dominates Russian politics.[66]

The Kremlin even created its own international NGOs that were supposedly focused on democracy promotion and seemed, from the outside, to be mirror images of Western groups like America's National Endowment for Democracy. But these Russian "NGOs" actually offered expertise and funding to foreign leaders to help them forestall new color revolutions.[67] In Kyrgyzstan, Russia allegedly helped launch several NGOs, such as the Coalition of People's Democrats, which mostly spent its time condemning the United States as well as opposition Kyrgyz politicians.[68] In Ukraine, an organization called the Russian Press Club and run by an adviser to Putin posed as an NGO and helped facilitate Russia's involvement in Ukrainian elections.[69] Moscow also copied a trick used for years by China, which has fought back against American criticism of its rights record by issuing its own annual survey of human rights in the United States, which often refers to historical abuses like slavery.[70] In 2008, Russia launched an "NGO" called the Institute for Democracy and Cooperation; its job was to monitor the human rights climate in Western nations like the United States and France. It produced a steady stream of articles and press briefings promoting Russia's style of "democracy" and taking apart America's democracy promotion efforts.

The Chinese leadership also wants to alter the meaning of democracy. In his report to the 17th Party Congress, held in October 2007, President Hu Jintao used the words "democracy" or "democratic" roughly sixty times, according to one analysis.[71] In its annual report on human rights, too, "Progress in China's Human Rights," Beijing featured a definition of human rights that emphasized economic rights and material gains for average people in China, twisting the traditional definition of human rights, which historically has focused more on social and political freedoms.[72] This altering of the definition of rights to focus primarily on economic gains was echoed by many elected autocrats, men and women like Cambodia's Hun Sen or Venezuela's Hugo Chavez. As the international monitoring organization Freedom House noted, Chavez has consistently touted Venezuela's (praiseworthy) economic gains on his watch, such as reductions in poverty, as indicators of the progress on rights the country has made—and as a means of avoiding discussion on political rights, which have gone backward during his time in office.[73] At the United Nations Human Rights Council, China has similarly made arguments that twist the traditional definition of human rights, while trying to change the way the Council operates so that only governments, and not human rights groups or other civil society organizations, could make reports on human rights to the Council.[74]

Many elected autocrats, like Cambodia's Hun Sen or Malaysia's Najib Tun Razak, have explicitly modeled their defenses of human rights on China's, claiming that, like China, they have brought significant economic progress and economic liberalism to their citizens, and that these gains overshadow any concerns about political repression.

9
Failure of the Emerging Powers

R EPRESENTING THE WORLD'S LARGEST DEMOCRACY, which has sewn together a nation of a billion people, as well as countless ethnic groups, castes, and languages, Indian officials long have boasted of their nation's deep and founding commitment to democracy. And as China and India increasingly have become global competitors—and China's gleaming infrastructure, rapid decision making, and high growth rates have outshone India's—Delhi has emphasized its rhetorical commitment to democracy only more.

But to Myo, a Burmese activist, democratic India doesn't look much different from authoritarian China.[1] Worse, maybe. "At least with China, you expect that they are going to support dictators, so it's not that surprising," Myo said. "But with India, it's not what I expected, so it was a slap to [Burmese activists.]"

After working as a democracy activist in Burma, underground, for many years, Myo fled the country in the mid-2000s to work in exile. Before he left, he sat in a dingy noodle shop in Rangoon, where customers slurped steaming bowls of Burmese mohingar noodles seasoned with bits of lime and cabbage and slices of egg. Myo picked a table wedged deep into one dark corner of the restaurant, where it would be hard for anyone to overhear conversation. He said he had been working for a publishing company in Rangoon, but he covertly had to smuggle political messages into the writings he published in magazines that focused on safe topics like soccer or Burmese rap.[2] "It's kind of a game everyone here plays, but after a while it gets so tiring," he said, as he stirred bits of oil into his soup broth. "I'd like to once not have to try to figure out how to fool the censors over a simple article."

At first, after leaving Burma Myo traveled to India, where he'd hoped that the world's largest democracy would prove hospitable to activists pushing for human rights and democracy in a repressive state on India's borders. "I'd heard that, before, India had been very welcoming to Burmese activists, particularly after 1988 [a period of antigovernment rioting in Burma], so I expected it would still be," he said. But Myo was wrong. In the 1990s, some Indian officials had tried to assist Burmese democracy activists, and India's then-defense minister George Fernandes, a prominent human rights advocate, even allowed some Burmese exiles to take shelter in his personal family compound.[3] But by the 2000s, Delhi had reversed its Burma policy 180 degrees. Rather than criticizing the Burmese junta, it now engaged the generals under a new policy it called "Look East," hosting Senior General Than Shwe on a state visit, during which, with no obvious irony, he visited the monument of the revered Mahatma Gandhi.[4] India ignored international resolutions condemning the Burmese regime's massive human rights abuses, and it launched a policy to boost Indian investment in Burma, particularly in the valuable petroleum industry. Delhi began providing arms to Burma, and in the fall of 2007, while tens of thousands of Burmese monks were protesting against the government in the streets of Rangoon, Burma's biggest city, India's petroleum minister traveled to Naypyidaw, the new capital of Burma that had been built by the military, to sign new agreements on oil and gas.[5] He made no mention of the massive protests going on in Rangoon, which ultimately would be put down with brutal force.

After Than Shwe's visit to Gandhi's monument, a Burma specialist for Amnesty International commented that "it was entirely unpalatable . . . that India could allow one of the world's most flagrant violators of human rights to stain the legacy of a man who led masses to peacefully overthrow a repressive colonial overlord . . . or to symbolically forsake its support for [Burmese opposition leader] Aung San Suu Kyi, herself a sort of Burmese version of Gandhi."[6] Amnesty could have launched a similar salvo at nearly every major emerging democracy around the world. It could have blasted South Africa, which Nelson Mandela vowed would make the promotion of democracy and human rights a pillar of its foreign policy, but which has for years tolerated Robert Mugabe's brutal regime next door in Zimbabwe.[7] It could have lambasted Brazil, which even as it has grown more powerful has cozied up to Iranian dictator Mahmoud Ahmadinejad as well as to local elected autocrats like Venezuela's Hugo Chavez.[8]

By the late 2000s and early 2010s, many Western officials still hoped that the big emerging democracies, the Brazils, Indonesias, and South Africas, would eventually become regional and global champions of human rights and democratization. To some Western observers, this made natural sense, since these countries themselves had fought hard for their own democracies, and surely saw the importance of strengthening democratic systems in the countries around them. And yet, as India showed with Burma, such hopes often proved naive. Unlike, say, the Netherlands or Canada, countries like India and Indonesia suffered decades of foreign interventions during the Cold War that left their leaders skeptical of any policies that might violate other countries' sovereignty. And more often than not, these major emerging democracies shared as many strategic interests with their undemocratic neighbors, whom they actually had to live next to, as with the faraway West.

The end of the Cold War may have sped up the emergence of new democracies in the world, but it was not until the late 1990s and early 2000s that the United States, and other Western nations, began aggressively trying to enlist emerging powers like India in global democracy promotion. Working with the leaders of several new democracies, including India, the Clinton administration helped establish the Community of Democracies, a global meeting of nations that first convened in Poland in 2000.[9] The group was supposed to help promote an expansion and deepening of democratic norms throughout the world, and it eventually expanded, in 2004, to create a democracies' caucus at the United Nations.[10] Still, despite a request from Washington, India declined to serve as the leader of the UN democracy caucus.[11]

The community of democracies established some shared democratic norms and, at the UN, created a fund to help support civil society groups that monitor elections and take other steps to promote freedom.[12] At roughly the same time, America's National Endowment for Democracy, working with civil society groups in many other nations, launched the World Movement for Democracy, which brought together democracy activists from around the globe to support prodemocracy organizations within autocratic nations, as well as groups operating in existing democracies. And some regional democracy organizations sprung up as well, from the Inter-Parliamentary Caucus of the Association of Southeast Asian Nations to the Office for the Promotion of Democracy of the Organization of American States. At one gathering of the World Movement for Democracy, held in Jakarta in the spring of 2010, Indonesian President Susilo Bambang Yudhoyono struck all the right rhetorical notes. "I am convinced," Yudhoyono declared, "that ultimately the 21st century instinct is the democratic instinct. . . . No political system can ignore this."[13] Indonesia also hosted the annual Bali Democracy Forum, at which representatives of many different emerging democracies come together to share their experiences and learn from each other's stories.[14]

In 2008, Arizona Senator John McCain would propose a League of Democracies that would strengthen cooperation among democratic nations.[15] This concept previously had been outlined in several essays by foreign policy specialists James Lindsay and Ivo Daalder, who argued that a "Concert of Democracies" could work together on a range of security and economic challenges that require multilateral cooperation, as well as on promoting democracy and human rights.[16] Such a concert, they noted, need not be a formal structure, with a permanent infrastructure, but could be more of an informal grouping of democracies.

Enlisting emerging powers like Brazil, India, or Indonesia in an international partnership of democracies made obvious sense; the concept of a Concert of Democracies, in theory, could promote more effective multilateral cooperation. Not only would the emerging powers' cooperation in such an initiative reduce any fears that democracy promotion was a stealth American plan for regime change around the world, but the emerging powers often wielded far more influence in their own regions than the United States or other Western democracies did. The United States slapped sanctions on Burma in 1997 that, since that time, have significantly reduced America's role in the country, but India, Thailand, and Indonesia, three democracies near Burma, implemented no sanctions, and enjoy sizable trade and security relationships with the Burmese junta.[17] South Africa provides Zimbabwe with electricity, food aid, and other lifelines, and so Pretoria carries by far the most weight in Harare, no matter how much Robert Mugabe rails at imagined diabolic American and British intervention in his country.[18] And while the United States wields enormous influence in the imagination of many Latin American leaders, due to Washington's history of interventions in the Western Hemisphere, it is Brazil's increasingly powerful economy, and left-leaning leaders, that now have greater influence over many South and Central American leaders, particularly those from socialist backgrounds like Venezuela's Hugo Chavez and Nicaragua's Daniel Ortega.

At times, the enthusiasm responsible for concepts like a League of Democracies has seemed warranted. Besides the growth of these new international organizations of democracies, some emerging powers had taken a stand, at times, in their own neighborhoods. In the late 1990s, under the government of Prime Minister Chuan Leekpai, Bangkok took a tougher approach to the Burmese junta than it had under any previous administration. Distancing itself from other Southeast Asian countries' engagement with Burma, Chuan's government began criticizing the junta's human rights abuses and offering measured support for Suu Kyi and her National League for Democracy.[19] Chuan himself told American officials, "As prime minister he never visited Burma. . . . He didn't want to demonstrate any form of support or sense of legitimacy to the [Burmese] regime."

But these examples are relatively rare. Besides its see-no-evil Burma policy, India took a hands-off approach to its neighbor Sri Lanka, which under the government of President Mahinda Rajpaksa crushed the Tamil Tiger rebel movement in the spring of 2009, and in the process tried to destroy Sri Lanka's press, civil society, and opposition parties, as well as indiscriminately shelled Tamil civilians in the north of the country.[20] At the UN, Delhi blocked a resolution tabled in the Human Rights Council that would have condemned Rajpaksa's actions.[21] Instead India praised the Sri Lankan government for its handling of the aftermath of the war against the Tigers, during which the Sri Lankan government allegedly executed Tigers who surrendered and garrisoned tens of thousands of Tamil civilians in prison-like camps.[22] And after Chuan's party lost in the 2001 national elections to Thaksin Shinawatra, Thailand once again launched close ties with the

Burmese military regime and all but ignored human rights abuses by its neighbor. Thaksin claimed his government "worked to bring Myanmar [Burma] in from the cold," and helped push the junta to draft a proposal for a transition to democracy—a proposal widely criticized by international human rights groups as actually paving the way to a sham election in Burma that installed the military's favored party in power.[23] Under Thaksin, Thailand also drastically increased its trade with and investment in Burma: Between 2003 and 2008, Burma's exports to Thailand more than doubled, including sizable exports of natural gas.[24]

After a coup deposed Thaksin in 2006, a military-backed government in Bangkok continued the policy of engagement, with Thai companies in 2010 making a $13.3-billion investment in a new Burmese deep-sea port, the largest-ever Thai investment in its neighbor.[25] Indeed, in 2010 and 2011, Burma received some $20 billion in new foreign investment, the highest year-on-year figure in its history; the vast majority of that investment came from neighboring nations, including democracies like India, Thailand, and South Korea.[26] Thailand, which during the Vietnam War era sheltered tens of thousands of Indochinese refugees, in 2009 also forced some three thousand Hmong, an ethnic minority group, back to Laos, even though many of the Hmong, who once fought against the communists in Vientiane, might face persecution back at home.[27] And in fact, after being pushed back to Laos many of the Hmong were corralled into areas that appeared to be prison camps, and foreign reporters who attempted to visit these areas were banned. Some of the Hmong refugees simply vanished.[28]

Like Thailand and India, South Africa, Turkey, and Brazil sometimes mouth the rhetoric of rights and democracy promotion. After the end of apartheid, many human rights activists had high hopes for South Africa's ruling African National Congress (ANC), which after all had benefited from a global pressure movement when its members were fighting against white rule. Under Mandela, the ANC passed one of the most progressive constitutions in the world, and South African leaders helped broker an end to conflicts across the continent. ANC leaders at times condemned atrocities in Zimbabwe, as well as abuses in other countries like Burma and Sri

Lanka.[29] Yet in recent years Pretoria has used its influence at the UN, and at African organizations, not only to protect the regime in Zimbabwe but also to veto a UN Security Council resolution condemning rights abuses in Burma.[30] Asked during a visit to Harare about Zimbabwe's coalition government, in which Mugabe used security forces to intimidate and kill members of the opposition Movement for Democratic Change, South African President Jacob Zuma blithely told reporters that "it is indeed very encouraging to note the significant progress that has been made under the auspices of the inclusive government" in Zimbabwe.[31] Perhaps unable to conceal his delight, Mugabe, speaking after Zuma, declared, "The inclusive government is alive and well."[32] Mugabe's allies would continue beating supporters of other political parties, using trumped-up criminal charges to intimidate opposition politicians, and persecuting independent-minded judges, reporters, and civil society activists, according to a comprehensive investigation by Human Rights Watch.[33]

In 2011, Zuma seemed to take a slightly tougher line toward Zimbabwe, declaring at a regional conference in March 2011 that state violence against opposition politicians must stop; one of Zuma's top advisers, Lindiwe Zulu, declared that "people [in Zimbabwe] want to see democracy." Still, Zuma took few concrete actions to pressure Zimbabwe to hold free and fair elections, even as Zimbabwean researchers released reports showing that voter rolls in the country were stuffed with at least two million ineligible voters, all likely to "support" Mugabe's party.

Pretoria also opposed the multinational effort to end the brutal regime of Libya's Muammar Qadaffi, ignored international efforts to bring Sudanese leader Omar al-Bashir to justice for crimes against humanity at the International Criminal Court, and generally remained mute about reports of massive rights violations in other young African democracies, from Kenya to Nigeria.[34] Even after Qadaffi's regime had already fallen, and the dictator and his family were on the run, Zuma's government refused to recognize the new, transitional government of Libya and played a lead role in getting the African Union to delay recognition. The South African leadership refused even to allow the Dalai Lama to make a visit to the country in 2009 for a conference of Nobel laureates, presumably for fear of angering China—a decision that drew the rebuke of Archbishop Desmond Tutu, South Africa's own Nobel Peace laureate.[35]

While Brazilian President Lula did speak out against some egregious human rights abuses, and offered asylum to an Iranian woman sentenced to be stoned to death for adultery, his government mostly ignored democracy promotion and human rights in other nations. Lula called on Venezuelan leader Hugo Chavez to tone down his fiery anti-American rhetoric, according to one U.S. embassy cable released by Wikileaks, but he did not push the Venezuelan to address some of his autocratic tendencies.[36] Questioned by a *Newsweek* reporter about why Venezuela was allowed to participate in a South American trade bloc that is supposed to be open only to full democracies that respect human rights, Lula responded, "Give me one example of how Venezuela is not democratic." When the reporter listed Chavez's crackdown on independent media, trade unions, and political rivals, Lula casually said, "That's not the [Venezuelan] government's version."[37] On another occasion, Lula called Chavez "the best president of Venezuela in the last 100 years."[38] And even though Lula himself got his start in trade unions and opposition politics during what was a relatively repressive atmosphere in Brazil at that time, he also pointedly refused to join regional condemnation of human rights abuses in Cuba. When a prominent Cuban political prisoner named Orlando Zapata Tamayo went on a hunger strike (he ultimately died in the midst of his strike, approximately two and a half months later), Lula seemed to ridicule Tamayo's struggle, likening the activist to a criminal who was trying to gain publicity to get out of jail. Meeting with Cuban leader Raul Castro, Lula pointedly declined to even mention the hunger strike or other abuses.[39] Along with Turkey, Lula also took a similarly accommodating view toward Iranian leader Mahmoud Ahmadinejad, even after Ahmadinejad's government crushed the Green protest movement that erupted in mid-2009, jailing hundreds of opposition supporters and allegedly torturing and even killing some of the most prominent opposition leaders.[40] Together, Lula and Turkish Prime Minister Recep Tayyip Erdogan traveled to Tehran, where they appeared in an embrace together with Ahmadinejad after allegedly brokering a solution to the Iranian nuclear program—one that most experts on Iran believed simply bought Tehran more time to develop a nuclear weapons program.[41] Lula's successor, Dilma Rouseff, who also had been persecuted by past military governments in Brazil, stepped back from some of Lula's most obvious embraces of abusers, such as his courting of Iran. But she continued the country's close ties to Chavez, rarely criticizing the Venezuelan leader.

There are exceptions to the emerging powers' abdication. Poland, the largest and most powerful of the newer entrants to the European Union, and a country that had its own democratic revolution, has used its influence to support reformers in other Central and Eastern European nations, such as Belarus. As the Belorussian government cracked down on opposition movements in the winter of 2010–11, Poland's leaders decried the repression and called for the European Union to enact strict punishments against Belarus, including travel bans on its leaders and bank account freezes. Poland also bankrolled opposition radio and television stations broadcasting uncensored news into Belarus.[42]

But Poland is an exception; Brazil and South Africa are the norm. Often, these weak policies drew international condemnation, like Amnesty's chastising of India for is approach to the Burmese junta. Even President Obama, who wanted to consolidate his predecessor's historic outreach to India, chided Delhi mildly during a trip to India in the fall of 2010. "If I can be frank, in international fora, India has often shied away from some of these issues [like Burma]," Obama said, to the annoyance of his hosts.[43] (The Obama administration would later launch its own engagement with the Burmese government, but would take a cautious approach, retaining sanctions on new investment in the country and keeping American aid flows into Burma to a trickle.) But the most stinging critiques came from the citizens of affected countries themselves, men and women like Myo who had hoped for more from the new democratic powers. "I am saddened with India. I would like to have thought that India would be standing behind us. That it would have followed in the tradition of Mahatma Gandhi and Jawaharlal Nehru," Suu Kyi told the *Indian Express* newspaper.[44] Or as another Burmese exile said, after years of living like a fugitive in Thailand and watching the Thai government coddle the Burmese generals: "Thai people will protest for democracy here [in Thailand] but in Burma they'd just as soon watch us die."[45]

The emerging powers' abdication of interest in international human rights or democracy did more than just hurt the efforts of activists like Suu Kyi or Myo. By taking a limited—or nonexistent—role in international democracy promotion efforts, countries like South Africa or Brazil or Turkey made it easier for autocratic leaders to paint democracy promotion as a Western, and alien, activity, or even to portray it as an illegal intervention similar to Western meddling in the Cold War in such places as Iran, Guatemala, and Chile, where Western intelligence organizations backed coups against left-leaning leaders. Eva Golinger, a prominent Venezuelan-American attorney who often advocates the worldview of Chavez's government, charged that democracy promotion was the latest American excuse for forceful regime change, a view echoed by leaders of many other autocratic regimes.[46] Again, as Western powers bombed Libya in the winter and spring of 2011, to assist rebel forces battling Muammar Qadaffi's regime, many emerging democratic powers harshly criticized the intervention, creating space for some of Qadaffi's closest friends, like Venezuelan leader Hugo Chavez, to condemn the intervention as neo-imperialism.[47] Turkey, for example, strongly opposed the Libya intervention, with Turkish Prime Minister Erdogan calling it "unthinkable" and "absurd." South Africa did the same, calling for an investigation into the war crimes committed in the toppling of Qadaffi, and mostly ignoring that Qadaffi himself had not only committed massive abuses over his forty-year rule but also played a role in stoking sub-Saharan African conflicts from Chad to Liberia.

Indeed, by studying the voting patterns of the major emerging democracies at the United Nations, the Democracy Coalition Project and Ted Piccone of the Brookings Institution clearly show that most of these new giants adhere to strict principles of nonintervention and sovereignty.[48] India's voting record at the United Nations—the General Assembly, the Rights Council, and the Security Council—shows that while it occasionally supports democracy, it "maintains that democracy must not be imposed on other countries" and so still favors nonintervention, the study revealed. Indonesia's voting record reveals that it opposes nearly every human rights and democracy initiative at the United Nations, even though within the Association of Southeast Asian Nations, where Indonesia is the leading member, Jakarta has forcefully pushed for the creation of a human rights body. Brazil's voting patterns, though more unpredictable, also tend to favor nonintervention, unless "supporting democracy or human rights will help [Brazil] to further its own goals of consolidating regional leadership," Piccone's study notes. Turkey, which benefited significantly in the 1990s and early 2000s from democracy assistance from Europe and the United States, also generally has avoided pushing for rights in its UN votes, although in the past year it has become more critical of Arab autocracies, such as Syria, that have brutalized their own citizens. (In October 2011, Turkish Foreign Minister Ahmet Davutoglu criticized the UN for not forcefully condemning Syria's crackdown on its citizens, saying, "What is taking place in Syria is not a domestic issue of Syria. It has become a tragedy for the humanity.")[49] And South Africa is perhaps the most disappointing in the study of UN voting records. Repeatedly at the United Nations, South Africa's postapartheid leadership has allied itself with autocratic regimes in votes, generally ignoring democracy movements in these authoritarian countries.[50] Like India and Indonesia, South Africa normally just abstained from any resolutions scrutinizing human rights abuses in other nations, even in such extreme examples as North Korea and Sudan, whose governments allegedly had committed massive crimes against humanity including, potentially, genocide. South Africa also refused to join a call for a special UN Human Rights Council session on Burma, whose abuses ranked on par with those of North Korea and Sudan.[51] Among emerging democratic powers studied by Piccone, only South Korea consistently voted for resolutions condemning authoritarian regimes like Burma and Sudan, or for resolutions creating mandates to monitor human rights abuses in these authoritarian states.[52]

Though they attracted criticism, the policies of these emerging democratic powers made some sense—in their own domestic contexts. The concept of nations' absolute sovereignty, promoted by authoritarian nations like China, also resonated intensely with the new emerging democratic powers. Many of them, like India and Indonesia, had been leading members of the nonaligned,

anti-imperialism movement during the Cold War, and felt extremely uncomfortable joining any international coalition that sought to undermine
other nations' sovereignty, even if potentially for a good reason.[53] "The internal anticolonial strain in the newly independent India morphed into sustained anti-imperialist posturing within the political discourse on world
affairs [during the Cold War]," notes India specialist C Raja Mohan.[54] India
allied itself with the Soviet Union, while the United States tilted toward
Pakistan. Though the end of the Soviet empire, and the bankruptcy of India's state-dominated economic model in the early 1990s, would undermine
some Indian leaders' faith in nonalignment and socialism, among Indian
elites and, particularly, older members of the Indian left this antipathy
toward any international efforts led by Western powers, and this defense of
absolute sovereignty, remained strong. What's more, India—like China,
Indonesia, and many other newer powers, democratic or not—still worries about maintaining its own territorial integrity, particularly in relation
to Kashmir, and so it wondered whether any international effort, even on
democracy or human rights, might eventually rebound against Delhi.

India's attitudes were hardly unique. Other emerging powers, including Indonesia and Turkey, want to avoid criticism of their own human rights
abuses, in restive regions like Papua, a province in eastern Indonesia where
security forces have harshly repressed dissent, or in Kurdish regions of Turkey. And during the Cold War, African National Congress leaders like
Zuma and his predecessor, Thabo Mbeki, watched as the United States
vetoed congressional legislation that would have punished apartheid, and as
Western nations pursued a relationship with South African scientists even
as some government-linked apartheid era scientists pursued programs to
poison ANC leaders.[55] Not surprisingly, many ANC leaders developed an
intense animus toward the West; some close associates of Mbeki believed
that his fear of outside powers, including scientists, trying to destroy the
ANC was one factor behind his strange, highly counterproductive beliefs
about AIDS, including questioning whether HIV causes AIDS and allowing his government to recommend natural remedies, including garlic and
lemons, to treat HIV.[56] Other emerging powers today also were victimized
by Western interventions during the Cold War: the Eisenhower administration backed an ill-fated rebellion by outlying Indonesian islands against

the Sukarno government in the late 1950s. So, in countries like Indonesia, where a younger, post–Cold War generation of political leaders has not yet taken power, most of the political class still instinctively views aggressive democracy promotion—and virtually any Western initiatives that threaten countries' sovereignty—with suspicion, even if some Indonesian liberals supported efforts like the Bali Democracy Forum.

Combined with this lingering suspicion of the West, leaders in many emerging powers realize that, on issues other than democracy and human rights, their interests do not always coincide with those of established democracies—and that, even on democracy promotion and rights advocacy, the institutions and structures were created by Western powers, during the Cold War, with little input from countries like Brazil or India. If democracies are going to challenge autocracies' sovereignty, nations like South Africa, Brazil, and India want to have the authority to help decide when such challenges to sovereignty are appropriate and when they are not. And as long as they are not granted that authority, whether through the United Nations or other international institutions, Pretoria or Brasilia will take stands at the United Nations supporting the sovereignty of even atrocious regimes like Burma or Iran. At summits of the so-called BRIC nations (Brazil, Russia, India, and China), these emerging powers have challenged many established international institutions, including the makeup of the UN Security Council and the use of the dollar as the world's reserve currency.[57] Though two of these BRIC members are autocracies, the democratic members supported challenges to international institutions just as strongly.

Indeed, as a developing nation that does not want to be penalized for polluting the environment as severely as a developed country, India has allied with China to push developed nations, like the United States, to play a larger role in reducing emissions, and to argue that Delhi and Beijing cannot afford prohibitive emissions caps, which would undermine their growth. India also has allied itself with China and Saudi Arabia, among other autocracies, in trying to reduce the power of the International Monetary Fund in managing global financial crises.[58]

In many cases, too, these new democratic powers, less secure in their regional environments than, say, Britain or Norway, are more willing to live with stable but autocratic neighbors than to risk destabilizing their regions.

The British and Norwegian governments need not fear, today, that problems in Sweden or Ireland could destabilize the United Kingdom or Norway. But India and South Africa do not enjoy such luxury. The chaotic border between India and Burma allows a myriad of armed insurgent groups, including several fighting for their own homelands in India's fractious northeast, to smuggle weapons, people, and narcotics; the porous frontier between South Africa and Zimbabwe includes large networks of people smuggling.[59] And, the instability that already exists makes leaders in these emerging democracies very wary of encouraging any more change, even if that change might ultimately benefit a vast majority of people.

Democracy advocates inside Burma or Zimbabwe would argue that these autocratic regimes, by their nature, foster instability—massive refugee outflows that suck up neighbors' resources, waves of popular unrest that occasionally spill over borders, illicit economic activity like drug smuggling. After all, at least a million Burmese refugees already have fled to Thailand (the real number is probably much higher), and some two million Zimbabweans have crossed the border into South Africa.[60] Yet despite the dangers Burma or Zimbabwe exports, sizable fear exists among leaders in Bangkok or Delhi or Pretoria that, in a political transition, the chaos and instability exported would be far worse. "The situation [on the Thai-Burmese border] isn't good now, but it's been mostly the same for decades," one Thai official said. "So no one wants to mess with it."[61]

Of course, in some cases, certain constituencies within the emerging powers prosper from their relationships with autocracies, and so have no reason to support democracy promotion and human rights advocacy. The Thai military and police, for example, long have utilized their presence along the Burmese border, and their connections in Burma, to exploit natural resources and drugs that trade across the border. (In the 1950s, Thai Police General Phao Sriyonand allegedly became one of the largest opium traffickers in Asia.)[62] Brazilian construction companies have established a large presence in Venezuela, a presence that necessarily requires some courting of Chavez's government.[63] Such interests exist in Western democracies, too: American oil firms do business in Equatorial Guinea, where they lavishly support that petro-state's thuggish regime, and French oil companies prosper from their ties to Gabon, where they enjoy a cozy relationship with Gabon's nepotistic regime.[64] But in these longer-established democracies, businesses' relationships with authoritarian regimes often are balanced by the advocacy of well-established human rights groups, democracy promotion organizations, muckraking journalists, and other civil society associations. American oil firms may invest in Equatorial Guinea, but *Mother Jones* will write a biting story chronicling their dealings, and human rights groups will make sure this article gets into the hands of congressional investigators probing Equatorial Guinea; French oil companies may do business in Gabon, but oil transparency organizations based in Paris and London will make sure that sunlight is thrown on their corporate practices. But in younger or weaker democracies like Thailand or South Africa or even Brazil, civil society and the press are not necessarily so strong, and so powerful groups that favor doing business with authoritarian neighbors can prevail more easily. In Thailand, offering any criticism in the media of the army's policies, even over a subject like doing business in Burma, could prove hazardous to a reporter's health.

All these concerns—that change fosters instability, that Indian or Brazilian or South African business groups will be hurt by their governments advocating democracy, that democracy promotion will link leaders too closely with the United States—are exacerbated by having to compete with authoritarian powers for the resources and the friendship of nations like Burma, Venezuela, or Iran. In the early 1990s, the period when some Indian officials like George Fernandes more strongly backed the Burmese prodemocracy movement, Delhi could in some ways afford to antagonize the Burmese government. At that time, the Burmese junta was still struggling to attract investment following years of xenophobic socialism, and India's potential rival, China, had not yet established a sizable economic presence in Burma. But by the early 2000s, when India sharply altered its Burma policy, engaging the generals, it did so in large part because it feared it was losing to China in a battle for Burma's resources　its oil, gas, deepsea ports, and other attractions. In the 2000s and early 2010s, Chinese companies built a new petroleum pipeline for annually transporting roughly 240,000 barrels of oil to China per day, as well as some twelve billion cubic meters of gas. Smaller Chinese firms came to dominate business across northern Burma, where they imported electronics, industrial goods, and virtually every other finished product and exported gems, logs, and other natural resources to China.[65] Chinese firms built a port in Burma that could help Chinese intelligence gather information on Indian activities and, feared some Indian strategists, could be part of a larger plan to encircle India with Chinese ports.[66]

Concerned it was losing out strategically, economically, and diplomatically, India changed course with Burma. The Burmese regime made sure that its giant democratic neighbor received some benefit from its policy shift, though India certainly never gained the type of economic influence in Burma that China has. India obtained the right to build several hydropower dams in Burma, and was given a chance to modernize a different Burmese port.[67] "This is a major strategic victory for us," Indian power and commerce minister Jairam Ramesh told Indian reporters.[68]

This fear of losing out to China on business and strategic deals if an emerging democracy focused too much on promoting democracy was hardly restricted to Burma. Indian concerns about China's growing influence in Sri Lanka, where Beijing also was building new ports, added to Delhi's decision to remain quiet, in 2008 and 2009, as Colombo committed massive human rights abuses in the waning days of the battle against the Tamil Tigers.[69] A desire to push back against the rising influence of China in Central Asian states like Kyrgyzstan and Kazakhstan, where many people are of Turkic heritage and have cultural ties to Turkey, surely was a factor in Ankara's diplomatic overtures to the region, which also make little mention of democracy or human rights abuses, even though Turkey routinely positions itself as a kind of model Muslim democracy. And China's rapid and sizable investments across sub-Saharan Africa, where it has gone from having little presence two decades ago to being the continent's largest trading partner and greatest source of finance and aid, has made other emerging powers in Africa, including South Africa and India, reconsider whether they might lose commercial deals if they prioritize human rights and democracy in places like Angola and Congo, two countries where China has made billions in investments.[70]

In Delhi, Pretoria, Brasilia, and other capitals of emerging powers, some opinion leaders argue that, in the long run, democracy would be these states' competitive advantage, and that they would devalue that advantage by seeking to out-China China, which they could never do anyway. "We came to be seen as no different from China in pursuing a policy of unconditional support to the [Burmese] junta," wrote Indian strategic analyst B Raman, a former senior official in the Indian intelligence agency—a sentiment confirmed to me by many Burmese activists, who wonder why India would try to match China's policy toward Burma when it could naturally appeal to Burma's reformers, who one day, most likely, will run the Burmese government.[71] After all, China's support for the Burmese government, along with an influx of Chinese businesspeople into central Burma, led to a spike in anti-China sentiment, symbolized by a near-riot in the Burmese city of Mandalay in the spring of 2011, after an argument between Burmese and Chinese gem traders.[72] Activists instead urge their leaders to look back to their nations' democratic heritage, or to their history of opposition to their own military dictatorships. And they suggest that, in the long run, when citizens of nations like Zimbabwe or Iran or Burma have freed themselves of their current autocratic rulers, those democrats now in power would remember—and reward—nations that stood by them when they were fighting in opposition. But how could they be so sure? After all, when they, the leaders of the ANC, or the Brazilian trade union opposition, had finally reached the presidential palace, they quickly seemed to forget democrats in other countries.

IO

Failure of the West

A s WE HAVE SEEN, democracy in the early part of the twenty-first century faces a serious range of threats, from empowered authoritarians to conservative middle classes to emerging giants uninterested in democracy promotion. Yet the idea that democracy eventually, ultimately, will be the end state of every nation on earth remains a powerful concept. This idea of the inevitability of progress has existed for centuries, since the Enlightenment, but in the past twenty years it was enunciated so clearly by Fukuyama—an inevitability still publicly embraced by nearly every major Western leader, despite the global democracy recession of the past decade, and despite the West's own unwillingness to actually come to the aid of embattled democrats around the world. Obama himself, in a 2010 speech to the United Nations General Assembly captured this concept of the inevitability of democratization, even if he was not prepared to stake his presidency on promoting this idea in the Middle East. "History is on the side of liberty," Obama told the gathering of world leaders. "Democracy, more than any other form of government, delivers for our citizens."[1]

As we will see in the next chapter, in the long run democracy probably is the best political system—not only because it allows people essential freedoms but also because it provides the transparency and rule of law that in the long run foster prosperity. Still, it is a mistake to assume that just because democracy has survived previous reverse waves in the 1930s and late 1960s—and in other times when undemocratic governments gained global power and nascent democracies in places like Germany and Latin America and Greece fell prey to coups and other government takeovers—it is predestined to survive in the developing world today. As political scientist

Azar Gat notes in his study of the history of democracy, the Allies did not win the Second World War because (excepting the Soviet Union) they were democratic and held some moral high ground. They won because they were the world's industrial powers, facing off against two medium-sized powers, Germany and Japan, which had nowhere near the industrial might or the population of the Allies.[2] Similarly, the Soviet Union collapsed in the late 1980s not primarily because of its lack of political freedom, though its collapse did trigger democratic change in other Eastern European states, but because its noncapitalist economic model, always flawed, had reached its limits and finally had begun to die.

What's more, today democracy faces greater challenges than in the previous two major reverse waves mentioned above. Though the Cold War is now long over and some of the strategic factors that led the United States and other Western powers to support autocratic rulers around the world have vanished, other developments have empowered autocracy, including the growing power of China, the global economic crisis, the decline of the West, and the poor leadership of emerging democracies. These challenges have no easy solutions, particularly when the United States' democracy promotion efforts have proven so shortsighted and inflexible.

We have touched upon some of the reasons why this current reverse wave of antidemocratization may be more serious than the reverse waves in the 1930s, 1960s, and early 1970s. But it is important to look at these threats to democracy today together, and at how Western nations are failing in their democracy promotion efforts. For one, the third and fourth waves are vulnerable partly because democracy proliferated to a larger, more diverse group of countries—in parts of the developing world like the Middle East and Africa that had not played a part in the previous waves. In some ways, of course, this spread strengthens democracy—when only a tiny handful of countries, primarily in Europe and North America, fit the definition of democracies enunciated in the first chapter, the possibility always existed that, due to war or political change, democracy could be wiped off the planet entirely. This is not going to happen today, since democracy, at least in some form, has spread so widely around the globe. But, as we have seen, in the third and fourth waves, democracy came far faster to many nations than in the previous waves, to countries that had only recently gained independence, or still lacked the foundations for solid growth, or remained quite poor, or had such a weak rule of law that democratization made graft worse. Because their democratic foundations are so weak, these third and fourth wave nations are far more vulnerable to reversals than are many of the countries in the first and second waves of democracy's spread, many of which had more time to consolidate change and create stable democratic institutions before facing the reverse waves of the 1930s and 1960s.

Because of the weakness of the newest democracies, the duration preceding the reversal of some of their gains has shortened, compared with previous reverse waves. And since the reverse waves come so much more quickly today, they pose a serious threat to these young democracies. While third wave nations like Thailand took more than a decade before recalcitrant, conservative elements of the middle class, combined with an aggressive military, were able to undermine even the most nascent reforms, in countries that have seen the Arab uprisings, such as Egypt, this reversal took less than a year to occur. In other third wave nations like the countries of Eastern Europe, working class anger at the lack of improvements in economic well-being during the democratic, post–Berlin Wall period, eventually led, over a decade or more, to growing dissatisfaction with democracy and, in some countries like Russia and Ukraine, a revival of authoritarian leaders who promised higher growth and stability in exchange for weakened democratic freedoms. In fourth wave countries like Malawi and Indonesia, this dissatisfaction with the lack of equitable growth, and the rise and spread of corruption, led to popular sympathy for authoritarian rule in less than a decade from the time of democratization. Only a year after the initial uprisings in Egypt, Libya, and Tunisia, weak growth, crime, chaos, and growing corruption already led to authoritarian nostalgia among the middle and upper classes.

Although the role of outside actors in democratization can be overstated, they can play a substantial part; American democracy promotion does matter, especially in states where the United States historically has wielded outsized influence, such as Thailand or Liberia. "The strong, positive incorporation of democracy as a mutually reinforcing goal alongside US economic and security interests in some places . . . has helped firm up the idea in these countries or regions that democracy is the normal, expected outcome," writes Thomas Carothers of the Carnegie Endowment for International Peace. In addition, he notes, during the 1990s, American assistance for reform-minded civil society groups helped promote democracy in many nations, and American diplomatic involvement at times helped stop threatened coups in places like Ecuador and Paraguay.[3] Indeed, a study of American democracy aid in the 1990s by researchers from Vanderbilt University found that U.S. democracy assistance generally helped speed the pace of successful democratization in developing nations.[4] Meanwhile, the European Union's increasingly aggressive democracy promotion, as well as the allure of joining the EU itself, created powerful incentives for nations in Eastern Europe in the 1990s to maintain reformist policies and alter their laws to conform to the progressive norms of the EU. After the end of the Cold War, the EU also provided substantial economic assistance to former Eastern bloc countries like Poland, offered expertise in creating new political institutions, and monitored their progress toward democracy, as part of the preparation for future EU accession.[5]

Yet Western nations have too often made critical mistakes in their democracy promotion: they have focused too much attention on whether countries hold regular national elections, on the emergence of one charismatic and reform-minded "big man" leader like Susilo Bambang Yudhoyono in Indonesia or Ellen Johnson-Sirleaf in Liberia, and on the ability of new democracies to follow a process of democratization that has become a one-size-fits-all routine. This one-size-fits-all democratization strategy rarely takes into account local cultural and economic conditions. What's more, Western powers, including the United States, too often do not look at either the quality of the elections, the strength of other institutions besides elections, the complex characteristics of their favored "big man," or—perhaps most important—the level of public support in that nation for democratization.

Often, the focus on regular elections conveniently makes it easier to argue that a developing country is a success and move on; the West has been relatively comfortable with weak democracies. As democracy theorist

Larry Diamond notes, "Despite . . . political scientists warning of 'the fallacy of electoralism,' the United States and many of its democratic allies have remained far too comfortable with this superficial form of democracy."[6] Counting a developing nation as a success thus allows Western nations to justify an alliance with that country, or providing aid to it, or investing there. This despite the fact that, in many developing nations, transitioning from authoritarianism local citizens recognize that regular elections, even if held freely and fairly, might not be the highest priority at the outset of their democratic era. Two months after the collapse of Hosni Mubarak, a poll of Egyptians, taken by the Pew Research Center, found that only about half of Egyptians thought "honest, multiparty elections" were most important in the country's transition. Nearly 80 percent, by comparison, believed that "a fair judiciary" was most important, and over 80 percent believed that "improved economic conditions" were most important.[7]

It was in Cambodia in the late 1990s and early 2000s that I first noticed this easy acceptance of elections as the end-all of democratic change. Nonprofit workers at that time gathered most evenings at one of the bars in Phnom Penh along the slow-moving, chocolaty Mekong River to drink Tiger beer over ice and snack on bowls of sliced chicken flavored with piquant sliced ginger and tiny, powerful chilis. In the run-up to the election in 1999, Cambodian human rights groups and opposition parties had been reporting numerous instances of intimidation, from beatings of opposition campaigners to money being handed out to village chiefs to convince people to vote for the ruling party. This type of intimidation had become common in Cambodia during the 1990s, where the legacy of the Khmer Rouge genocide had left a shattered and traumatized population, a high incidence of violence, and a surplus of weapons. The crime pages of the local newspapers read like horror scripts, with stories of villages beating to death petty thieves, or people handling disputes by taking an axe to the other person.[8]

All of the aid workers, many of whom had lived in Cambodia since the beginning of the massive UN assistance program in the early 1990s, which ultimately cost over $3 billion and was charged to Western donors, had heard about the intimidation; some had traveled to villages and had seen the effects in person. The enormous reconstruction effort was partly due to

Western nations' guilt over having done nothing during the Khmer Rouge era, and partly because of a desire to court Cambodia as a new strategic ally. Many of the aid workers remembered that, back in 1993, Prime Minister Hun Sen of the ruling party had actually lost the national election and then used the threat of force to convince the real winner to allow him to form a coalition government. Only two years earlier, in 1997, a group of Americans working for the International Republican Institute (IRI) had attended a rally of the opposition Sam Rainsy Party, along with around two hundred party supporters. In what seemed to be a well-planned attack, someone tossed four grenades into the crowd, and the explosions killed at least sixteen people and maimed at least a hundred, scattering limbs and other body parts in the street.[9] The leader of the IRI mission in Cambodia was seriously wounded in the attack.

But when anyone brought up the problems with the elections, and the general chaos, intimidation, and thuggery that was coming to characterize all of Cambodian politics, no one wanted to respond. Turning the conversation to the unpleasant, even brutal nature of Cambodian politics would force people to put down beers or stop talking about the latest affairs in Phnom Penh's incestuous foreigner society, or to admit that their massive reconstruction effort was failing. As in Afghanistan later, the Cambodia effort came to revolve around national elections, one big man, and a process—a certain sequencing of elections, list of laws to be passed, and other proscribed reforms—developed in post-Soviet states, but which bore little resemblance to the people and problems of Cambodia, where local-level government, and basic education about democratic processes, were in far greater need than in Eastern Europe. "Look at how far they [Cambodia] have come since the Khmer Rouge era," one aid worker said. "You have to admit it's impressive—even if there are problems with the election, they are having an election, one generation after a genocide." "Sure, there are some problems," said another aid worker who'd spent considerable time in villages where opposing the ruling party could be tantamount to a death sentence. "But they're still holding an election."

Of course, compared with the past—in this case a past that constituted one of the most genocidal regimes in history—elections where people campaigning are only sometimes beaten up or harassed rather than murdered en masse were a step forward, but how long could the country be measured against that low standard? How would any free elections be preserved in the long run if the country's political culture became more and more violent and repressive? How could Western donors push a democratization process on Cambodia developed in post-Soviet Eastern Europe, where countries were far richer and more stable, and had more experience with democratic politics? How could any donors put their trust in Hun Sen, leaving no other political options other than the big man?

When I put these questions to foreign aid experts in Cambodia, or even to local human rights activists, no one wanted to answer. And ten years after my experience, in the late 1990s, Cambodia had not made much more progress. As veteran journalist Joel Brinkley shows in *Cambodia's Curse,* an exhaustive investigation of the country's current troubles, the UN and other Western donors in Cambodia are still falling into "the fallacy of electoralism"— they have focused almost exclusively on holding elections as a sign of progress, all but ignoring the other, more important, foundations of a free society. As long as the Cambodian government holds regular elections, even elections with no pretense of fair competition, Western donors continued to support the government with aid, and mostly ignore it otherwise: in 2010, donors pledged over $1 billion to Cambodia, even while at the same time noting that corruption had become endemic in the country. And in this vacuum of any external influence, Cambodia's big man, long-ruling prime minister, Hun Sen, and his cronies have robbed the country blind, sold off much of its valuable land to China, and used unfair laws and outright thuggery to crush the opposition.

The opposition parties that existed in the 1990s, during the early part of the UN period, have crumbled in the face of persistent pressure from Hun Sen's Cambodian's People's Party, which now dominates the legislature as a one-party giant like Mexico's old Partido Revolucionario Institucional. Other opposition politicians are simply bought off: Brinkley describes a common stratagem in which opposition politicians who agree to throw in with the ruling party are given control of parts of certain ministries, which allow them to loot public coffers.

Meanwhile, powerful men and women act with total impunity—they can grab land, steal from the public treasury, or even kill peasants without facing any repercussions. In one too-common type of incident that occurred in August 2008, a nephew of the prime minister ran down another man on a motorcycle with his Escalade SUV, tearing off the other man's arm and leg and leaving him bleeding to death in the middle of a crowded street in the capital. As the motorcycle driver expired on the street, military police comforted Hun Sen's nephew and took the license plates off of his car, making it difficult for anyone to report the crime.[10]

If Cambodia illustrated the failure of electoralism, perhaps nowhere has the reliance upon one big man been more disastrous than in Afghanistan, a country that theoretically has been the center of the Obama administration's foreign policy efforts, despite the fact that it fits few of the qualities of other countries ready for democratization, like Thailand, Russia, or Venezuela—stability, urbanization, a history of some democratic institutions. From early after the victory over the Taliban, the United States pinned its hopes on Hamid Karzai, a man believed to combine Pashtun legitimacy and Western liberal ideals—he and his family had lived in the West for decades.[11] As in Liberia, Nigeria, Indonesia, and many other developing nations, in Afghanistan American officials failed to invest time studying and connecting with a broad range of opinion leaders, and identifying a wide range of potential democratic allies after the fall of the Taliban. Consequently, the White House wound up personifying hopes for reform in the being of one supposedly transformative leader—Karzai.

Karzai's power would be legitimized through national presidential and parliamentary elections, which he and the West could point to as obvious signs of Afghanistan's progress. But the focus on him, and legitimizing him through national elections, even if they were fraudulent, distracted attention—and funding—from fostering deeper democratic institutions, such as investing in creating a stable judiciary like the one that was critical to the development of democracy in Israel's early years, a decentralized series of local and village elections like those that have transformed Indonesia, or a vibrant civil society of NGOs like those that emerged in Taiwan's early years of transition. The United States and NATO developed some small programs in all of these areas, but they were downplayed compared with the military offensive, the backing for Karzai, and the holding of regular national elections, which could be held up to Afghans and Americans, and to the media, as a sign of progress toward democracy.

In fact, Afghanistan, like Indonesia, could have been perfect for decentralization—giving more power to local leaders through village and township elections. The country had a tradition of local consultation and governance, through the *jirga* process, and was as ethnically diverse, if not as geographically spread out, as a place like Indonesia. Indeed, in many villages across Afghanistan local leaders in the mid-2000s had themselves established such types of decentralized democracy, often with some help from foreign aid organizations. Called local development councils, these small groups managed local infrastructure projects that the central government ignored, addressed local social welfare issues, and sometimes took the place of the local courts in adjudicating disputes. The local development councils proved enormously popular, despite their meager funding from the national government and a few foreign NGOs. As the *Economist* reported, in some parts of the country they had become so popular that, when central government funds for the councils ran out for one year, villagers worked together to petition foreign NGOs for aid.[12] But Karzai apparently saw even these local councils as a threat to his rule, and the kind of progress made through these local-level efforts—new wells, more effective annual audits of local government—rarely got much attention in the international media, and were hard to tout in a speech explaining Afghanistan policy to the American public.

Perhaps these failures of democracy promotion might have mattered less, but unlike the reverse waves of the 1960s and early 1970s, nascent democracies today have new models of development that mix successful capitalism with undemocratic rule. As Gat points out, from the end of World War II until very recently such alternative models did not exist; the only alternative for smaller countries that chose capitalism over communism (itself not a successful economic model) was to embrace democratization.[13] But as we have seen, that is no longer the case: smaller countries can copy the example of China—and, to a lesser extent, Vietnam, the United Arab Emirates, Qatar, or other successful authoritarian capitalists—and thus delink prosperous free market capitalism from democratization. At a time when the quality of governance in Western democracies has plummeted, reflected by the constant partisan deadlock in Congress, the two decades of paralysis in Japan, and the European Union's inability to agree on effective measures to resolve its financial crises, these alternative options of governance seem ever more alluring. After all, Western citizens themselves seem to be losing faith in their own governing models, resulting in waves of popular protest on both the left and the right, from the Occupy movement to the Tea Party movement to the somewhat anarchic violent antistate protests in Greece and Italy. As Charles Kupchan notes in an essay on the governability crisis, and the rise of the authoritarian model, Western nations will essentially have to copy some of the Chinese strategies, such as "strategic economic planning on an unprecedented scale [in order to prevent political and economic collapse]. . . . State capitalism has its distinct advantages, at least for now."[14] And certainly, Kupchan notes, as citizens of developing nations see the West's leaders floundering, and Western living standards eroding, and Western publics protesting and rioting, they will wonder why they should listen to anything Western democracy promotion advocates say. Or as one State Department official focusing on democracy promotion said, "How can with a straight face we be telling countries in Africa and the Middle East that they need to develop better systems for governing when we can't even pass a budget [in Congress]?"[15]

In the long run, the lack of transparency and openness may hinder the rise of these authoritarian capitalists. China, for one, already faces a corruption epidemic so large that one China scholar estimates puts the cost to government at $86 billion annually, and the lack of sunlight in Dubai's financial and real estate markets helped precipitate a massive crash in the emirate in the late 2000s.[16] Still, in the short run most of the authoritarian capitalists, and particularly China, have amassed relatively successful economic records, and so smaller countries no longer have to choose between democratic capitalism and authoritarian noncapitalism. No longer having to take into account conservative middle classes—which, as we have seen, now have serious doubts about democracy—they can enjoy economic benefits without allowing political freedom for all their compatriots, which is an increasingly attractive bargain. Many members of the People's Alliance for Democracy, the conservative middle class Thai organization that, through street protests and other demonstrations, has debilitated democracy and called for a return of unelected leaders, spoke favorably of China's model of development, a model that would allow them to maintain their businesses and their wealth without having to deal with the popular power of the working classes.[17] This sentiment praising China's model is heard over and over from middle class men and women in Malaysia, Singapore, Indonesia, Cambodia, and many other countries.

In the aftermath of the Arab uprisings, such sentiments were heard, too, in places like Egypt, where growth collapsed in 2011, partly because tourists, so critical to the economy, were scared away, and partly because crime, graft, and uncertainty undermined business and drove some of the brightest talents out of the country. But having seen the successes of Gulf states like Qatar, and of China, an increasingly powerful investor in Egypt, Egypt's business community increasingly wondered whether it might not have prospered more under Mubarak, said Egypt expert David Schenker of the Washington Institute for Near East Policy. The dictator, after all, had in the 2000s committed to liberal economic reforms. Or, Schenker said, some Egyptian business elites wondered whether they might do better under some future Chinese-style autocratic government, even if that meant tolerating a far less open political system than in the year after Mubarak's fall.[18]

Though the exigencies of the Cold War are a memory—the divide into Soviet and American camps that led the United States to back dictators from Zaire to Indonesia—other strategic changes have not necessarily proven more hospitable to democracy. The war on terror in many ways mimics the Cold War, with Washington offering new pledges of support to undemocratic nations, like Malaysia or Morocco, countries whose leaders can more readily hold prisoners indefinitely and conduct brutal interrogations of suspects.[19] I recent years, in fact, as the Malaysian government has launched a wide crackdown on hundreds of opposition activists trying to hold rallies promoting clean and fair elections, with riot police beating demonstrators including longtime opposition leader Anwar Ibrahim, the United States and other Western governments have barely paid notice. The Clinton administration had explicitly criticized the Malaysian government's Internal Security Act, which allowed Kuala Lumpur to detain people indefinitely. But the Bush and Obama administrations muted that critique as Malaysia's ability to hold detainees became a valuable tool in combating terrorism.

Afghanistan again has been the apex of how exigency has trumped democracy—even as the United States receives few benefits for making supposedly "strategic" decisions. In Afghanistan's 2009 presidential elections, it became obvious months before the actual vote that Karzai and his allies would rig the election, preventing Abdullah Abdullah, the former foreign minister and a man generally viewed as more stable and liberal than Karzai, from having any chance of winning. Karzai had handpicked an election commission totally biased toward him, and on voting day it became clear that whole regions had voted for one candidate, normally Karzai. In many cases, polling sites counted their votes without ever opening them in public view.[20] An independent election monitor concluded that 1.3 million votes had clear evidence of fraud; of these, 900,000 were for Karzai.[21] Before the vote, the government had made little real effort to create an independent election watchdog, a court system that could scrutinize election violations, or even a national apparatus to get polling places open. There was no legislation designed to handle the fact that many candidates had criminal, even murderous, backgrounds; indeed, the entire electoral system lacked credibility among most voters, according to an analysis of the process by Scott Worden of the Afghanistan Electoral Complaints Commission, a UN-appointed body during the 2009 vote.[22]

But the White House, and American diplomats on the ground, portrayed the election as a triumph for democracy, since Karzai, for all his fraud, finally allowed a runoff between him and Abdullah—which Karzai won handily. Diplomats from other countries pushed the United States to condemn the election; Canadian ambassador to Afghanistan William Crosbie apparently told the Americans in early 2010 they should be "prepared for a confrontation with Karzai" in order to stop him from rigging the 2010 parliamentary elections as he had the 2009 presidential election.[23] American officials mostly ignored this advice, and no top American leader condemned the cheating and fraud in the election.

Indeed, the United States remained convinced that Karzai alone could deliver effective counterterrorism cooperation, help cement the offensive against the Taliban, and keep some kind of order. As in many other developing nations, U.S. officials seemed to feel that, once they had bet so much on a "great man," they had to double and redouble that bet; there was precious little willingness to step back and examine whether any possible alternative would be better both for American strategic aims and for the future of Afghanistan's democracy.[24] They did so even after Karzai handed over control of much of southern Afghanistan to his brother, who was reported to be one of the largest drug traffickers in the country (before he was killed by insurgents), and after the Afghan president pardoned or simply ignored other drug traffickers moving massive quantities of opium in and out of the country, thereby undermining a major initiative of the NATO program to reduce opium production and create alternative economic strategies.[25] In the vacuum of leadership, the Taliban grew bolder and bolder, putting more and more of the weight of fighting the insurgency in the hands of the United States and its NATO allies, and allowing the Taliban to gain de facto control of more and more territory.

Too often, the Obama administration, like the Bush administration before it, fell into another democracy promotion problem: failing to work with developing nations' leaders to manage their citizens' expectations of what democracy, and assistance, would actually do for them. Rarely did the White House work with developing world leaders to approach democracy promotion a different way, like a permanent political campaign. Approaching it like a campaign would have meant, for one, trying to help manage popular expectations about what gains in the standard of living and effective governance democracy actually would bring to a developing country, at least in the early years of democratization. It might have meant admitting that now there are viable, serious alternatives to democracy in authoritarian states like China, and that the West's crises of governance have undermined some of the appeal of liberal democracy to developing nations.

But American presidents and many leaders of developing nations instead often promised to developing nations not only that democracy would sweep the globe, bringing enormous political *and* economic benefits to average people, but that the United States would greatly assist that transformation. As Bush declared in his second inaugural address, "The policy of the United States [is] to seek and support the growth of democratic movements and institutions in every nation and culture.... The survival of liberty in our land increasingly depends on the success of liberty in other lands. The best hope for peace in our world is the expansion of freedom in all the world"[26] In 2005 Secretary of State Condoleezza Rice promised, during a trip to Egypt, that the United States would abandon its policy of backing Arab autocrats, saying, "We are supporting the democratic aspirations of all people.... Our goal instead is to help others find their own voice, to attain their own freedom."[27] When democracy had spread to developing nations, Bush— and, later, Obama—repeatedly suggested it would pacify civil conflicts, unleash new waves of prosperity, and reduce inequality.

Fostering these perceptions of democracy's infallibility mattered. A Pew Research poll taken only months after Egypt's initial Tahrir Square uprising showed that more than half of Egyptians believed that democratization would make Egypt more prosperous—56 percent of Egyptians expected the economy to improve over the next year with Mubarak gone, even though Mubarak actually had pursued relatively liberal economic policies during the last decade of his rule.[28] Similarly, numerous studies of African states in the early 2000s showed that large majorities of people believed democracy would increase growth rates and reduce societal inequality. Yet as we have seen, in the early period of democratization growth often stagnates as newly empowered parties push populist measures and compete for spoils, graft can get worse, and civil conflict can intensify.

Both the Obama and the Bush administrations knew democracy could come, in the early stages, with such problems.[29] Many American officials working on democracy promotion had read the literature showing that, in its early stages, democracy is not necessarily more linked to higher growth than is authoritarian rule; some had worked in places like Kenya or the Balkans where the initial period of democratization had made civil conflict worse; quite a few had read the literature, such as the books and articles by Edward Mansfield and Jack Snyder, suggesting that countries initially transitioning to democracy may actually be more likely than authoritarian states to engage in conflicts because they fall prey to nationalism, ethnic conflict, and interclass strife, without the stable institutions to rein in bellicose leaders like Vladimir Putin or Slobodan Milosevic.[30] But neither Western officials nor leaders of developing nations tried to manage public expectations for what democracy would bring.

And partly because hopes had been raised so high in many developing nations, the reality of democracy's early stages proved such a letdown—a major reason, as we have seen in places from Malawi to the Philippines to Russia, why public support for democracy dropped in many developing nations in the 2000s and early 2010s. Even in the countries of Central and Eastern Europe, which were far wealthier than nations like the Philippines, the economic downturn of the late 2000s and early 2010s, combined with populations' overestimation of how joining the EU and building democracy would help stabilize their economies, led to precipitous drops in public support for democracy in many Central and Eastern European nations.

Conversely, in countries where the first group of postauthoritarian leaders made a serious effort to manage expectations, the population often has been willing to accept slower growth, slower attempts to reduce inequality, and a longer time frame for effective economic reforms. In South Africa, for example, shortly after assuming the presidency in 1994 Nelson Mandela made clear, in a series of speeches, that he would not begin a rapid program of land redistribution, that white capital remained necessary to the economy, and that serious inequality would remain for years due to the adjustments of the postapartheid era. South Africa's poor were not thrilled by these speeches, and some did demand a more rapid land redistribution program than the moderate one that was designed. But public support for Mandela's administration stayed strong and, more importantly (since one could attribute that support to Mandela's enormous reserve of public goodwill), support for democracy as the preferred political system remained high throughout the terms of Mandela and his far less beloved successor, Thabo Mbeki. When questioned in polls, poor South Africans expressed anger about how democracy had not led to equitable growth, enriching mostly a small, new black middle class, but they remained committed to democratic governance—and often told pollsters that they understood the slow nature of change in a new democracy, exactly the message Mandela had emphasized. Even under the term of Mbeki's successor, Jacob Zuma, as grievances over the lack of redistribution built up and led to larger public protests against the government and against Zuma himself, they never seriously threatened South Africa's democracy.

Along with some local leaders' failure to cater to the poor, the Bush and Obama administrations further alienated working classes critical to successful democratization by failing to make their democracy promotion efforts as inclusive as possible. This lack of inclusion went beyond simply focusing on one big man. "It was made clear to USAID and other embassy staff working on the ground in Jordan that, if there was civil society, democracy promotion programs that the [the government] didn't want, those would be gotten rid of," said Tom Melia, a specialist on democracy assistance at Freedom House who later went to work for the State Department.[31] Indeed, a comprehensive Freedom House report, released in 2009, found that American officials "have sought to distance themselves from civil society and human rights leaders who were not favored by the host government," even though the very definition of civil society often places its leaders in opposition to government.[32] In many cases, the Obama White House now refuses to provide funding to any local NGOs that were not registered with host governments, even though many governments have used registration laws as a means of weeding out civil society groups they disapproved of.[33]

And when American diplomats visited developing countries, they shied away from meeting a broad swath of political parties, which they would not have thought twice about if they had been in France or Germany or Canada, where American diplomats and officials have regular contacts with parties currently in opposition, such as Canada's Liberals. Many of the parties ignored by Western officials in developing nations—Thailand's Thai Rak Thai, for instance—tended to be those representing the working classes, and led by men and women who did not speak English or have much knowledge of the United States, compared with more traditional liberal, secular, and elite parties. But as in Thailand, those more populist parties eventually would triumph in the democratic system since they appealed to large majorities of the population, leaving American diplomats, and American democracy promotion efforts, largely unprepared for their assumption of power. When Assistant Secretary of State Kurt Campbell visited Thailand in 2009 and 2010, he occasionally tried to meet leaders not from the ruling Democrat Party but from other, more populist parties. Many Democrat Party leaders objected to Campbell's breakfasts with the opposition, saying that American officials had set no precedent of meeting anyone but top government officials. They were right—Campbell's breakfasts were unique, and few other American officials followed his lead.[34]

This myopia also suggested to working classes in many countries that the United States did not care to support democratization if elections did not lead to outcomes Washington felt comfortable with. At its worst, this myopic focus on only one or two elite-led parties in developing countries led to at least tacit American support for extraconstitutional efforts by conservative middle classes to overthrow democratically elected, if unsavory, leaders. As pressure built up in Thailand in 2006 among middle class Thais unhappy with the government of Thaksin Shinawatra, American officials said little publicly about the possibility of a coup. Many privately told Thai peers that it would not be a disaster to see Thaksin replaced, since it might result in the return of Abhisit's Democrat Party, the favorite of the military and the crown.[35] The American ambassador at the time, Ralph Boyce, clearly saw a potential coup coming and warned officials in Washington and in other Western embassies. But even after the coup occurred, in September 2006, the United States did little to sanction Thailand, continuing to hold high-profile joint military exercises with the Thai armed forces, which senior Thai leaders interpreted as support for their actions. (The United States did make some token downgrades of its ties with Thailand.) In one diplomatic cable released by Wikileaks, the U.S. ambassador in Thailand met privately with the coup leader shortly after the putsch. Though the ambassador had not been in favor of the coup, he knew that Washington was not going to punish the Thai government severely, and he advised the coup leader on how he could quickly show the United States and other Western nations that Thailand was still on a democratic track, which would result in completely restored diplomatic relations.[36]

Similarly, in Venezuela the Bush administration in 2002 refrained from condemning a coup attempt against President Hugo Chavez; before the attempt collapsed, press secretary Ari Fleischer seemed to be blaming the coup on Chavez and quickly welcoming the coup leaders as legitimate. Chavez has since been able to portray the United States' Venezuela policy as decidedly undemocratic, undermining any efforts by the United States to reach a broad swath of Venezuelans beyond anti-Chavez middle classes and elites with aid programs or other democracy assistance. Then, in 2011 the Obama administration risked making the same mistake in another region, with administration officials privately briefing reporters and suggesting that the administration was not happy with the victory of Islamic parties in Morocco and Tunisia and other Arab states, before enough time had passed to determine whether these parties were willing to govern within secular and liberal democratic norms, and sometimes without distinguishing between more hard-line and more moderate Islamic parties.

Even if the White House had developed a masterful democracy promotion strategy, any policy requires funding to back it up. But too often rhetoric, as in George W. Bush's Second Inaugural Address, was not matched by resources, or at least the wise use of resources. In most years the Bush administration did increase budgets for democracy promotion, but it drastically undermined the use of those funds by linking the war in Iraq to democracy promotion, as well as by undercutting Bush's rhetoric with undemocratic practices such as rendition and torture. Bush's policies essentially equated democracy promotion with military intervention and regime change, poisoning the idea of democracy promotion by suggesting that it could be touted as a reason for the United States, unilaterally, to overthrow governments that Washington opposed. Bush himself reportedly said in April 2004, a time when American marines were fighting a bloody battle in Fallujah, "If somebody tries to stop the march to democracy, we will seek them out and kill them!"[37]

While the Bush administration had welcomed many dissidents to Washington, a strategy that at least helped pacify some middle class and elite opinion leaders from developing countries, the Obama administration seemed strangely aloof to dissidents, which only further alienated opinion leaders from countries like Thailand, Malaysia, China, or Egypt. When several prominent Iranian dissidents came to Washington in the summer of 2009 following the massive Green uprising in Tehran, they could not obtain meetings with any senior Obama administration officials.[38] Similarly, many Uighurs, Tibetans, Cubans, and other dissidents found it hard to get a meeting with administration officials. Rabeeya Kadeer, the Uighur equivalent of the Dalai Lama who had met with George W. Bush, found herself shunted off to low-level State Department officials by Obama.[39] Even when the Dalai Lama visited Washington in 2009, the Obama administration did not allow him to meet the president, the first time the Tibetan leader had come to Washington and not seen the president in nearly two decades.[40]

Determined to take a new and less confrontational approach to democracy promotion, the Obama administration shifted away from Bush's bellicose tone, which was probably a wise idea. Added to the desire of drawing a line between himself and George W. Bush, and the weakened position of a debt-ridden, febrile American economy, Barack Obama himself seems to have a natural inclination toward pragmatism and consensus. As historian Walter Russell Mead notes in a lengthy essay on Obama's foreign policy, the president fell into the Jeffersonian tradition of American leaders who want to "reduce America's costs and risks overseas by limiting U.S. commitments [and] believe that the United States can best spread democracy and support peace by becoming an example of democracy at home."[41]

But the new president, too, failed to match rhetoric with the effective use of resources. Between 2009 and 2011, the Obama administration repeatedly cut funding for core democracy promotion programs in some of the biggest battlegrounds for democratization, despite the fact that several of these programs had performed well in both internal and external audits of finances and delivery of results. Although the White House in fiscal year 2011 and 2012 asked for funding to support some five hundred new State Department positions, these were primarily in consular departments. The

White House repeatedly cut democracy funding to Egypt, halving it to $25 million annually in 2009, and then cut it again in 2010 and 2011, while slashing the State Department's broader Democracy Fund by 21 percent in early 2011. The administration also cut the most important government-affiliated democracy promotion organization, the National Endowment for Democracy, reducing subsidies for it in 2011 by roughly 12 percent.[42] "The administration was looking across the board, and looking for places to cut, and they were choosing to cut democracy assistance, and prioritizing other areas, it wasn't just democracy assistance getting cut along with everything," said Tom Melia of Freedom House, who later went to work for the State Department.[43] The White House also eliminated high-level positions on the National Security Council that, under the Bush administration, had been devoted to democracy promotion.[44] At the State Department, the administration appointed an Assistant Secretary for Democracy, Human Rights, and Labor, Michael Posner, who in his previous work had been mostly focused on cleaning up America's own abuses.[45] This was not a bad thing—the Bush administration indeed left major issues to resolve. But it meant that the top official in the State Department focused on democracy promotion actually had had little experience with promoting democracy abroad before he came to the job.

To be sure, in a tough fiscal climate, and dealing with a Congress controlled by the opposition party beginning in 2010, the Obama administration was constrained, and the White House did not necessarily always cut democracy funds in exchange for worse-performing or less useful programs. But in many cases, it did. Overall, foreign aid funding decreased in the 2012 budget, and congressional staffers made clear that there was little chance for increases in the 2013 budget. And the White House was not exactly getting a lot of help from its friends and allies: consumed by its own fiscal crises, the European Union failed to agree in 2011 to create its own version of the National Endowment for Democracy, a longtime goal of European democracy advocates.[46] At the United Nations, the new secretary-general, Ban Ki-moon, seemed uncomfortable with the rhetoric of democracy, and often took a soft line. In dealing with some of the most recalcitrant nations, Ban usually just backed down: Ban meekly left Burma in 2009 and 2010 after the regime refused to allow him to meet opposition leader Aung San Suu Kyi.[47] By contrast, when Kofi Annan served as secretary-general, he was far more willing to criticize autocratic leaders who denied the UN human rights rapporteurs access to their countries.

But of all foreign aid, democracy promotion funding has been but a rounding error in the federal budget, and it might well not have been held up in Congress because, of all foreign aid programs, democracy promotion has tended to be the most popular on the Hill and with constituents, and it also had been thoroughly examined by internal and external auditors, far more than most other foreign aid programs. Indeed, in interviews with senior staffers for GOP senators and representatives working on appropriations, most said that they would have gone along had the administration pushed hard for stable or higher levels of democracy funding.[48] "If the administration had come to us, and made clear that wanted to restore [i.e., maintain] funding for democracy aid in the budget, I don't think that would have been a problem on appropriations," said one senior congressional staffer. "No one wants to look like they are cutting money for democracy and for protesters and activists."[49]

Even when the Obama administration did maintain or even increase funding for democracy promotion programs, it failed to shift programming toward local needs, and away from USAID and State Department formulas. I compared USAID democracy assistance strategies in twelve developing nations, including countries as diverse as East Timor, Mozambique, and Bosnia. Almost without exception, the strategic planning documents, the priorities for the programs, and the actual methods of implementation were the same for each country. Successful democracy promotion must be flexible, adapting to local conditions and involving a wide range of local actors. But in country after country, this was not happening with USAID and State.

This survey was hardly unique. In a similar study of American democracy promotion efforts, Matthew Alan Hill of the University of London found that USAID rarely employed case-specific strategies, in part because it knew that if it used strategies that already had been vetted throughout the entire bureaucracy and procurement process, it was unlikely to be criticized later. "Afghanistan had four years of drought, famine, and a greater level of absolute poverty than Bosnia, but Bosnia had lost over half its population during the conflict. . . . Despite these differences there was an assumption that democracy could be developed using the same strategy in each case," he found.[50] "The sub-program areas [i.e., the specifics of assistance on the ground] are nearly identical." Or, as Thomas Carothers of the Carnegie Endowment noted after participating in multiple USAID assessments, American democracy promotion remained wedded to process, leading to "lamentable patterns of inflexibility, cumbersomeness, lack of innovation, and mechanical application."[51]

At times, Western leaders like Obama simply seemed to abdicate democracy promotion, assuming that the spread of new technology would take on the burden of fomenting political change. Indeed, many Western leaders and writers argue that technology is a new factor and will strengthen the third and fourth wave democracies, smoothing their paths to freedom. Cell phones, the Web, Internet calling technologies like Skype, and social media sites like Facebook will, in theory, allow activists to organize large numbers of people quickly and easily, and without subjecting their communications to government surveillance. In some respects, Western leaders seem to want to believe in the power of transformative technology because technology, combined with globalization, would let them off the hook—if the Internet is going to change societies, then all Washington has to do is support Internet freedom in other nations, without the kind of hard choices of publicly backing real activists in countries like Thailand or Malaysia, where the American government has close ties with ruling governments.

What's more, techno-optimists believe, the spread of the Internet and mobile communications will make it nearly impossible for governments to censor information from their publics, since savvy netizens could always access free, unfettered information online or by calling outside the country. The new technology also theoretically will make it easier for activists to share their thoughts with the wider public, without having to use traditional platforms like television and the print media. "The networked population is gaining greater access to information, more opportunities to engage in public speech, and an enhanced ability to undertake collective action," wrote Clay Shirky of New York University, one of the most prominent techno-optimist writers. In 2000 President Bill Clinton said, "In the new century liberty will spread by . . . cable modem," and other prominent Western leaders followed up with similarly optimistic projections. Clinton's successor, George W. Bush, promised, "If the Internet were to take hold in China, freedom's genie would be out of the bottle," and, under President Obama, Secretary of State Hillary Clinton launched a new American initiative to promote global Internet freedom. Announcing the initiative, Hillary Clinton declared, "Now, in many respects, information has never been so free. There are more ways to spread more ideas to more people than at any moment in history. And even in authoritarian countries, information networks are helping people discover new facts and making governments more accountable."[52] Some cyberactivists even got the Internet nominated for the 2010 Nobel Peace Prize, theoretically for its transformative impact on global political life.[53]

The media, too, are hardly immune from techno-exuberance, touting the growth of the Internet as a de facto sign of political opening and exuberantly highlighting the use of new technology in virtually every political protest or civil society gathering. Even *New York Times* columnist Thomas Friedman, a longtime cynic regarding change in the Middle East, wrote, "The Internet and globalization are acting like nutcrackers to open societies."[54] Friedman's colleague, columnist Nicholas Kristof, wrote that in "the quintessential 21st century conflict . . . on one side are government thugs firing bullets [and] on the other side are young protesters firing tweets."[55]

The impact of technology is so great, both for activists and for authoritarian governments, that it should be neither celebrated as a revolutionary tool destined to promote democracy nor feared as a powerful device of autocracy. Instead, technology can cut both ways, a prospect few of the new techno-utopians seem to realize. Some successes by activists organizing through the Web, or through cell phones, have stoked this enthusiasm. Filipino activists gathering in Manila in early 2001 to protest corruption organized their marches through text messages, a template that later rallies in Manila would follow.[56] In the Orange and Rose revolutions in Ukraine and

Georgia, many activists used mobile phones and text messages to organize demonstrations, while in Moldova in 2009, protests organized largely by text messages, Facebook, and the microblogging site Twitter helped restore a legitimate government after a clearly fraudulent election.

In the winter of 2010–11, Tunisian and then Egyptian and Bahraini activists used social media and mobile technology to organize antigovernment protests and disseminate articles that chronicled the corruption and repression of the governments of Zine el Abidine Ben Ali and Hosni Mubarak. In January 2011, Ben Ali's government collapsed, and he fled the country, followed soon after by Mubarak.[57] In the central areas of Tunis, activists painted graffiti that read, "Thank you Facebook."[58] One of the heroes of the anti-Mubarak revolution was a local Google executive, Wael Ghonim, who was detained for over a week by Mubarak's security forces.[59]

Activists in other Arab-Muslim countries employed similar usage of cell phones, text messages, and social media, and major technology companies like Google launched divisions designed to develop tools that might help democratic activists around the world.[60] By the early 2010s, some activists in developing nations began to travel to other countries to share information on the best ways to use new technology for organizing.[61]

The impact of the Internet, social media, and mobile communications technology on democratic change is far too nuanced, and complex, to be explored in depth here—there are entire books dedicated to this question. But it is clear that while social media, the Internet, and mobile phones have helped activists push for greater democracy in some developing nations, they also at times have enabled governments to monitor and censure activists, and even to forestall democratization entirely.

Simply the spread of Internet access certainly has not ensured freer politics or democratic consolidation. Technology often matters most in the early stages of democratic change, when activists can use social media or cell phones to organize public protests and other high-profile activities, which rouse people out of their everyday routines, and require less long-term commitment. But in societies that have already begun transitions to democracy, and where what is required for democratic consolidation is sustained, diligent reformist advocacy—such as monitoring government transparency, launching NGOs and independent media outlets, and maintaining pressure on government officials, judges, or other civil servants—these emerging technologies, which do not develop bonds as close as those in old-fashioned organizing, appear less effective. The weak bonds built by technology's new tools such as social media often wilt under pressure from governments, and are not strong enough to keep citizens coming back to the regular, more mundane institutions of civil society critical for a democracy—town hall meetings, ongoing public demonstrations, or elections for local offices. Writer Malcolm Gladwell has dubbed this "slacktivism"—the idea that the Internet leads to casual participation in groups, since the barriers to entry are very low, compared with old-fashioned organizing, which requires people to leave their homes, attend meetings in another place, and participate in rallies where they would potentially face physical danger. "The platforms of social media are built around weak ties. Twitter is a way of following, or being followed, by people you may never have met," Gladwell writes. "Weak ties seldom lead to high-risk activism."[62] In his native Belarus, writer Evgeny Morozov, author of the prominent new techno-skeptic book *The Net Delusion: The Dark Side of Internet Freedom,* saw the effect of such weak bonds. Belorussian activists, he found, focus on the Internet, which appears to them capable of doing "politics remotely, anonymously, and on the cheap."[63] But, he finds, no social media or online organizing in Belarus has been able to match the government's control, or generate the type of grassroots movement necessary to seriously challenge the government through consistent and repetitive actions.

Authoritarian governments, and even elected autocrats like Hun Sen, Putin, or Chavez, increasingly understand that, outside of charismatic street protests, technology often creates weak bonds—bonds that they can exploit or crush. In Thailand the growth of the Internet, while allowing some degree of discussion of topics like labor rights, environmental concerns, corruption, the future of the powerful Thai monarchy, and military repression, has not clearly helped boost opposition politics, except when the opposition has used technology to help organize rallies in Bangkok. Thai opposition activists admit that, in getting participation for regular activities like petition-writing or weekly protests, old-fashioned methods like calling friends and

neighbors have proven more effective. The Thai Internet, which has penetrated most Thai households, also has given rise to hard-core, nationalist,
royalist, and progovernment activists who use the Web to attack—and
sometimes to cause the arrest of—opposition politicians who do try to discuss the future of the monarchy, even if they make only the most benign
comments about the royal family.[64] And during the Arab uprisings of 2010
and 2011, many autocratic Arab regimes launched similar types of attacks
on opposition leaders. Bahrain's government used Facebook to create a
smear campaign against Mohammed al-Maskati, a prominent human rights
activist, while Sudan's government allegedly used Facebook to barrage
opposition movements, and anyone else, with reams of false information
about prodemocracy movements' aims and gatherings.

Many authoritarians and elected autocrats also have developed highly
sophisticated methods of monitoring and filtering websites, often based on
China's comprehensive "Great Firewall," which make it harder for people
to use technology to organize or gain access to free news. Unlike older forms
of communication, like face-to-face organizing in dissident Eastern Europe, the Internet's bonds often prove weak enough that filtering and blocking successfully prevent activists from organizing. Thailand now blocks some
100,000 websites, according to an analysis by one Thai NGO; theoretically,
this blocking is to prevent online discourse harmful to the Thai monarchy,
but in reality it serves to censor a wide range of political opposition.[65] Since
Thailand's Internet laws banning content offensive to the monarchy are so
broad that they could be used against virtually any Internet user, they scare
all users, keeping many even from exploring sites that mention the royal
family but that otherwise are devoted to criticism of the Thai government.
Even some of the most prominent Thai academics and writers who'd considered themselves immune from political pressure now report that they
increasingly watch what they say and post online.[66]

Other nascent democracies, like Malaysia, have attempted or considered
similar blocks to prevent opposition parties or other civil society groups from
organizing online, or they apparently have used "denial of service" attacks to
shut down opposition groups' websites and forums.[67] Singapore has drafted
broad Internet laws that could implicate many Web users, and has reinforced

paranoia by occasionally notifying the public that the government-linked Internet provider has snooped through users' Web accounts.[68]

Some authoritarian or elected autocrat governments also use state-backed commentators to control online discourse and threaten political opponents. After all, activists have no monopoly on the Web. In emerging democracies, as in the West, most Internet users are not logging on to join a political cause but to play games, read soccer scores, download music, or watch pornography. And governments can use the Internet to promote their messages, to flood the Net with progovernment writings, to swamp the blogs and other accounts of activists, or simply to create enough mindless entertainment that average people do not focus on online politics. The Internet is perfect for these kinds of distractions. As writers like Cass Sunstein have noted, the Internet is particularly well suited to disseminating false and unreliable information, since it has no fact-checking and tends to create echo chambers, in which people with similar beliefs search for information that confirms their ideas.[69]

Russia seems to have particularly perfected using the Internet to distract and confuse the populace. The Kremlin has its own funded "Web brigades" that attack liberals and praise Prime Minister Putin, and the Kremlin also apparently is considering creating a "national search engine" modeled on Google but that will filter out content that Moscow considers dangerous to the state.[70] The Kremlin also has launched many other strategies to co-opt bloggers by creating state-controlled online forums for them. As Morozov notes in *The Net Delusion,* the Russian state not only has co-opted bloggers but also has played a role in producing a wide range of online entertainment programming that is both highly enjoyable and clearly nationalist and pro-Kremlin. This entertainment includes a beautiful blonde blogger named Maria Sergeyeva, who both praises Vladimir Putin and blogs about her personal life like Paris Hilton or some comparable American celebrity.[71] "At some point, economies of scale begin to kick in," writes Morozov. "The presence of paid commentators [advocating for the government online] may significantly boost the number of genuine supporters of the regime, and the new converts can now do some proselytizing of their own."[72]

Worse, by creating their own personal Web pages or Facebook pages, activists are building the kinds of dossiers about themselves that, in the old days, government security services had to work hard to piece together, using timely legwork and bugging of dissidents' homes, which could take months or even years. Now this information is easily available online. It also has become easier for the security services to follow dissidents, since they can track groups of them online rather than having to infiltrate actual meetings of dissidents in people's homes or bars. Many Syrian and Iranian protesters, for example, believe that Damascus and Tehran use protest leaders' Facebook pages and other online identifiers to find them and their friends during anti-government demonstrations.[73] Similarly, in Thailand, many activists believe that the government has used monitoring of social media to follow and, in some cases, detain people opposed to the military-backed government.[74]

The technology that became available in earlier waves of democratization was not so easy for regimes to adapt for their own purposes. Part of the challenge for activists and foreign powers trying to support democracy is to develop ways that new technology can mimic the strong bonds and effective penetration of older communication technologies. Fax machines, which dissidents in Eastern Europe used before 1989, and shortwave radios were basically an upgrade on old-fashioned printing presses that could circulate samizdat literature or advertisements for rallies, but they did not allow governments to collate massive amounts of information about democracy activists. And although the fax machine was more modern than state-controlled radio and television—communication methods that people in authoritarian states tended to find boring and consequently often ignored—regimes found that faxing was neither a more complete nor more sophisticated way to flood their country with their own propaganda and entertainment. The oldest tool of all, oral messages relayed from person to person, among small groups of friends and neighbors, remains the most effective form of communication; when a close friend or neighbor invites someone to participate in an activity, the likelihood that he or she will do so is high, since the person will have to see that friend or neighbor again, and since he or she can experience a real sense of close community by joining friends in such group activities. Indeed, recent experiments by political scientists Aaron Strauss and Allison Dale have found that text messaging and e-mails—particularly when sent from strangers and not from friends or relatives—are relatively ineffective in voter mobilization, in terms of increasing voter turnout. Numerous other studies have found similar results, concluding that e-mail and other similar tools are ineffective in voter mobilization. But, if activists can transform social media or cell phone networking to mimic the effects of more traditional organizing, authoritarian governments will have much more to fear.

11

Prescriptions for the Future

THE FAILURE OF YOUNG DEMOCRACIES in so many regions of the world, a decade-long trend that was not halted by the uprisings in the Middle East, has had enormous consequences. Most obviously, the renewed strength of authoritarian rule today, including the many "elected autocrats" who dominate what are nominally democracies, means that billions of people around the world continue to live under repressive or pseudodemocratic hybrid regimes, deprived of the social, political, and economic freedoms most in the West take for granted. It means that Thai webmasters and bloggers will continue to go on trial and face long prison sentences merely for posting critical comments online, that Belorussian opposition activists will continue to vanish, and that Russian journalists will continue to be beaten and even killed by pro-Kremlin goons.[1] It means that, whoever ultimately winds up in control of Arab countries like Libya, Syria, Egypt, Tunisia, and Bahrain, those leaders will find it easier to use repression to crush their enemies, making it more likely that they will turn into the kind of "elected autocrats" who have come to dominate countries like Thailand and Ukraine.

With the increasing conservatism of the middle class in many developing countries, journalists, union leaders, opposition politicians, and other threatened civil society leaders find fewer local supporters who can protect them, bail them out, or bring their cases to the media or the international community. And with many developed nations distracted by their own domestic problems—even with Middle Eastern nations rising up against their rulers, polls in the United States have shown that most Americans want their government to play a smaller role in the Arab-Muslim world—these rights advocates, journalists, and other groundbreaking reformers have fewer champions in the international community as well. While in the 1990s attacks on human rights activists in Thailand drew the concern and support of many middle-class-led Thai civil society organizations, by the early 2000s, with the middle class increasingly siding with authoritarian rulers, many of these same groups ignored attacks on pro-poor and pro-ethnic minority rights activists. Developed nations, consumed by their own economic problems and governance crises, also often ignored rights crises, with serious human consequences. When Joe Gordon, an American citizen who emigrated from Thailand more than three decades ago, returned to his native country for a visit in 2011, he was jailed for the "crime" of translating part of a book that critically examined the country's royal family. Gordon received little support from human rights groups or even from the U.S. State Department, according to several former American officials who closely followed his case. "The State Department, shall we say, is not too interested in Joe Gordon," said one former U.S. official. "They don't want to offend the Thai government, they don't feel they are in a strong position [like in the 1990s], so they didn't get him out of the country or do much."[2]

Beyond anecdotes, several studies capture the human consequences of this democracy recession. The Committee to Protect Journalists (CPJ), a global press monitoring organization, found that the years 2008, 2009, and 2010 were among the deadliest in history for reporters around the world; it was hardly coincidental that increased attacks on the press occurred as democracy retreated around the world. Several of the countries that had become the most dangerous in the world for journalists, including Russia and the Philippines, are states that have regressed from democracy. CPJ has noted that many democratic leaders and many international organizations—in particular, the United Nations—had been pitifully silent about the threats to journalists.[3] Indeed, Secretary-General Ban Ki-moon seemed uncomfortable even using the rhetoric of democratization and human rights in meetings with world leaders. The United Nations' cultural organization, UNESCO, even launched an annual prize funded by and named for Teodoro Obiang, the longtime dictator of African petro-state Equatorial Guinea and one of the worst oppressors of the press in the world.[4] (Obiang's state media memorably once declared that he was "in permanent contact with the Almighty" and thus could kill whomever he wanted.)[5]

Other international and local monitoring organizations revealed the human consequences of democracy's decline. In Cambodia, local human rights group Licadho, and global monitoring organization Freedom House, found that human rights defenders experienced a rising number of threats, beatings, and even killings as the overall state of Cambodia's democracy declined.[6] In Thailand, human rights organizations noted that the number of blocked websites has spiraled steadily upward since 2006, the year of Thailand's last coup.[7] Human Rights Watch, probably the most respected global monitoring organization, found in 2011 that attacks on human rights defenders rose sharply internationally, and that civil society groups were increasingly threatened across the developing world. Again, notes Human Rights Watch and other organizations, the fact that this rise coincided with a democratic rollback was hardly coincidental—the weakening of democratic protections in many countries left rights activists exposed.[8]

But beyond its obvious human toll, does the antidemocratic renaissance have real economic and strategic consequences, both for the countries themselves and for the United States and other established democracies? Indeed, failed attempts at democratization can make these countries worse strategic partners for the United States, as they become consumed with internal political struggles and unable to advance any coherent foreign policies of their own. One such country is Thailand, which is formally an American treaty ally and long was one of the most stable and reliable strategic partners in Asia. But both the Bush and the Obama administrations have struggled to work with the Thai government on many important issues, including counterterrorism, a free trade deal, and regional naval balance. "Our relationship with Thailand has basically been in a holding pattern, it's not like it was in the 1960s or 1970s," said former U.S. ambassador to Thailand Ralph Boyce. "We don't know what policies are going to be continued from government to government [in Thailand] so the alliance has kind of withered."[9] The Obama administration now is dealing with the same type of uncertainty with many nations in the Middle East, and even some of the most ardent democrats in the White House are wondering whether American strategic priorities,

including Israel, the free flow of trade, and access to oil, have been threatened in the short run by the change in the Middle East.

To be sure, democracy is not necessarily a panacea and can bring with it
serious consequences; at times, authoritarian nations have grown faster than
their democratic peers. We must rethink the boundless optimism about the
benefits of democracy—optimism so common in Western policy makers'
speeches and among protesters fighting authoritarian regimes. Autocrats
sometimes are able to make hard political choices that might generate protest in a democracy—such as China's decision to invest hundreds of billions
of dollars in clean energy projects, which in a democracy might have been
fought mercilessly by older energy industries and their lobbyists.[10] But it is
important to distinguish between the short-term effects of democratization
in the developing world, which can be destabilizing as compared with some
types of autocracy, and the longer-term effects of democratization, which
ultimately can create the kind of stability that countries in the second and
third waves of global democratization have enjoyed. Indeed, most of those
countries that built solid democracies in the second wave of global democratization have managed, over decades, to pursue strategies of balanced
growth, combat inequality, and respond to public opinion in a way that has
brought them long-term stability that is difficult to attain with authoritarian rule. Less than 5 percent of the countries that were in the second wave
of global democratization now are not established democracies, and none
seem likely to regress in the future.[11]

To understand the longer-term benefits of democracy, and to set reasonable standards and expectations for how the United States can help with
democracy promotion, it is critical to examine not only growth figures but
also other indicators of the health of society. It then becomes clear that, in
the long run, democratic governments more often make choices that foster
broader development and stability. Take child mortality, for instance—one
of the best indicators of whether a country is prioritizing health care and
social welfare. In a comprehensive study of different types of regimes and
rates of infant mortality, an indicator of governments' focus on well-being.
political scientists Thomas Zweifel and Patricio Navia found that "almost

without exception, democracies made more of their inhabitants better off than did dictatorships"; perhaps, then, it is not a surprise that, on average, residents of democracies today live longer than residents of authoritarian regimes.[12] Democracies' superior social performance, they theorized, was the result of the demand, by voters, for their governments to invest in human capital, a demand fostered by greater freedom of association and expression, and by the greater accountability of democratic governments over time. (As a result, democratic governments often initially tend to have higher rates of inflation than their nondemocratic counterparts, partly because they run higher fiscal deficits in order to invest in their populaces.)[13] Other, broader studies suggest the same. In a World Bank analysis of its lending across a broad range of nations, the Bank found that the rate of return on its assistance increased by as much as 22 percent in recipient nations that had strong freedom of association and expression, as compared with those with weak protections of human rights.[14]

Those countries that fostered democracy, too, tended to be more stable in their growth rates, even when those rates, over time, were roughly equivalent to authoritarian peers. In perhaps the most thorough analysis of democracy's benefits and demerits, political scientists Morton Halperin, Joseph Siegle, and Michael Weinstein found that even in the poorest countries in the world, sustained democracy over decades is linked to "less volatility in growth rates than autocracies. . . . The strength of democracies' economic performance is as much their ability to maintain steady growth [i.e., avoid disastrous outcomes] over time as it is to achieve relatively rapid progress."[15] They found that, since the 1960s, only five of the twenty worst-performing economies in the world, in terms of per capita growth rates, were democracies. The rest were all authoritarian regimes. And even when democracies did face serious economic challenges, the research by Halperin and his colleagues suggested that they respond more rapidly and effectively than most authoritarian nations. Following the Asian financial crisis of the late 1990s, democracies in East Asia generally recovered from the crisis more rapidly than autocracies and hybrid regimes. In part, these studies suggest, the solid democracies recovered more quickly because they used elections to restore confidence in their governments, confidence that spread through the population and ultimately led to confidence in government reforms, which helped rebalance the economies and put them on a path back to growth.[16]

It remains to be seen whether democracies will recover more rapidly from the current global economic slowdown, but this past history suggests some reason for optimism. Even in those undemocratic countries that invested in human capital and improved average people's lives, those enhancements have tended to happen during the most politically open eras in these countries' histories. For example, as economist Yasheng Huang has noted, China's growth during the 1980s, a period when the country implemented the most liberal political reforms in its modern history, benefited a broad swath of Chinese society, including farmers, small businesspeople, and companies in big cities. China at that time was led by relatively liberal senior party officials, including Hu Yaobang and Zhao Zhiyang, who embraced reforms that would be anathema to most of their successors. During that era of Hu and Zhao, Chinese citizens' personal income rose faster than GDP, and income distribution actually grew more equal. But after the 1989 Tiananmen crackdown, China reversed many of the political reforms of the 1980s: it stopped many plans for self-government in rural areas, tightened restrictions on civil society groups, purged the party of many liberals, including Zhao (Hu had died), and reimposed more controls over the domestic media. The Communist Party abolished many of the committees that, in government agencies, had provided for some degree of feedback about government policies. As Huang found, in the 1990s and early 2000s, though China continued to grow, the quality of growth for average Chinese was not as high as in the more liberal 1980s. Income inequality rose, wealth became concentrated in cities, and other measures of social welfare, including literacy and immunization rates, actually declined, a shocking trend in a country where growth continued at rates of 8 to 10 percent per year.[17] Labor's share of China's GDP fell, as compared with the 1980s. With the party retaking more control of politics and the economy, there was less need for the government to respond to the demands of the broader public. Access to capital for farmers and small businesses in rural areas shrunk; tax revenues flowed increasingly to the center, potentially reducing investments in infrastructure and social welfare in rural areas; urban governments, flush with cash, wasted huge sums on massive projects, with no one to stop them.[18]

By the 2010s China had, despite its overall high growth rates, regressed in terms of the quality of life, in many respects. Income inequality now was among the highest in Asia, approaching the historically high rates of Latin American nations like Brazil; but other than traveling to Beijing to beg the central government to listen to them or launching violent protests, which erupted frequently in rural areas, most Chinese had no way to express their discontent to the government. Extreme poverty among farmers and other sectors of the working class actually was growing, and private entrepreneurs found themselves increasingly marginalized by high barriers to loans, competition from state enterprises, and other obstacles put in place by the party. Despite continued growth, capital was increasingly misallocated, undermining the country's economic future. Indeed, one study by economists at the University of Bari in Italy and BBVA bank group found that while state-owned enterprises in the late 2000s contributed only about 25 percent to China's economy, they got roughly 65 percent of all Chinese bank loans. By funding poorly performing state enterprises Chinese banks actually were taking money from Chinese savers and transferring it, in the form of unnecessarily cheap capital, to enterprises that did not perform well enough to deserve these loans. Inflation continued to soar, while banks offered such low returns on deposits that most Chinese saw whatever savings they had lose value year after year, along with their quality of life.

On an intuitive level, this misallocation of resources in China should be hardly surprising, despite Beijing's overall reputation for wise economic management. Autocrats have few limits on their actions, so they can lavish money on wastes like Putrajaya, an enormous new capital for Malaysia that was the brainchild of longtime autocrat Mahathir Mohamad in the 1980s and 1990s, even though the country really did not need a new capital. Today much of Putrajaya stands empty, a high-tech ghost town where vacant luxury hotels wait for information technology investors who will never arrive.

When it comes to indicators of societies' health and overall well-being, democracies that succeed in consolidating their political transitions fare better on all of them, over the long run, than do their autocratic peers. In a comparison of democracies and autocracies using data compiled by the United Nations Human Development Report, my team of Council on Foreign Relations research assistants and I found that, with only a few exceptions, democracies have higher rates of literacy, greater access to basic health care and safe drinking water, greater enrollment in primary school, and less malnutrition than autocracies with similar per capita incomes. This gap is largely the result of democratic countries' openness, which fosters sharing of information about these serious problems, as well as the result of political consequences that democratic leaders face for failing to improve these basic standards.[19] The value of this openness, in times of crisis, was first examined more than thirty years ago by Indian economist Amartya Sen in his famous essay on famine and political systems. He showed that, even when they face serious crises like famine, democratic governments are better equipped to handle them, ensuring that their citizens do not starve. Democracies have more incentive to learn from their mistakes and adapt, he showed, and are designed to take in information and respond to it, making it highly unlikely that a democratic government could simply ignore a famine or other catastrophe.[20] Halperin, Siegle, and Weinstein call this ability to take in information and respond "horizontal and vertical accountability"— democratic governments, unlike autocrats, are moderated by checks on the regime's power, and by their need to obtain the support of much of the population to continue governing. Largely because of democracies' ability to adapt and handle all types of crises, as well as their investment in public welfare, citizens of even the poorest democracies tend, on average, to have a longer life expectancy than citizens of authoritarian nations with similar levels of income. Studying World Bank data, Halperin and his colleagues found that citizens of poor democracies had a life expectancy that was eight to twelve years longer than their peers in poor autocracies, though more recent analysis of the data, by Council on Foreign Relations researchers, suggests that the life expectancy gap is more like seven years—still a very sizable gap.

If, over the long run, democracy fosters societal well-being, consistent growth, and greater accountability, will it also make countries into better strategic partners for the United States? Again, the answer lies somewhere between the Cold War–era preference for stability at all costs and the overly optimistic idea that democracies will always make better partners for the United States. The United States has important undemocratic partners in several regions, from Vietnam to Saudi Arabia to Pakistan; and it has democracies or hybrid regimes with whom Washington maintains prickly relations, such as Venezuela or Bolivia. As we have seen, in the near term, the dislocation and uncertainty created by political opening can make a country less stable, and thus a less attractive partner, as Thailand has become while its political system disintegrates. It can bring to the fore groups that, while genuinely popular, tend to be more anti-American and potentially illiberal, as is occurring in Egypt today, where both moderate and hard-line Islamists have gained considerable power through parliamentary elections. It can lead to the rewriting of long-standing laws on investment and trade to the detriment of foreign companies, as has happened in Venezuela and Bolivia.

Comparing a broad spectrum of nations' interactions with the United States, we can see that, in general, and over time, democracies tend to work more effectively with, and share the interests of, the United States. The North American Treaty Organization, one of the longest-lasting alliances in the world, has succeeded in large part because of the members' shared democratic cultures.

But one could argue that the countries of NATO are almost all wealthy, Westernized democracies, and so share more than a political system—they share culture, language, and a way of life. Yet we can examine other regional and global organizations, with a wider range of nations, and still find that, on average and excluding NATO members, democracies tend to work more closely with the United States. At the UN Security Council, democracies have over the past decade been more than three times more likely to vote with the United States on any resolution than authoritarian nations were, a rate roughly matched in votes in the broader UN and at the UN Human Rights Council. Again, this does not mean that every democracy always will prove a more reliable ally: France and several other powerful Western democracies were major impediments to the United States' desire to launch war against Iraq in the early 2000s, while India has on a number of occasions proven a major obstacle to U.S.-led initiatives at the World Trade Organization. But the voting patterns do suggest that, most of the time, democracies share similar interests. And even though some of the emerging democratic powers, like India and Brazil, often did not support democracy and human rights initiatives at the UN, they still were more likely than authoritarian states to throw their backing behind these initiatives.

Examining the voting patterns at regional organizations suggests a similar trend. The Association of Southeast Asian Nations (Asean), the major Asian regional organization, contains members that are democracies, such as the Philippines and Indonesia and Singapore; members that are hybrid regimes, like Cambodia, Thailand, and Malaysia; and members that are autocracies, like Burma and Laos. Although Asean tends to operate by consensus, reaching agreement on any issue internally, over the past decade the most democratic Asean members—the Philippines, Singapore, and Indonesia—have been the most vocal in support of leading American initiatives in the region, including antipiracy efforts, greater regional trade integration, a renewed U.S. defense presence in Southeast Asia, and freedom of navigation in the South China Sea. "We share the most in common with these countries, and it's just easier to sit down ahead of time and work out where we have in common, where we can present a joint front," said Boyce. "That's a lot harder to do with a place like Cambodia or even Vietnam."[21]

Many of the developing democracies that have repeatedly voted with the United States at the United Nations and in regional organizations also provide some hope that, whatever the dislocating effects of democratization, over time democratic consolidation tends to reduce anti-American sentiment. In the Philippines and South Korea, for example, the transition to democracy in the 1980s and 1990s uncorked a great deal of pent-up anti-American sentiment, anger at past American support for dictators and the establishment of U.S. bases in the countries—a situation roughly analogous to the anti-American anger pouring out of Egypt and other Middle Eastern nations today. The Philippines forced the United States to remove its forces from two bases outside Manila, while a series of left-leaning anti-American politicians, including eventual prime minister Roh Myun-hun, gained popularity in South Korea. But over time, anti-American sentiment in the Philippines and South Korea cooled, just as it has in other young democracies such as Indonesia, Thailand, Chile, and South Africa—a situation that offers hope for American relations with the Middle East today. The most strident anti-American groups in newly democratic countries like Indonesia or the Philippines, some of which were Islamist organizations or political parties, slowly muted their rhetoric because they had to compete for a broad swath of voters in national elections, and they lost voters to other groups that were not as well-organized at first. A study published in the *Journal of Democracy* analyzed the performance of Islamic parties going back three decades and concluded that, over time, their vote totals usually fell from an initial high point in the first postauthoritarian elections, and that their political platforms also tended to become more moderate.[22]

Over time, too, many opinion leaders in these emerging democracies see that, whatever the faults of their countries' past relationships with Washington, as democracies they share certain core values with the United States— especially when they contrast the United States with China and other authoritarian powers. In the Philippines, some of the most stridently anti-American organizations in the 1980s and early 1990s were labor unions and other left-leaning civil society groups, but over time, as they have interacted more with counterparts in the United States while also gaining exposure to China, leaders of these organizations have changed their tune. Many have built at least informal links with American unions and other civil society groups while simultaneously increasing their protests against labor and environmental abuses by Chinese companies operating in the Philippines. Indeed, today some of the Philippine politicians and activists who two decades ago called for the United States to leave the archipelago and abandon its bases now call for U.S. forces to return to the country, as a defense against China.[23]

Over time, democracies also tend to provide the kind of transparency and stable growth that investors desire. In the World Bank Group's most recent rankings of countries by ease of doing business, all of the countries in the top ten were democracies except for Hong Kong, which is a unique city that has maintained many aspects of a democratic system even though it is ruled by China.[24] Even China, supposedly the great outlier, able to provide a climate ideal for foreign investors, is not truly so ideal. While many foreign businesses initially embrace the welcome they receive in China, where the physical infrastructure is marvelous (at least in coastal regions where multinationals mostly invest), permits for joint ventures and investments are quickly delivered, and local politics is streamlined, over time they often realize that such an autocratic system actually is not best for foreign businesses, either. Without real public support for many of the Chinese government's initiatives, foreign investors always run the risk that their projects will be targeted by protesters, or undermined by officials, or simply canceled outright, since the central government has few restrictions on how it can handle its activities. What's more, since the central government does not enjoy the legitimacy of being democratically elected, it often looks for other ways to win some degree of public support, such as whipping up nationalism, which can easily lead to targeting foreign investments and foreigners in general through policies to protect local companies, unfair judicial rulings, or even outright nationalizations. In 2009 the European Union Chamber of Commerce in Beijing, normally just a cheerleader for closer EU-China relations, issued a surprisingly harsh condemnation of the Chinese government's increasingly nationalistic treatment of foreign investors. China, the EU Chamber noted in a lengthy report, was instituting new trade barriers and other types of protectionism, and also was favoring Chinese state companies in bids for contracts in China, even when foreign companies clearly had made far more attractive proposals.[25]

In the longer run, too, despite the challenges that Washington faces in working with emerging democracies, the openness and transparency of these nations' politics will make them more natural partners for the United States. Even if the United States today has differences with India or South Africa on some issues, like trade or climate change, over the long run democracies tend to work better together, since their decision-making cultures are more parallel than those between democracies and authoritarian nations. Despite some tensions with India, often relating to Cold War antagonisms, American policy makers generally agree that it is easier to understand Delhi's decision making, even if that decision making winds up in choices that do not benefit America, than it is to understand how policy is formulated in Beijing. Simply the process by which the Chinese government chooses its next senior leaders remains opaque, even to the most senior foreign China watchers. How, for example, did Xi Jinping, the vice president and presumed heir to Hu Jintao, ascend to that position? Even the top China specialists within the U.S. government could only guess.[26]

Because emerging democracies generally are more likely to work with the United States over the long run, this does not mean that, in critical strategic regions, the White House should shun nondemocratic partners, such as Saudi Arabia. Instead, Washington must at least consider in any long-term relationship with a developing country whether, in not promoting democracy in that country, it is helping only to postpone a political transition that could lead to a backlash against the United States in the short run but also might eventually create a more solid and stable relationship with that nation.

We have examined how democracy has regressed in the developing world, and found that the culprits are, most often, to be found in developing nations themselves. The responsibility for reversing this decline will fall primarily on the shoulders of the leaders, and citizens, of countries from Thailand to Russia that have witnessed the democratic recession. It will not be easy, but they could follow seven critical steps that would help stop the decline.

Manage Expectations

As we have seen, part of the problem in young democracies is not merely that citizens have expectations of greater social and political freedoms, many of which they do obtain. They often have high expectations that democracy will bring growth and equity—expectations that, in many nations, have not been met. As in a political campaign, then, managing the public's expectations in the early years of an emerging democracy is critical to maintaining public support and preventing "authoritarian nostalgia." We earlier saw how the initial generation of postapartheid South African leaders managed expectations, delivering modest economic promises in the

1990s—promises that could be met—on land redistribution and job creation. A few other leaders in emerging democracies have taken similar,
wise steps: in Taiwan in the late 1990s and early 2000s, officials in the government of Lee Teng-hui and, later, Chen Shui-bian, both of whom were
pushing to deepen democracy and make Taiwan increasingly independent,
admitted that these strategies could have economic consequences, at least in
the short run. In other words, they leveled with voters.

Prevent Growth from Stagnating

Probably the most important job for developing world democrats is to
prevent their growth rates from stagnating or declining. As we have seen in
previous chapters, when working class citizens of emerging democracies
have become disillusioned with democratic government, they do so more
likely than not because growth has stagnated and/or inequality has risen
sharply. The current global economic slowdown has further damaged faith
in democratic government. Indeed, the Community of Democracies, a global
talk shop of democratic governments, has repeatedly warned that economic
stagnation is the biggest threat to democracy; many of the "elected autocrats"
detailed in this book never could have won office if not for severe economic
downturns that darkened the reputations of other, more politically and economically liberal, politicians in their countries. In Thailand, for instance,
Thaksin Shinawatra, who won his first national election as prime minister
in 2001, was victorious in part because of his great wealth, which allowed
him to deploy sophisticated advertisements that blanketed the country. But
he also won because many Thais blamed the existing government, which
was led by a man named Chuan Leekpai—who had a far better record on
human rights and democratization than Thaksin—for the Asian financial
crisis. In reality, Chuan's government took many initial steps that helped
bring Thailand out of the crisis, but voters punished them anyway for the
country's economic stagnation, and Thaksin's advertisements mercilessly
portrayed Chuan and his cabinet as economically inept.

Of course, every nation in the world, developed or developing, wants to
avoid a severe economic downturn. But the grave danger of stagnation to

emerging democracies' political survival means that, the developed world and its aid organizations must think more carefully about whether economic policies they prescribe are likely to depress developing economies, at least for the near term—and thus possibly harm the chance of democratization's success. Austerity programs, like those imposed upon developing Asian nations in the late 1990s and early 2000s, or on Greece and some Eastern European and Baltic nations in the late 2000s and early 2010s, may have some utility in reducing government debts, rebalancing budgets, and trimming fat from bloated state enterprises. But at the same time, they are likely to lead to slowing growth rates, at least temporarily. In a developed democracy, this growth slowdown might lead only to a change of parties in the next election, or to protests against the president. But in a less stable, nascent democracy, slowing growth and the resulting economic stagnation can lead to distrust of the idea of democracy itself, authoritarian nostalgia, and even the return of authoritarian rulers, like Thaksin, Vladimir Putin, or Ukraine's Viktor Yanukovych, who essentially promise higher growth in exchange for restrictions on personal and political freedoms.

Instead of always relying on standardized austerity programs for developing nations facing economic downturns, the international community could be more willing to let developing nations' leaders try more unorthodox measures. For example, during the Asian financial crisis, Malaysia's then-leader, Mahathir Mohamad, attracted harsh criticism from international financial institutions, leading bankers, and many finance ministers for instituting capital controls designed to deter the outflow of capital from his staggering country and stabilize the economy. Yet in retrospect, Mahathir's unorthodox and widely condemned actions appeared to have worked. Following the crisis, a study by the Asian Development Bank, hardly a paragon of unorthodox economics, found that Malaysia's capital controls had been effective in restoring stability to its economy.

Keep the Middle Classes Onboard

Although economic stagnation affects all classes in a developing nation, middle classes worry that democracy will produce leaders elected by the poor who will trample on private property rights and generally undermine the economic and social power that the middle class had accrued over time. In Thailand, Pakistan, the Philippines, and many other countries, these middle classes have become so disillusioned with democracy that they have supported extraconstitutional efforts to overthrow elected, if flawed, leaders. And without this middle class business community support, as we have seen, countries not only go into democracy recessions but also often struggle to grow, as business leaders leave the country (like those who fled Venezuela) or invest elsewhere (such as Indonesia's business leaders who temporarily parked much of their capital in neighboring Singapore).

Retaining the support of the middle classes requires several important steps. First, as emerging democracies' votes become dominated by the poor, elected leaders must take pains to reassure the middle class and elite business community that they will be committed not only to elections but also to the protection of private property, the rule of law, trade rights, and other commercial rights. They can do so while also pursuing relatively pro-poor economic policies, as long as the middle class trusts that these policies, while designed to reduce inequality and extreme poverty, are not highly redistributive and do not threaten established economic powers in that country.

It is not an easy balance. But in Brazil, Luiz Ignacio Lula da Silva, in his two terms as president, succeeding in doing exactly this—he maintained the support of the middle class even as he pursued pro-poor policies that were, in many ways, relatively similar to the policies of someone like Thaksin Shinawatra. When he first took office in 2003, Lula had a reputation as a left-wing populist; he came from the union movement and had for years fought the country's conservative dictatorships. In office Lula took major steps to fulfill progressive campaign promises, including providing government incentives and direction to major state companies, decreasing extreme poverty through new cash transfer programs, and focusing greater government resources on primary education. But at the same time, he and his senior-most advisers took pains personally to reassure the business community in São Paulo that he would continue the liberal macroeconomic policies of his predecessor, including appointing orthodox monetary authorities, taking the regional lead on fostering trade ties with other high-growth economies like Chile, and reducing red tape.[27] Under Lula, economic growth soared and the country began to make a dent in extreme poverty, and he left office as the most popular president among Brazilians—including the middle class—in modern history.

Because Lula's policies helped reduce inequality in Brazil, he made another contribution to the consolidation of democracy in his country. In studies of a range of developing countries Ethan Kapstein and Nathan Converse, writing in the *Journal of Democracy,* found that "inequality was indeed significantly higher in democracies that eventually underwent a reversal. Likewise, the poverty rate is on average higher in countries where democratization was reversed than in those where it was sustained."[28] In other words, higher income inequality in a developing nation made the survival of its democracy unlikely.

Create Mechanisms to Foil Elected Autocrats

As part of keeping middle classes onboard, emerging democracies will need to find stronger, more effective means to prevent the rise of "elected autocrats" like Thaksin or Hugo Chavez. Some possible ways to forestall elected autocracy would be to create high-level courts, enshrined in a national constitution that is nearly impossible to change and that would be tasked with adjudicating major election fraud, graft among senior government leaders, and other government-related crimes.

Similarly, emerging democracies might consider altering their voting systems in order to make "elected autocracy" less likely. Many of the countries with elected autocrats, like Thailand, have parliamentary systems that now favor two large parties, and under which the eventual prime minister can become—in a system with weak courts and other institutions—a de facto autocrat. Consequently, changes that reduce the power of a prime minister would, overall, reduce the possibility of elected autocracy. These could include switching to a presidential/parliamentary hybrid system, in which an elected president (or, in countries such as Bhutan or Cambodia, a king) also has some minimal powers to check the prime minister, as in Singapore today. Indeed, Kapstein and Converse found that, of the 123 nations they studied, those with weak constraints on executive power were nearly twice as likely to regress from democracy as those with strong constraints.[29]

Retire the Army for Good

As we have seen, in many developing nations middle classes dissatisfied with their democratically elected leaders have looked to other alternatives. Most often, this has meant a military intervention or, in the case of places like Thailand and the Philippines, placing a great deal of political power in the hands of the armed forces even if they do not actually stage a coup.

Of course, middle classes could become disillusioned with democracy even in a country, such as Hungary, where the military completely falls under civilian rule. But the fact that the armed forces in so many developing nations remain major political actors adds to middle class disillusionment by constantly providing a potential alternative to civilian rule, as in Thailand, where leaders of the armed forces frequently criticize the civilian government and suggest that they could handle many matters far better. Without the military involved in politics, middle classes would have fewer places to take their grievances, and their complaints about democracy would be less likely to result in the overthrow of an elected government.

Despite the challenges it still faces, Indonesia has succeeded dramatically in asserting civilian control over its armed forces. Under Suharto the military was the central institution in the country and had a philosophy called *dwifungsi,* or dual function, which meant that the army should take a leading role not only in defense but also in domestic politics. The armed forces had reserved for themselves a percentage of seats in Suharto's parliament, and regional commanders in outlying parts of Indonesia, such as Aceh or Timor, had so much power that they were like warlords.

Indonesia's realization of establishing effective civilian control of the armed forces, reducing the military presence in many conflict zones (though not in Papua), removing the armed forces from centers of political power, and generally inculcating in rising officers the idea that the military is divorced from politics, is cited by many Indonesian opinion leaders as the greatest triumph of the democratic period. (To be sure, Indonesia's current president is a retired general, but he is not influenced by or linked to the armed forces as Suharto was; he acts in a civilian capacity, placing civilian interests first.) The civilianization was the result of both concerted efforts by Indonesian leaders, including Yudhoyono, to reduce the power of the army, as well as to make broader structural changes in Indonesian politics, and public discontent with the armed forces. Civilian leaders after Suharto generally convinced military leaders that, in order to retain the armed forces' national reputation, it would have to divorce itself from politics. Civilian leaders in Indonesia then made several other critical decisions in the early 2000s. They split the armed forces from the police. This emphasized to the public that the police were responsible for domestic matters, including counterterrorism. The public came to trust some of these elite police divisions, which were able to disrupt Jemaah Islamiah, the most potent terrorist group in the country, in large part because the police had cultivated a vast network of informants and public tipsters. Eventually, the Indonesian government also removed the military's reservation of seats in parliament, the most important entrenched privilege it enjoyed. Still, civilian leaders privately reassured the military that, although their business and political interests would be reduced, the government would steadily increase the defense budget as a kind of compensation. Indeed, the military budget did increase from roughly $1.18 billion in 2003 to over $3.6 billion in 2010.[30]

At the same time, civilian leaders in Indonesia made clear to the uniformed military that, if they went along with this transition, certain privileges and rights would be reserved to the armed forces. This was a realist decision in Indonesia that, ultimately, may have to be repeated in nations like Egypt and Syria where the armed forces historically have played such a large role in society. Civilian leaders in Indonesia made it clear that, despite legislation passed in the early 2000s that created the possibility of human rights tribunals, no national government was going to prosecute former senior officers for abuses committed in Timor, Aceh, or Papua, or during campaigns against communists, Islamists, or other political opponents during Suharto's time.

Understand the China Model

As Western nations have faced a governance crisis while China has largely sailed through the global economic downturn, the appeal of the China model to many developing nations has grown. We have seen how the China model's appeal has spread from dictators to a broader range of opinion leaders in many emerging democracies, who contrast their own weak governments with the supposedly strong, wise, and rapid decision-making qualities of the Chinese government. In particular, the China model has grown in appeal in Southeast Asia, where opinion leaders from most of the countries in the region actually have been to China for business or leisure, and so have personally witnessed China's enormous economic gains.

But even in Southeast Asia, most governments and opinion leaders do not have a particularly comprehensive understanding of the China model. If they did, they might not view it so highly. Most developing nations have few diplomats fluent in Chinese, or with the ability and financial means to travel outside Beijing or Shanghai and see the many challenges China faces, including extreme income inequality. To obtain a more nuanced understanding of the China model, and China itself, developing nations will have to shift some of their diplomatic priorities. In most Southeast Asian nations, the senior-most and most acclaimed diplomats eventually rise to postings in the United States and Western Europe, a legacy of the Cold War era. This leaves middle-ranking diplomats, partway through their careers, in China, but few stay for several tours of the country.

This must change: for developing nations, and particularly those in Asia, postings in China must be given the same prestige, pay, and support that a diplomat would get in London or Washington, in order to create a group of officials with nuanced, thorough knowledge of China. With that knowledge, developing nations can make a true assessment of whether China's model of authoritarian capitalism will work, in the long run, for China itself, and whether the model could be transferred to their own countries.

Declare War on Graft

Of all the problems that emerge in democratic transitions, the spread of graft, as we have seen, often is the most corrosive both to business confidence and to popular opinion of democracy. The spread of graft, in a society where graft was once highly centralized, causes the impression that corruption is skyrocketing, even if that is not the reality. Combined with a freer media that is more likely to report on government corruption, the perception that corruption has become a serious plague on government is a nearly universal problem in young democracies. Emerging democracies that are successful in reducing corruption over time tend to enjoy higher levels of public support for democracy as a political system. One strategy may be to pay higher salaries to senior ministers and civil servants, an approach pioneered in Singapore, where ministers' salaries are indexed to the pay of high-earning professional in the private sector. By paying ministers and civil servants well, the government may reduce the impetus for high-level government corruption. (Of course, these salaries can get out of hand, too; Singapore's leaders recently took a pay cut, in recognition of economic tough times, but they still make more than twice as much as the president of the United States.)[31]

This reward for senior ministers and civil servants could be combined with an independent anticorruption watchdog that is constitutionally protected from political meddling, something few emerging democracies have been willing to try. The anticorruption watchdog, which must have independent investigating powers, could even be made up in part of foreign experts, perhaps from organizations such as Transparency International, in order to further guarantee its independence. It might seem radical, or a loss of sovereignty, to have foreigners investigating corruption in an emerging democracy, but it is hardly a radical idea: corporations appoint independent directors to their boards to ensure a similar type of autonomous, outside opinion. And a few developing countries already have tried to create such an independent watchdog: tiny East Timor, aware of the potentially corrupting effects of oil wealth in a young democracy, has created an oil-financed sovereign national fund. But unlike governments in many other developing countries, East Timor's is, by its own laws, prohibited from spending much of the fund now, except on investments in education and other types of social welfare, and a group of both Timorese and outside experts monitor how the fund is managed and publish regular reports about its usage.[32]

The United States also will have a role to play in stopping the democratic decline in the developing world. Western democracy promotion is not the biggest factor in fostering democratization, but as we have seen it can be important, and its absence—or failed implementation—often has negative consequences. One recent study of authoritarian regimes found that autocracies had the best chance of surviving "in countries where Western leverage is limited and where linkages with the West are low."[33] Indeed, during the initial periods of the second, third, and now potentially fourth waves of global democratization, Western pressure, and Western aid, have played an outsized role in offering models, money, and rhetorical support to emerging democracies in many countries.

At the same time, American democracy promotion specialists should have reasonable expectations of what they can accomplish; after all, the hard work of democratization has to be done by developing nations themselves. But as we have seen, at certain times in a developing nation's transition outside actors can have a real impact. What's more, by focusing on the core strengths of American democracy promotion, the United States can have its largest impact in developing nations. To successfully revitalize democracy promotion, the United States will have to make several important changes in how it operates. Following are ten steps that are critical to improving democracy promotion.

Understand the Opportunities

As we have seen, outside actors can have the greatest impact on democratization at three critical points in the process. First, when countries are still under authoritarian rule, outside actors can play a significant role through rhetorical criticism, funding of prodemocracy dissident groups inside the country, or just publicly providing a different model of governance to authoritarianism, one that average citizens of an autocratic state can see. This role was played, most notably, by the United States and Western Europe in the 1980s. After decades of détente, both the United States and Europe increased their rhetorical condemnation of the Eastern bloc's rulers, boosted their support for groups that broadcast into the Eastern bloc, provided exchange programs for Eastern bloc intellectuals, and helped promote labor rights and other civil society in the Eastern bloc. And, as the divide between

West and East began to crumble slightly, the freedoms, prosperity, and pop culture of the West became more accessible to Eastern bloc citizens, many of whom eagerly embraced it. In other words, simply the idea of Western Europe and the United States, which seemed appealing to some Easterners, accelerated the ultimate decline of the Eastern bloc.

Once a developing nation has begun to make a transition to democracy, outside actors have their second chance to make a significant impact. In the early years of the transition, when countries normally are more aid-dependent, political culture and institutions are still in flux, and the possibility of a regression to authoritarianism remains, the United States and other major donors can play a large role. With these countries, outside actors can play a dual role: they can continue using aid money and rhetoric to demand that the countries do not regress to authoritarian rule, while simultaneously offering critical expertise in areas like developing civil society, fighting corruption, and holding and monitoring elections. With these countries' democracies so nascent, this expertise is far more likely to be needed, and absorbed, than later on, when countries like Tunisia would develop their own cadres of experts, and when their politicians, labor leaders, and journalists might be more resistant to training programs from foreign nations. Meanwhile, the United States, and other leading democracies, can be using their aid money, and their bully pulpits, to try to ensure that elements from the previous authoritarian regimes do not return to power: the United States can warn armies in places like Thailand not to launch coups, link aid to benchmarks of democratization, and work with developing nations to create reasonable systems of accountability for former authoritarian leaders. Of course, the United States, which is widely unpopular today in countries such as Egypt, needs to be cautious—if its pressure on developing nations to stick to a democratic transition becomes counterproductive, then it may be better to stay quiet, at least for a time.

Finally, as developing countries' democracies become more stable and mature, the United States and other donors can play a third role. By this point, as in Indonesia, the Philippines, or South Africa today, the process of democratization is unlikely to be reversed, and is less dependent on aid as a percentage of its national budget. The country now has its own cadre of experts in everything from social media to election monitoring to investigative reporting. At this point the United States and other developed democracies can help solidify these nations' democracies by recognizing their progress and including them in international institutions like the G-20 and other groups, citing them as examples of democratic change, and working alongside local democracy promotion specialists from these countries on the ground, as equal partners. So while the United States and other donors might have launched a national election observer project in Indonesia, by the time the country's democracy is on firmer ground, those foreign staff would be serving only as advisers and technical experts, having given over control of the program to Indonesians. The United States might also increasingly call on these democracies, like Indonesia or South Africa, to send *their* experts—in elections, budgeting, media, or many other topics—to developing countries that are still at a much earlier stage of democratic development.

Focus Spending on the Best Prospects

To be effective, American democracy promotion also must become more concentrated. Specifically, it must focus more clearly on countries where the United States can make the largest impact with limited democracy promotion dollars. This is not an easy trade-off, and any decision to ignore potential democratic change somewhere will open up the White House to criticism. But it is a necessary selectiveness in an era of diminished resources and significant existing global threats including terrorism and nuclear proliferation, both of which much be addressed as well, at significant cost. The United States should be consistent in rhetorically upholding democracy and human rights, but Washington could, due to necessity, focus its democracy promotion aid on a certain spectrum of countries where democratic consolidation seems most feasible, American assistance can make a greater difference, and American aid can be packaged with multilateral assistance from other donors.

The United States, and other leading democracies, can identify the nations ripest for democracy promotion assistance by examining them on a range of indicators, such as those used by Freedom House or the Economic

Intelligence Unit, to rank countries that have begun transitions from authoritarian rule to democracy.[34] These indicators can be compiled and combined with historical data to analyze which nations have the best chances of consolidating their democratic transitions. Countries that are above a certain level of income, that have only modest economic inequality, and that have some experience with inclusive government are most likely to complete a successful transition to democracy. By comparing developing nations using these standards, it is possible to identify the most promising cases for democracy promotion assistance. These nations may not be the poorest, but providing democracy promotion aid to nations like Thailand does not preclude humanitarian assistance to the neediest countries. And in the long run this humanitarian assistance may help poorer nations achieve some of the conditions that, historically, have made them riper prospects for stable democracy.

By evaluating nations eligible for democracy assistance using these criteria, American policy makers also will be better equipped to decide whether to prioritize democracy promotion when it potentially conflicts with U.S. strategic interests. These criteria for evaluating potential democratic success stories thus will help create a kind of sliding scale. On one end of the scale are countries such as North Korea where, judging from historical data and current criteria, the likelihood of successful democratization is very low. Yet North Korea is critical to American strategic interests—it has nuclear weapons and the potential to destabilize all of Northeast Asia. Given the unlikelihood of democratic change anytime soon, U.S. policy toward countries like these should revolve around critical strategic interests, hard-hearted though that may be. On the other end of the spectrum are nations, like Thailand, that fulfill many of the conditions that, historically, have proven essential to successful democratization. In these cases, it may make sense for Washington to prioritize democracy promotion, even when it conflicts with American strategic interests, such as alienating an autocratic-minded leader.

The balance of democracy promotion and strategic interests will prove the most difficult in the middle ground of countries on this sliding scale—a country like Egypt, which fulfills only some of the criteria that historically have suggested a successful transition to democracy, but where the ruling regime, not yet truly democratic, also has been historically a close partner on many high-priority strategic issues. Should the White House throw all the weight of its office behind democratic change in Egypt, given that a democratic transition is hardly assured, and the strategic issues—the peace with Israel, the Suez Canal—are so weighty? It is beyond the scope of this book to provide answers to every such conundrum. But at least by having the kind of established, quantifiable criteria of democracy's chance of success that we have examined here, American officials can make informed judgments on when to make decisions that could threaten the United States' strategic interests.

Move Beyond the Big Men

As we have seen, when it comes to democracy, American administrations, whether Democratic or Republican, too often tend to associate reform with one supposedly groundbreaking leader in a developing nation, a supposedly democratic "big man." In rare cases, such a leader exists, someone like Nelson Mandela, who not only is truly dedicated to reform but also possesses such moral authority and total control of his political party and allies that he or she really can, almost singlehandedly, push a country through transition. But such a unique individual is very rare: there is only one Mandela. More often, even a truly reform-minded "big man" like Indonesian President Susilo Bambang Yudhoyono requires many factors to go in his direction to push his country successfully toward democracy, and can be hindered by recalcitrant leaders from the old regime, endemic poverty, a restive army, or many other factors. In worse cases, like Nigeria's Olesegun Obasanjo or Senegal's Abdoulaye Wade, once in power "big man" leaders who initially look like reformers, perhaps because they spent years in opposition fighting authoritarian rulers, turn out to be as corrupt or autocratic as the men and women they replaced.

American administrations thus must avoid the temptation to personalize reform, and to confuse supporting change and institutions in a country like Nigeria or Indonesia with supporting one leader. At the least, this personalization can allow such a leader to kill quality foreign-funded programs, from civil society building to anticorruption initiatives, that might go against his or her interests. This "big man" theory of democracy promotion also leads U.S. diplomats to ignore a wide range of opinion leaders in an emerging country. Failing to make contacts with many other potential democrats thus leaves the United States unprepared if the favored reformer loses an election. At worst, it makes the United States appear to be choosing sides and directly meddling in the politics of an emerging democracy.

Respect Election Winners—If They Play Fair

The United States, and other leading democracies, also will have to make a habit of respecting the winners of elections, as long as those winners adhere to certain guidelines of a democratic society, such as not using their victory to then legitimize authoritarian rule, as in Germany in the early 1930s. If the winners of democratic elections show, in good faith, their commitment to democratic norms and values, the United States and other leading democracies should not isolate or remove them. This commitment will probably mean dealing with political parties that win elections and contain noxious beliefs within their party platforms. But such problematic parties have gained power in many countries, without destroying those nations' political systems; for example, in Austria the far-right Freedom Party gained a good deal of power in the mid- and late 2000s, while in India elements of the Bharitya Janata Party, which ran the government between 1998 and 2004, were implicated in anti-Muslim pogroms that left thousands dead.[35] And over time, as has occurred in countries like Indonesia and India, extreme parties' participation in the political system tends to moderate their views as they seek to gain larger numbers of voters.

However, if elections are clearly flawed, or simply preempted by a democratic reversal such as a coup, the United States needs to be willing to take a stronger stand. In 2006, for example, following the coup in Thailand, the United States did not cancel joint military exercises with the Thai military, a sign of de facto acceptance of the coup. "The minimal sanctions we put on Thailand after the coup were like a sign that we did not dislike the coup, and then meeting with the coup leaders immediately after the coup was another sign," said one former U.S. official in Thailand.[36] Unfortunately, many Thai military officers—and army men in other parts of Southeast Asia—interpreted the United States' reaction to the 2006 coup as a potential signal that the United States still does not condemn military takeovers. Indeed, in early 2012 a similar group of conservative middle class Thais that helped push for the 2006 coup was once again publicly agitating for the military to take power, in order to force out the elected government of Thaksin's sister Yingluck.[37]

Of course, in some cases, such as a potential coup in Pakistan today, American strategic interests would likely trump concern for Pakistani democracy. The United States likely would not punish Islamabad severely for a coup today, fearful that punishment would further degrade the relationship and cost Washington intelligence, drone attacks, and even its diplomatic ties with Islamabad. But even in such a special case, Washington can help put the country back on the path to democracy. In cases of coups or other democratic reversals, if the United States needed to continue aid to that country for strategic reasons, it should do so through emergency one-year programs authorized with Defense Department funding, and waiving only for a short period congressional controls on aid to authoritarian nations.

But Realize That Elections Are Only Step One

As we have seen in Cambodia, Russia, and many other nations, simply holding elections does not make a democracy. Effectively promoting lasting democracy will require investing in far more than national elections, even ones held freely and fairly. For one, donors should consider pushing aid-recipient developing nations to adopt some of the decentralization strategies used by Indonesia over the past decade. By decentralizing political and economic power, Indonesia devolved control from the capital, involved more citizens in the political process, and reduced threats of separatism. By funding and helping monitor Indonesian-style village, local, city, and provincial elections as well as national elections, donors would be contributing to the inclusion of larger numbers of citizens in developing nations in the democratic process.

Donors also should recalibrate their funding so that larger percentages of democracy assistance go toward building institutions and less toward organizing and holding national elections. For democracy to thrive in developing nations, it will need many of the institutions discussed above: constitutional courts, anticorruption commissions, an informed populace, a vibrant civil society, a reduced role for the army, and, possibly, a more fragmented political system. Building all of these foundations takes more time, and requires more sustained investment, than holding elections, but these factors are critical to democracy's success. To shift funding toward these foundations of democracy, donors could modify their budgeting for democracy promotion from renewal annually to every two or three years, a change some Scandinavian nations already have made. Moving toward funding democracy promotions over a longer cycle would allow projects on the ground to develop closer relations among local partners, set long-term objectives, and have the time to truly assess whether their projects are succeeding.

Donor nations also could expand their exchange programs for opinion leaders from emerging democracies, in part by relaxing visa restrictions for certain types of exchange involving religious leaders, civil society leaders, and politicians from developing nations. Diplomats and officials from donor nations also could make greater efforts to link civil society in developing nations not only to American officials but also to U.S. or other Western civil society organizations, serving as a kind of bridge. For example, in recent years diplomats at the U.S. embassy in Thailand have expanded traditional programs that brought Thai foreign ministry officials to the United States to learn about Congress or the State Department to include journalists, labor leaders, and other activists, who come to the United States and meet a wide range of their American civil society counterparts.

Get Better at Judging

Going beyond electoralism also would include conditioning a growing amount of American foreign assistance on criteria similar to those of the Millennium Challenge Corporation, a recent effort at tying aid to good governance pioneered during the George W. Bush administration. Historical data show that this is the right approach—that the foundations for a more participatory and inclusive government make democracy's success more likely. To take one example, in a comprehensive study of developing nations international political economists Hilton Root and Bruce Bueno Mesquita found that those that were the most inclusive—defined by the openness of the government and the ability of citizens to organize and compete on a national level, among other criteria, are more likely to promote frequent government turnover, a sign of democratic consolidation.[38]

By more effectively using criteria to judge recipients of democracy aid, and by limiting the number of recipients to only those countries where the aid is most likely to have an impact, Washington could maximize the effect of its assistance. What's more, by reducing the number of recipients, and conditioning aid on criteria, it could more effectively judge whether its democracy promotion efforts are actually successful, by using Freedom House, U.S. government, or *Economist* assessments of these criteria each year. Of course, it is impossible to say exactly how much democracy assistance is responsible for change in any developing nation, but by developing this list of criteria, and matching year-on-year change in the criteria with levels of American democracy promotion funding, any administration can at least see whether its aid seems to have having a measurable impact.

Be Flexible in Programming

Of all the complaints about U.S. democracy promotion offered by aid recipients in developing countries and by American officials working on the ground, the one that comes up most often in study after study by USAID and independent experts tasked to evaluate American aid is the rigidity of democracy assistance programs, which tended to be developed in Washington and then put into place, with little flexibility, in various countries. They are done in this one-size-fits-all way, notes Thomas Carothers of the Carnegie Endowment, primarily because developing one consistent plan is easier when working with Beltway contractors, is easier to present to appropriators who then get familiar with the structure of aid programs, and is easier for people working in the field to learn.

However, this type of plan usually does not work. For example, many plans that were based on projects developed in the late 1990s for supporting local and national governance, as well as civil society, in the Balkans were then brought, with few changes, to Afghanistan—even though Afghan society bore little resemblance to the areas where USAID and other agencies had worked in the Balkans. In fact, Afghanistan bore little resemblance to most of the emerging democracies where democracy promotion efforts are launched, countries like Croatia or Thailand that, when compared with Afghanistan, have much higher income levels, histories of participatory rule, and educated societies. Nevertheless, USAID and other aid organizations transplanted programs developed in places far more prepared for democratization directly to rural Afghanistan.

But Afghanistan is hardly the only example of this trend. In Cambodia the United States and other donors, working through contractors, have tried to implement programs on labor rights, women's rights, media, and other areas, using templates that were taken from earlier programs in countries like Thailand. But Cambodia, like Afghanistan, is far poorer, more rural, and much more dangerous than Thailand—journalists and labor leaders are routinely beaten and killed in Cambodia. Consequently, donor-funded programs on media and labor rights in Cambodia often failed because the program organizers did not provide enough security, assumed that attendees had the same level of knowledge as those in Thailand, or committed numerous other mistakes caused by a one-size-fits-all mind-set.

Instead, U.S. democracy promotion programs, whether implemented through USAID or contractors like the National Endowment for Democracy and the International Republican Institute, must become more attuned to local conditions. Like companies thinking about entering a new market, USAID and its contractors should use a small amount of their funding to first conduct extensive surveys of the countries in which they are planning to launch programs, asking questions about the labor environment, the media environment, and the political culture. Before launching new programs, they also could hold donor groups' meetings with other donors to make sure American programming is not duplicating others' efforts. Currently, these types of donor group meetings are held in many countries, including

Cambodia, but they often are not held until after the major donors already have planned and launched projects—at which point many of the projects may actually duplicate each other.

Work with Multilateral Democracy Actors

Stronger democracy promotion also should include boosting cooperation with multilateral efforts to promote civil society and to improve the quality of democracy, such as the United Nations Democracy Fund. Some 85 percent of UN Democracy Fund monies are allocated for nongovernmental organizations.[39] The fund was launched in 2006 but remains underfunded and poorly utilized; it could be drastically expanded and, with greater American support, made into a powerful tool of aid to civil society in emerging democracies. Other multilateral democracy organizations also tend to be poorly funded and relatively unknown, such as: the Bali Democracy Forum, a group that brings together primarily Asian democracies to discuss ways to foster democracy in the region; the Community of Democracies, an intergovernmental group of democracies from all regions of the world that mostly serves to share information on how to improve the quality of democracy; and several others. Although the United States participates in many of these organizations, it tends to play a minimal role. But with only modest financial assistance (less than $5–$10 million annually) and perhaps higher-level U.S. participation, some of these organizations could play a larger regional role in promoting democracy. The Bali Forum, for example, eventually could become not only a talk shop but also an organization that utilizes experts from emerging democracies like Indonesia to lead democracy promotion projects such as journalism training workshops, anticorruption seminars, and legal clinics in other parts of Asia.

Enlist the Emerging Giants

As we have seen, many of the most powerful democracies in the developing world, such as India, Brazil, and South Africa, have thus far been reluctant to engage in democracy promotion themselves, or even to stand up for democracy and human rights at international forums like the United Nations. Besides their Cold War histories, which made them adherents of absolute sovereignty, many of these emerging giants still do not see the gains they would accrue by promoting democracy. But what have these emerging giants gotten from their defense of sovereignty, their support for autocratic regimes like Zimbabwe, Sudan, Libya, and Burma? American officials, and activists in the emerging giants themselves, must work harder to convince these new powers that, no matter how they defend sovereignty, China still always will have an advantage over them in making business deals and strategic alliances with autocratic nations. As we have seen, from the 1990s, when many of its leaders rhetorically supported the democracy movement in Burma, India reversed its policy, so that by the end of the 2000s it was working closely with the Burmese junta, and inviting Burmese leader Senior General Than Shwe on state visits. But China still was able to gain a far larger share of Burma's oil and gas resources, partly because even as the Indian government shifted its Burma policy, activists, writers, and some retired Indian officials continued to criticize India's relations with the Burmese junta—criticism that is allowed, of course, in Indian democracy, and that slowed the process of rapprochement and, possibly, made the Burmese generals less comfortable dealing with Delhi. By contrast, in China there was no space for open criticism of Beijing's relationship with the Burmese regime, and Burma's top leaders, though wary of any major power, clearly were more comfortable dealing with the Chinese government.[40] China obtained not only the majority of Burma's petroleum contracts but also a prime naval port.[41]

India, South Africa, Brazil, or other emerging democratic powers could establish themselves as models of democratic rule for other developing nations—and thus reap the strategic benefits of being seen as a model when other nations solidify their democracies. Both the emerging democratic powers and the United States, in fact, must realize that despite China's powerhouse economy and rising military might, they still have enormously valuable benefits to offer developing nations. If the United States criticizes the Philippine government's human rights abuses, Manila is not going to immediately replace its defense relationship with the Pentagon with one with the People's Liberation Army: America's officer training programs, weapons systems, and other military benefits are far superior to China's. If South Africa took a harder stance against Robert Mugabe's attempts to prevent real democratic rule in Zimbabwe, Mugabe could not just turn to China, though he already has tried to do so—South African food, energy, and other supplies are too inexpensive, since South Africa is right on Zimbabwe's borders, to be replaced.

Turkey already is reaping this benefit of being seen as a democratic model, despite recent concerns that its government has jailed growing numbers of journalists who disagree with Ankara's policies. As nations in the Arab-Muslim world throw off their tyrants, and then look for models of democratic consolidation that promote secular and liberal rule, the "Turkey model"—Turkey's successful evolution from a shaky, army-dominated nation to a solid and vibrant democracy—frequently tops the list.[42] Turkish leaders were among the first foreign powers to advise Egyptian autocrat Hosni Mubarak to step down, and, as unrest continued, many top officials and democracy activists from across the Middle East visited Ankara to learn from Turkey's successes and to enlist Turkish leaders to help mediate their crises.[43] And having already established ties to Egypt's Muslim Brotherhood, Turkey's ruling AK Party may play a direct role in helping the Brotherhood prepare for a more democratic Egypt.[44] Ankara has become "a potential powerbroker in post-Mubarak Cairo," wrote Turkey expert Soner Cagaptay of the Washington Institute for Near East Policy. "Turkey [has gained] access to hitherto unimaginable power in the Egyptian capital."[45]

Show Some Humility

Even while reviving aggressive advocacy for democracy and human rights, established democracies also need to become more humble. Humility means accepting, and trying to remedy, the crisis of governance in established Western democracies today. As we have seen in the previous chapter, this governance crisis has not only damaged support in Western nations for democracy but also has made it harder for Western nations to promote democracy abroad. Beginning to solve the partisanship and economic drift that plagues American governance today will help the United States in democracy promotion abroad. Righting the United States' economy, coming to a solution on entitlements, and reducing the partisanship and gridlock that has paralyzed Washington would help present the United States as a finer model to developing nations. In the meantime, while the United States and other Western nations struggle with their own governance problems, American leaders, and officials working in developing nations, should not avoid talking about the United States' current troubles; certainly, anyone they interact with in developing nations who has taken even a cursory glance at the news in the past three years would know anyway. And, while talking about American exceptionalism on the presidential campaign trail may be a political imperative, admitting that even developed democracies face governance challenges—and can resolve these challenges through public discussion, nonviolent protest, political campaigns, and elections—should hardly degrade the "brand" of American democracy. These gestures also demonstrate to foreign audiences that the United States recognizes that, while there are certain core values and norms of democracy, there are different approaches to making democracy work.

Though the rhetoric, and the ideas, of democracy promotion and rights advocacy sometimes can become abstract, interactions with activists on the ground, working and sacrificing in countries where politics could be deadly, usually bring any theoretical discussion back to the concrete. In early 2011, as citizens on the streets of Tunisia and Egypt were celebrating and planning for their futures, Thai activists focused on democracy and freer media in their country were far more somber. Their government had arrested a cherubic but tough young woman named Chiranuch Premchaipoen, who is the editor of the popular but contentious Thai politics site Prachatai.[46] The authorities charged her with insulting Thailand's monarchy—the charge used as a catch-all to silence government opponents—simply because an anonymous poster on Prachatai's Web board had made slightly prickly comments. Though she normally projected a sunny glow, and had become known for wearing skirts studded with sparkles and other fake jewels, when faced with

the actual prospect of going to prison Chiranuch lost her sunniness. In interviews she seemed stunned by the real possibility of spending the rest of her
life in Thai jails, not exactly known for their safety or cleanliness.[47]

Chiranuch's case became a cause célèbre among Thai progressives,
men and women who, in the 1990s, had helped pass a reformist constitution and who had resisted the urge to join many middle class Thais in
celebrating the coup in 2006 that overthrew the elected autocrat Thaksin.
They took up donations for her, helped foreign reporters meet and interview her, and pressed the United States and other foreign governments to
condemn Thailand, just as Washington would condemn other backsliding
developing democracies that were not so friendly to Western strategic interests as Thailand.

But if in the 1990s these progressive Thais had been hopeful, and could
shrug off arrests, bribes, or beatings as the price of trying to establish a free
political system, now many of them just despaired, since their sacrifices did
not seem to be getting them anywhere, but rather just costing them their
closest friends and relatives. Thai academics critical of the government found
themselves ostracized, or going into exile in London, Washington, or Sydney;
but even in exile they were followed by government allies reporting on their
activities.[48] Thais who tried to find out what had happened to relatives and
friends during the bloody crackdowns on the streets of Bangkok in spring
2010 were warned not to look harder or were detained until they got the
message.[49] Thai journalists who tried to probe how, and why, Thailand's
democracy had regressed into a kind of soft authoritarianism were silenced
by fearful editors, or condemned as unpatriotic and disloyal to Thailand's
monarchy.[50] A few foreign news outlets continued to focus on Thailand's
deteriorating political climate, but with news budgets stretched thin many
of the reporters who had come to the country during the bloody crackdown
in spring 2010 returned home. And with policy makers in the West finding
it hard to believe that, despite the protests in the Middle East, democracy
was still in dire danger throughout the developing world, the trial of one
website editor in Bangkok—or news of many other democracies that were
sliding backward even as Egyptians danced in the streets—did not get much
attention.

Image has always been critical in Thailand—creating a perfect exterior image, even if inside you are angry, depressed, or unkempt, is a central part of Thai culture. As democracy fell apart, the Thai government seemed determined to uphold this concept. On the streets of Bangkok, there were few signs that, in spring 2010, the center of the city had disintegrated into a war zone complete with rooftop snipers, Molotov cocktails, street to street fighting, and sieges at one major Buddhist temple, where soldiers apparently shot up the house of worship and left pools of blood from the victims in its courtyard.[51] The government's suave, American-educated spokesman insisted that democracy had been restored. The city seemed reminiscent of Phuket Island in southern Thailand a year after the powerful 2004 tsunami had ripped apart its coast and killed some five thousand people. Through efficient rebuilding, and powerful marketing campaigns, hotels on the island had patched up the coast so that a casual observer could not notice that the tragedy had happened, and groups of tourists flocked back to the bars, noodle houses, and massage parlors—even though one only had to probe a bit to find that families on the island were still shattered, divided, and in mourning.

One similarly had to push a bit harder to find the damage in Bangkok and other parts of Thailand, the destruction of democratic culture and institutions, and the malaise, the popular fatigue with politics, which would make restoring democracy that much harder. "People [foreigners] aren't paying any attention to what's happening here, with what's going on in the Middle East, and people think Thailand is just back to normal, Thailand has a reputation as a friendly, lovely place," one Thai academic said. "So the [Thai] government just gets away with it, and they know they are getting away with it, and we are putting off a final explosion [in Thai society] just a bit longer." His face, lined and taut, betrayed years of trying to navigate the political climate, keeping his job at a top-tier university and trying to stay true to his beliefs at the same time. "We are just giving up."

Appendix: Egypt

As this book was going to press, Egypt's dramatic revolution took what appeared to be another turn. In the summer of 2012 the country's elected president, Mohamed Morsi, from the Muslim Brotherhood, seemed to strike a dramatic blow for Egyptian democracy and constitutional rule. He sacked the army head, Field Marshal Hussein Tantawi, who had led the junta that had ruled the country in the year after the ouster of Hosni Mubarak. Morsi's decision appeared to be a striking move in a country that for six decades had been dominated by the army and its top men. At the same time, the president also fired the heads of the country's other branches of the military, officers who also had been in the junta and who had long ties to Mubarak's regime. In response to the sacking, the military accepted the decision without threatening a coup or other disruption, even though earlier in the year the generals had wielded so much power that they had effectively dissolved Parliament. In their place, Morsi appointed two other generals who appear to have closer ties to him.

In so doing, Morsi apparently demonstrated the power of civilian rule, as well as the legitimacy of being elected by the public, which Tantawi had not been; many Egyptians celebrated the sacking, which appeared to end the army's desire to continue to play the role of kingmaker, even after the fall of Hosni Mubarak. And Morsi made other decisions that appeared to be ushering in an era of more open and free Egyptian politics. He oversaw the creation of a website for the presidency, enabling citizens to provide feedback on his performance and on the country's direction. Morsi, using his presidential powers, announced new laws giving defendants greater rights in court cases, a welcome change in a country where Mubarak had for decades used emergency laws to arrest critics at will.

Morsi also appeared to understand one of the critical lessons of democratization in other developing countries: If the new government does not produce rapid growth, particularly at a time when the population is expanding, the public may soon lose patience with democracy. Morsi quickly reached out to the International Monetary Fund and other potential lenders to help rescue Egypt's ailing economy, before the combination of a high birthrate, low productivity, and the government tradition of subsidizing staples like bread completely destroyed the economy. Morsi even appeared to take a relatively pragmatic approach to Israel, despite the fact that the peace deal with Israel was popular neither in his party nor among the Egyptian public at large.

And yet Morsi's actions did little to quash the fears of many middle class Egyptians and minorities, the types of people who control much of the economy and who are critical to making democracy work, as we have seen in countries like Thailand and the Philippines. Though Morsi moved against the army, at the same time he and the Muslim Brotherhood, long the country's dominant party but outlawed and harassed for years, appeared to be emulating Mubarak in their actions to centralize power. The government charged one of the country's most prominent journalists for insulting the president, and also charged a leading television personality for insulting the Muslim Brotherhood. Both acts only heightened fears that the Muslim Brotherhood was insensitive to constitutional liberties, and eventually would seek to completely dominate the political sphere. Reporters at several of the new TV and print outlets that had sprung up after Mubarak's demise publicly worried that they would be next, or that their coverage now would have to be altered to keep them out of jail.

Morsi himself did nothing at first to address the charges, but as protests mounted in the streets, including many by the same people who had demonstrated in Cairo against Mubarak, the president moved to release one of the journalists from pretrial detention, though the charges against him remained. Meanwhile, other leaders of the Muslim Brotherhood issued dire warnings for the country's religious minorities like Christians, intensifying an already toxic interreligious brew that, in the wake of Mubarak's ouster, had led to riots in several cities between Muslims and Coptic Christians.

Ultimately, public confidence in Morsi, and in Egypt's democracy, continued to be mediocre at best. Though no one wanted Mubarak back, the number of Egyptian emigrants continued to rise in 2012, an exodus dominated by middle class men and women, and by minorities. Meanwhile, public support for democracy as the best system of governance remained tepid. In one major study, about 40 percent of Egyptians did not believe democracy was the best system of governance for the country—an especially troubling finding given that the country's reforms were very young and that people therefore had had little time to become cynical about popular politics.

Notes

1. Democracy Goes into Reverse

1. Author interviews with Thai officials, Washington, DC, June 2010.

2. Thomas Fuller and Seth Mydans, "Thai General Shot; Army Moves to Face Protestors," *New York Times,* 13 May 2010.

3. "Bangkok in Pictures," British Broadcasting Corporation, 20 May 2010, www.bbc.co.uk/news/10130473, accessed May 2010.

4. Giles Ungpakorn, "Right-Wing Mob Riots Outside Government," *Asia Sentinel,* 7 Oct 2008.

5. Author interview with former U.S. ambassador to Thailand, Washington, DC, Apr 2010.

6. "Not Enough Graves," Human Rights Watch, 7 July 2004, http://www.hrw.org/en/node/12005/section/2.

7. "Court Condones Suffocation," Asian Human Rights Appeal, http://www.humanrights.asia/news/urgent-appeals/AHRC-UAU-012–2009, accessed Nov 2010.

8. Author interview with reporters and editors at the *Bangkok Post,* Bangkok, Mar 2005.

9. "Thai Protests Cancel Asian Summit," British Broadcasting Corporation, 11 Apr 2009.

10. James Kelly, "We Can Count on Thailand," speech to Asia Foundation Bangkok, 13 Mar 2002.

11. "Powell Hails Thai Ally in War Against Extremists," *Nation* (Bangkok), 29 July 2002, A1.

12. *Freedom in the World 1999* (New York: Freedom House, 2000).

13. Author interview with red shirt leaders, Chiang Mai, Feb 2010.

14. Thitinan Pongsudhirak, "Meaning and Implications of the General's Rise," *Bangkok Post,* 5 Oct 2010, http://www.bangkokpost.com/opinion/opinion/199699/meaning-and-implementations-of-general-rise, accessed Oct 2011.

15. "A Dubious Distinction: Thailand Blocks 100,000 Websites," *Bangkok Post,* 29 June 2010, For more on this, see FACT Thailand, http://facthai.wordpress.com.

16. Ibid.

17. Author interview with Thai official, Washington, DC, Mar 2010.

18. *Countries at the Crossroads 2010* (New York: Freedom House, 2010), 1–3.

19. *Freedom in the World 2011,* 2–13.

20. Arch Puddington, "Freedom in the World 2010: Erosion of Freedom Intensifies," in *Freedom in the World 2010.*

21. *2011 Annual Report,* International Federation for Human Rights, http://www.fidh.org/+-freedom-of-expression-+?lang=en, accessed Nov 2011.

22. Alina Mungiu-Pippidi, "EU Accession Is No End of History," *Journal of Democracy,* Oct 2007, 13.

23. Ivan Krastev, "The Strange Death of the Liberal Consensus," *Journal of Democracy,* Oct 2007, 57.

24. "Hungary: Media Law Endangers Press Freedom," Human Rights Watch, 7 Jan 2011, http://www.hrw.org/news/2011/01/07/hungary-media-law-endangers-press-freedom.

25. Carlos Conde, "Leftist Activist Is Slain in Philippines," *New York Times,* 5 July 2010, http://www.nytimes.com/2010/07/06/world/asia/06phils.html, accessed Oct 2011. Also, "Armed Forces as Veto Power: Civil-Military Relations in the Philippines," in *Democracy Under Stress: Civil-Military Relations in South and Southeast Asia,* ed. Paul Chambers, Aurel Crossant, and Thitinan Pongsudhirak (Bangkok: ISIS Chulalongkorn University, 2010), 142.

26. Author interview with Harry Roque, Manila, May 2006.

27. Al Labita, "Philippine Military Waits in the Wings," *Asia Times,* 11 Nov 2010.

28. Author interviews with Obama administration officials, Washington, DC, July 2010.

29. David Kirkpatrick, "Church Protests in Cairo Turn Deadly," *New York Times,* 9 Oct 2011, A1.

30. Leila Fadel, "Second Day of Clashes in Egypt Leads to Fears of Second Revolt," *Washington Post,* 20 Nov 2011.

31. Isobel Coleman, "Tunisia's Election Results," Council on Foreign Relations (Democracy in Development blog), 25 Oct 2011, http://blogs.cfr.org/coleman/2011/10/25/tunisias-election-results/.

32. "All Eyes on Al Nahda Party's Strategy," Associated Press, 22 Oct 2011.

33. Yasmine Ryan, "Tunisia's Vocal Salafist Minority," Al Jazeera, 11 Oct 2011, http://english.aljazeera.net/indepth/features/2011/10/20111011131734544894.html, accessed Nov 2011.

34. Rajaa Basly, "The Future of Al Nahda in Tunisia," Carnegie Endowment for International Peace, 20 Apr 2011, http://carnegieendowment.org/2011/04/20/fu ture-of-al-nahda-in-tunisia/6bqw, accessed Oct 2011.

35. "Tunisia: Police Inaction Allowed Assault on Film Screening," Human Rights Watch, 30 June 2011, http://www.hrw.org/news/2011/06/30/tunisia-police -inaction-allowed-assault-film-screening.

36. Husain Haqqani and Hillel Fradkin, "Islamist Parties and Democracy," *Journal of Democracy,* July 2008.

37. Adam Nossiter, "Hinting at an End to a Curb on Polygamy, Libyan Leader Stirs Anger," *New York Times,* 29 Oct 2011.

38. Rod Nordland and David Kirkpatrick, "Islamists' Growing Sway Raises Questions for Libya," *New York Times,* 14 Sept 2011.

39. Tara Barahmpour, "Libyan Authorities Struggle to Rein in Militias," *Washington Post,* 6 Oct 2011, A1.

40. Nordland and Kirkpatrick, "Islamists' Growing Sway Raises Questions for Libya."

41. Borzou Daragahi, "Democracy Fears over Libya Leaders," *Financial Times,* 27 Oct 2011, A2.

42. David Rosenberg, "Arab Spring Fails to Deliver Yet on Human Rights," *Jerusalem Post,* 1 Sept 2011.

43. Richard Joseph, "Democracy and Reconfigured Power in Africa," *Current History,* Nov 2011, 325.

44. Michael Schwirtz, "Former Prime Minister Set to Win Kyrgyzstan Vote," *New York Times,* 31 Oct 2011.

45. "The Discontents of Progress," *Economist,* 29 Oct 2011, 48.

46. Marta Lagos, "Latin America's Diversity of Views," *Journal of Democracy,* Jan 2008, 11–12.

47. *2010 Life in Transition Survey* (Brussels: European Bank for Reconstruction and Development, 2011), 3–21.

48. Ibid., 3.

49. Ibid., 71.

50. Paul D. Hutchcroft, "The Arroyo Imbroglio in the Philippines," *Journal of Democracy,* Jan 2008.

51. "Ugandan Opposition Pushing for Presidential Term Limit," Reuters, 12 May 2010.

52. Shaun Walker, "Medvedev Promises New Era for Russian Democracy, "*Independent* (UK), 13 Nov 2009.

53. Thomas Carothers, *Stepping Back from Democratic Pessimism,* Carnegie Endowment Paper No. 99, Carnegie Endowment for International Peace, Washington, DC, Feb 2009, 5, http://carnegieendowment.org/files/democratic_pessimism .pdf.

54. "Overview," in *Freedom in the World 2010* (New York: Freedom House, 2010).

55. Jan Cienski, "Belarus Juggles Lure of West and Reliance on East," *Financial Times,* 24 Dec 2010, 3.

56. Rajan Menon and Alexander Motyl, "Counterrevolution in Kiev," *Foreign Affairs,* Nov/Dec 2011, 137–39.

57. "Malaysia," in Freedom House, *Countries at the Crossroads 2010* (New York: Freedom House, 2010), 401–5.

58. "Malaysian Aide's July Death 'Probably Homicide,'" *Asia Sentinel,* 21 Oct 2009, http://www.asiasentinel.com/index.php?option=com_content&task=view&id =2111&Itemid=178, accessed Nov 2009.

59. "2009 Human Rights Report: Cambodia," 11 Mar 2010, U.S. Department of State, Washington, DC.

60. Juan Forero, "Venezuelan Judge Is Jailed After Ruling Angers President Hugo Chávez," *Washington Post,* 25 Apr 2010. Also, "Venezuela Orders Arrest of Anti-Chavez TV Boss," Reuters, 11 June 2010.

61. Larry Diamond and Marc Plattner, eds., *Democracy: A Reader* (Baltimore: Johns Hopkins University Press, 2009), x–xi.

62. Francis Fukuyama, "The End of History?" *National Interest,* Summer 1989, 3–16.

63. Robert Kagan, *The Return of History and the End of Dreams* (New York: Knopf, 2008), 4–5.

64. This comes from my own calculation of Freedom House data.

65. George H. W. Bush, speech to Congress, 6 Mar 1991.

66. George W. Bush, "Second Inaugural Address," 20 Jan 2005.

67. Bill Clinton, "America's Stake in China," *Blueprint,* 1 June 2000.

68. Stewart Patrick, "Irresponsible Stakeholders?," *Foreign Affairs,* Nov/Dec 2010.

69. For more on these earlier waves of democracy, see Samuel Huntington, *The Third Wave* (Norman, OK: University of Oklahoma Press, 1991).

70. "National Security Strategy of the United States," May 2010, www.white house.gov/sites/default/files/rss.../national_security_strategy.pdf. Also, author interviews with White House officials, Washington, DC, Nov 2009 and Dec 2009.

71. Author interviews with ASEAN officials, Washington, DC, Nov 2009, and Bangkok, Feb 2010.

72. "No Candidates Found for $5 Million Leadership Prize," Associated Press, 13 June 2010.

73. See Daniel Brinks and Michael Coppedge, "Diffusion Is No Illusion," *Comparative Political Studies,* Aug 2010, 1148–76.

2. How We Got Here

1. Babatunde Williams, "The Prospect for Democracy in the New Africa," *Phylon,* 2d quarter 1961, 174–79.

2. Jeanne Kirkpatrick, "Dictatorships and Double Standards," *Commentary,* Nov 1979, http://www.commentarymagazine.com/article/dictatorships-double-stan dards/, accessed Oct 2011.

3. Charles Kurzman, "Not Ready for Democracy? Theoretical and Historical Objections to the Concept of Prerequisites," *Sociological Analysis,* Dec 1998.

4. Author interviews with Malawian politicians, Blantyre, Feb 2005.

5. For more on this, see Alec Russell, *Big Men, Little People: The Leaders Who Defined Africa* (New York: NYU Press, 2000).

6. Bruce Reynolds, "The OSS and American Intelligence in Postwar Thailand," *Journal of Intelligence History,* Winter 2002, 46. Also, "Police Describe How Four Men Met Death Yesterday," *Bangkok Post,* 6 Mar 1949.

7. Henry Kissinger, *American Foreign Policy* (New York: Norton, 1977).

8. Francis Fukuyama, *The End of History and the Last Man* (New York: Free Press, 1992), 8.

9. Geoffrey Robinson, *If You Leave Us Here, We Will Die: How Genocide Was Stopped* in East Timor (Princeton, NJ: Princeton University Press, 2009).

10. Ibid.

11. "Spain: A Vote for Democracy," *Time,* 29 Nov 1976.

12. Per Freedom House Economist Intelligence Unit data.

13. Author interviews with Asia Foundation officials, Bangkok, Jan 1999.

14. Paul Wolfowitz, "The Aquino Legacy Is Peaceful Regime Change," *Wall Street Journal,* 4 Aug 2009, http://professional.wsj.com/article/SB10001424052970204 31360457432850285705892.html?mg=reno64-wsj, accessed Oct 2011.

15. Ronald Reagan, "Our Noble Vision: An Opportunity for All," speech to the American Conservative Union, 2 Mar 1984, reagan2020.us/speeches/Our_Noble _Vision.asp, accessed Aug 2010.

16. National Endowment for Democracy, "About NED," http://www.ned.org /grantseekers/application-procedure, accessed Aug 2010. Also, International Republican Institute, "History," http://www.iri.org/learn-more-about-iri/history, accessed Aug 2010, and National Democratic Institute, "What We Do," http://www.ndi.org /whatwedo, accessed Aug 2010.

17. Author interviews with National Endowment for Democracy program officers, Washington, DC, Mar 2010.

18. Ibid.

19. Douglas Brinkley, "Democratic Enlargement: The Clinton Doctrine," *Foreign Policy,* Spring 1997, 111–16.

20. Ibid.

21. Ibid.

22. "National Security Strategy of the United States," Feb 1996, http://www.fas .org/spp/military/docops/national/1996stra.htm, accessed June 2010.

23. "Examining the Clinton Record on Democracy Promotion," Carnegie Endowment for International Peace symposium, Washington, DC, 12 Sept 2000.

24. Thomas Carothers, "Examining the Clinton Record on Democracy Promotion," paper presented at Carnegie Endowment for International Peace symposium, Washington, DC, 12 Sept 2000.

25. Author interviews with former Clinton officials, Washington, DC, Sept 2010.

26. Brinkley, "Democratic Enlargement: The Clinton Doctrine," 111–16.

27. For more on the 1975 and 1999 comparison, see Robinson, *If You Leave Us Here, We Will Die.*

28. Robert Kagan, *The Return of History and the End of Dreams* (New York: Knopf, 2008), 5.

29. Kishore Mahbubani, "End of Whose History?" *New York Times,* 12 Nov 2009, http://www.nytimes.com/2009/11/12/opinion/12iht-edmahbubani.html?page wanted=all, accessed Oct 2011.

30. See, for example, Gordon G. Chang, *The Coming Collapse of China* (New York: Random House, 2001).

3. The Fourth Wave

1. "HIV/AIDS in Malawi," United States Agency for International Development, http://www.usaid.gov/our_work/global_health/aids/Countries/africa/malawi.html, accessed June 2010.

2. Kevin Hassett, "Does Economic Success Require Democracy?," *American,* May/June 2007, http://www.american.com/archive/2007/may-june-magazine-contents/does-economic-success-require-democracy, accessed Jan 2009.

3. My own analysis is based on the annual Freedom House data.

4. Peter Rosenbul, "Irrational Exuberance: The Clinton Administration in Africa," *Current History,* May 2002, 195–98.

5. Michela Wrong, *It's Our Turn to Eat* (New York: HarperCollins, 2009).

6. Wahaqb Oyedukun, "Nigeria Democracy Day: Which Date Is More Appropriate," *Leadership* (Abuja), allafrica.com/stories/200806250400.html, accessed July 2010.

7. Norimitsu Onishi, "Albright Vows to Increase Aid to Nigeria," *New York Times,* 21 Oct 1999, http://www.nytimes.com/1999/10/21/world/albright-vows-to-increase-aid-to-nigeria.html, accessed Oct 2011.

8. Fareed Zakaria, *The Future of Freedom: Illiberal Democracy at Home and Abroad* (New York: W. W. Norton, 2003), 19.

9. Ibid., 106.

10. Ibid., 107–13 and 117–18.

11. Robert Kagan, "The Ungreat Washed," *New Republic,* 7 July 2003.

12. Zakaria, *Future of Freedom*, 145–46.

13. For more on the 1976 Thammasat massacre, see "Thailand: A Nightmare of Lynching and Burning," *Time,* 16 Oct 1976.

14. Sabeel Rahman, "Zakaria Explores the Tyranny of the Masses," *Harvard Book Review,* Summer 2003.

15. For more on Cambodia's regression, see Joel Brinkley, *Cambodia's Curse* (New York: Public Affairs, 2011).

16. George W. Bush, "Renewing America's Purpose," speech at Boeing plant, 17 May 2000.

17. William J. Clinton, *Between Hope and History* (New York: Random House, 1996), 36.

18. John Williamson, "A Short History of the Washington Consensus," paper presented at From the Washington Consensus Toward a New Global Governance conference, Barcelona, 24–25 Sept 2004.

19. Dani Rodrik, "Goodbye Washington Consensus, Hello Washington Confusion? A Review of the World Bank's Economic Growth in the 1990s: Learning from a Decade of Reform," *Journal of Economic Literature* 44 (4), 973–75.

20. "World Bank Aims to Cut Poverty, Hunger in Half," Associated Press, 30 Nov 1993.

21. World Bank, "Economic Growth in the 1990s: Learning from a Decade of Reform"(Washington, DC: The World Bank, 2005).

22. From IMF data.

23. Author interview with Stephen Carr, Blantyre, Feb 2005.

24. Author interviews with agricultural consultants, Blantyre, Jan 2009.

25. Celia Dugger, "Ending Famine, Simply by Ignoring the Experts," *New York Times,* 2 Dec 2007, A1.

26. Author interviews with Malawian officials, Blantyre, Jan 2009.

4. It's the Economy, Stupid

1. For more on this thesis, see Dani Rodrik, *One Economics, Many Recipes: Globalization, Institutions, and Economic Growth* (Princeton, NJ: Princeton University Press, 2008).

2. Kevin Hassett, "Does Economic Success Require Democracy?" *American,* May/June 2007.

3. Adam Przeworski, Michael E. Alvarez, Jose Antonio Cheibub, and Fernando Limongi, *Democracy and Development: Political Institutions and Well-Being in the World, 1950–1990* (Cambridge: Cambridge University Press, 2000), 155–57.

4. Dani Rodrik, "Goodbye Washington Consensus, Hello Washington Confusion? A Review of the World Bank's Economic Growth in the 1990s: Learning from a Decade of Reform," *Journal of Economic Literature* 44 (4), 973–74.

5. Compiled from IMF data World Bank, World Development Indicators.

6. ROMIR Monitoring poll, 18 July 2003, www.cdi.org/russia/johnson/7255–3 .cfm, accessed Nov 2010.

7. Richard Rose, "Learning to Support New Regimes in Europe," *Journal of Democracy,* July 2007, 111–25; author interviews with Polish and Ukrainian activists, Washington, DC, Apr 2011.

8. Peter Lewis, "Growth Without Prosperity in Africa," *Journal of Democracy,* July 2008, 95–97.

9. *Transition Report 2010,* European Bank for Reconstruction and Development (Brussels: EBRD, 2011), 60–69.

10. Latinobarometro surveys, 1995–2009, available at .latinobarometro.org.

11. Owen Matthews, "The Breadbasket Becomes the Basket Case," *Newsweek,* 14 Mar 2009, http://www.thedailybeast.com/newsweek/2009/03/13/the-breadbasket -becomes-the-basket-case.html, accessed Oct 2011.

12. "Poll of 18 African Countries Finds All Support Democracy," WorldPublic Opinion.org,   http://www.worldpublicopinion.org/pipa/articles/brafricara/209.php ?nid=&id=&pnt=209&lb=braf, accessed June 2010. Also, Afrobarometer Survey, 2008/9 round of surveys.

13. I am indebted to Shelby Leighton for this analysis of Afrobarometer data.

5. The Middle Class Revolts

1. "Philippines Country Profile," British Broadcasting Corporation, news.bbc .co.uk/2/hi/americas/country.../1262783.stm, accessed Nov 2010.

2. "Philippine Poverty Statistics: Table 4," Philippine National Statistical Coordination Board, www.nscb.gov.ph/poverty/2006_05mar08/table_4.asp, accessed Sept 2010.

3. Benigno S. Aquino Jr., "The Filipino Is Worth Dying For" (reprint), *Manila Times,* 22 Aug 2010, A1.

4. Author interview with Roel Landingin, Manila, Mar 2007.

5. See, for example, "Gunmen, Eight Hostages Killed in Manila Bus Siege," Reuters, 23 Aug 2010, and Joel D. Adriano, "Foreigners Beware in the Philippines," *Asia Times,* 17 Aug 2010.

6. "Corruption," in "Enterprise Surveys: Philippines 2009," The World Bank, 9, http://www.enterprisesurveys.org.

7. Paul Hutchcroft, "The Arroyo Imbroglio in the Philippines," *Journal of Democracy,* Jan 2008, 148–49.

8. Eliza Diaz, "Aquino Taken to Task over Promises," *BusinessWorld* (Manila), 28 June 2011.

9. Central Intelligence Agency, *The World Factbook,* chapters on Singapore and the Philippines, https://www.cia.gov/library/publications/the-world-factbook/.

10. Paul Hutchcroft, *Booty Capitalism: The Politics of Banking in the Philippines* (Ithaca, NY: Cornell University Press, 1998), 240–41.

11. Yvette Collymore, "Rapid Population Growth, Crowded Cities, Present Challenges in the Philippines," Population Reference Bureau report, Aug 2007, http://www.prb.org/Articles/2003/RapidPopulationGrowthCrowdedCitiesPre sentChallengesinthePhilippines.aspx.

12. Linda Luz Guerrero and Rollin Tusalem, "Mass Public Perceptions of Democratization in the Philippines: Consolidation in Progress?" in *How East Asians View Democracy,* ed. Yun-han Chu, Larry Diamond, Andrew Nathan, and Doh Chull Shin (New York: Columbia University Press, 2008) 61–80.

13. Chang Yu-tzung, Yun-han Chu, and Chong-Min Park, "Authoritarian Nostalgia in Asia," *Journal of Democracy* 3, 2007, 66–80.

14. "Marcos Son Proclaimed Philippine Senator," Associated Press, 15 May 2010.

15. Norimitsu Onishi, "Marcos Seeks to Restore Philippines Dynasty," *New York Times,* 7 May 2010, A1.

16. According to reports by the Philippines Center for Investigative Journalism, PCIJ.org.

17. Author interview with Roel Landingin, Manila, Mar 2007.

18. For the classic overview of Huntington's views, see Samuel Huntington, *The Third Wave* (Norman, OK: University of Oklahoma Press, 1993).

19. "Most Folks See Themselves as Middle-Class," *Ad Week,* 24 Sept 2010, www .adweek.com/.../news/.../e3i0121638c1a14264a1858ae8b0e95981b.

20. For more on this thesis, see Amy Chua, *World on Fire* (New York: Doubleday, 2003).

21. *The Expanding Middle: The Exploding Global Middle-Class and Falling Global Inequality,* Goldman Sachs, Global Economics Paper No. 170, 7 July 2008, http://www2.goldmansachs.com.

22. *The Global Middle-Class: Views on Democracy, Religion, Values, and Life Satisfaction in Emerging Nations,* Pew Global Attitudes Project, 12 Feb 2009, http:// pewglobal.org/2009/02/12/the-global-middle-class, accessed June 2010.

23. "The New Middle Classes Rise Up," *Economist,* 3 Sept 2011.

24. David Beresford, "Row over Mother of the Nation Winnie Mandela," *Guardian,* 27 Jan 1989, http://century.guardian.co.uk/1980–1989/Story/0,,110268,00 .html, accessed Oct 2011.

25. Author interviews with DPP activists, Washington, DC, Jan 2004.

26. "Former First Lady of Taiwan Admits to Laundering $2.2 Million," Associated Press, 10 Feb 2009.

27. Jonathan Adams, "Three Taiwan Officials Quit in Diplomatic Furor," *New York Times,* 7 May 2008.

28. Joseph Kahn, "U.S. Says No to Overnight Stay for Taiwanese Leader," *New York Times,* 4 May 2006.

29. "Georgia," in *Human Rights Watch World Report 2008: Events of 2007* (New York: Human Rights Watch, 2008), http://www.hrw.org/sites/default/files/reports /wr2k8_web.pdf.

30. Compiled from Freedom House data.

31. "The Wrecking of Venezuela," *Economist,* 13 May 2010.

32. Ibid. Also, Simon Romero, "Venezuela, More Deadly Than Iraq, Wonders Why," *New York Times,* 22 Aug 2010.

33. "The Wrecking of Venezuela."

34. Simon Romero, "New Laws in Venezuela Aim to Limit Dissent," *New York Times,* 24 Dec 2010.

35. "IAHCR Concerned," http://www.cidh.oas.org/Comunicados/English /2010/36–10eng.htm, released 24 Mar 2010, accessed Nov 2011.

36. Juan Forero, "Documents Show C.I.A. Knew of a Coup Plot in Venezuela," *New York Times,* 3 Dec 2004.

37. Heba Saleh, "Security Vacuum Hurts Business," *Financial Times,* 3 Nov 2011, A2.

38. Negar Azimi, "In Egypt, the Lure of Leaving," *New York Times Magazine,* 26 Aug 2011.

39. Isobel Coleman, "Women and Democracy in the New Egypt," Council on Foreign Relations, Democracy in Development blog, http://blogs.cfr.org/coleman /2011/07/28/women-and-democracy-in-the-new-egypt, 28 July 2011.

40. Robert Malley and Hussein Agha, "The Arab Counterrevolution," *New York Review of Books,* 29 Sept 2011.

41. Ibid.

42. Author interviews with Thai politicians, Washington, DC, and Chiang Mai, Dec 2011.

43. "Fearing Change, Many Christians in Syria Back Assad," *New York Times,* 27 Sept 2011, A1.

44. Keith Bradsher, "Protestors Fuel a Long-Shot Bid to Oust Taiwan's Leader," *New York Times,* 28 Sept 2006.

45. Author interviews with Taiwanese activists, Taipei, Mar 2003 and May 2005.

46. "Chen Shui-Bian Gets Life," *Taipei Times,* 12 Sept 2009.

47. Author interview with Noppadon Pattama, Washington, DC, Mar 2010.

6. Graft, Graft, and More Graft

1. Keith Richburg, "Suharto Steps Down, Names Successor," *Washington Post,* 21 May 1998, A1, http://www.washingtonpost.com/wp-srv/business/longterm/asiae-con/stories/suharto052198.htm.

2. "Let Us All Collectively Unite," *Jakarta Globe,* 14 Aug 2009.

3. International Crisis Group, "Jemaah Islamiah's Current Status," released 3 May 2007, Jakarta/Brussels.

4. "The US-Indonesia Comprehensive Partnership," http://www.whitehouse.gov/the-press-office/us-indonesia-comprehensive-partnership, accessed Feb 2011.

5. Scott Wilson, "Obama Administration Studies Recent Revolutions for Lessons Applicable in Egypt," *Washington Post,* 14 Feb 2011, A1.

6. Barack Obama, "Speech in Jakarta, Indonesia," 9 Nov 2010, http://www.america.gov/st/texttrans-english/2010/November/20101109213225su0.4249035.html, accessed Jan 2011.

7. Matthew Lee, "Clinton: Indonesia Can Be Democratic Role Model," Associated Press, 25 July 2011.

8. "Indonesian Anti-Graft Officials Thieves: Official," Agence France Presse, 9 Sept 2011.

9. "Former Chief of Indonesia's Anti-Corruption Commission Found Guilty," http://www.demotix.com/news/245158/former-chief-indonesias-anti-corruption-commission-found-guilty, accessed Nov 2011.

10. Michael T. Rock, "Corruption and Democracy," DESA Working Paper No. 55, United Nations Department of Economic and Social Affairs, http://www.un.org/esa/desa/papers/2007/wp55_2007.pdf.

11. Ibid.

12. Ibid.

13. "Crucial 2007 Jakarta Governor's Race Taking Shape," U.S. Embassy Jakarta Cable, 12 Sept 2006, accessed through Wikileaks.org, Oct 2011.

14. "Kalla Wins Chair of Golkar," U.S. Embassy Jakarta Cable, 21 Dec 2004, accessed through Wikileaks.org, Oct 2011.

15. "Corruption Everywhere," *Economist,* 2 Sept 2011. Also, author interviews with Indonesian leaders, Washington, DC, Sept 2011.

16. "Indonesia Most Corrupt of Key Asian Nations: PERC," Reuters, 8 Mar 2010.

17. "Power to the People! No, Wait!" *Economist,* 17 May 2011.

18. Author interviews with American executives focusing on Asia, Washington, DC, Oct 2011.

19. "Google Seeks Exemption in Indonesia's Investment Procedure," Xinhua, 21 Sept 2011.

20. Richard Rose and Christian Haerpfer, "New Democracies Barometer V: A 12 Nation Survey," Studies in Public Policy 306, University of Strathclyde, Glasgow, 1998.

21. Hamid Mohtadi and Terry Roe, "Democracy, Rent Seeking and Growth: Is There a U Curve?," Bulletin Number 97-1, University of Minnesota Center for Political Economy, May 1997, http://ageconsearch.umn.edu/bitstream/7485/1/bu970001 .pdf.

22. Ibid.

23. For more on this, see Richard MacGregor, *The Party: The Secret World of China's Communist Rulers* (New York: Harper, 2010).

24. Mark Magnier and Tsai Ting, "China Damage Control over Reports of Bling," *Los Angeles Times,* 26 Dec 2007.

25. "Indonesia's Suharto Tops 'Worst-Ever' Corruption Charts," Agence France Presse, 24 Mar 2004. Tom Allard, "Yudhoyono to Address the Nation as Corruption Scandals Spread," *Sydney Morning Herald,* 24 Nov 2009.

26. Rock, "Corruption and Democracy."

27. "Indonesia Facebook's Second Largest Market," *Asian Correspondent,* 4 Nov 2010, http://asiancorrespondent.com/42231/indonesia-facebooks-second-largest-market -as-asia-surpasses-100-million-members, accessed Jan 2011.

28. I am grateful to Shelby Leighton for this research.

29. Eric Chang and Yun-han Chu, "Corruption and Trust: Exceptionalism in Asian Democracies?" *Journal of Politics* 68 (2006), 259–71.

30. I am grateful to Shelby Leighton for this research.

31. Daniel Armah-Attoh, E. Gyimah-Boadi, and Annie Barbara Chikwanha, "Corruption and Institutional Trust in Africa: Implications for Democratic Development," Working Paper No. 81, Dec 2007, Afrobarometer.org.

32. Ronojoy Sen, "The Problem of Corruption," *Journal of Democracy,* Oct 2009, 89.

33. Paul Collier, *Wars, Guns, and Votes* (New York: Harper Perennial, 2009), 41–42.

34. Michael Bratton, "Vote Buying and Violence in Nigerian Election Campaigns," Working Paper No. 99, June 2008, 4–7, Afrobarometer.org.

35. "Understanding Electoral Violence in Asia," United Nations Development Program, Asia Pacific Regional Center, June 2011, 7, http://www.snap-undp.org/eli brary/Publications/UnderstandingElectoralViolenceinAsia.pdf.

36. Thomas Fuller, "Democracy and Vote Buying Returning in Thailand," *New York Times,* 25 Nov 2007.

37. U.S. Library of Congress, "Country Studies: Indonesia," http://countrystudies .us/indonesia/91.htm, accessed Jan 2011.

38. Author interviews with Indonesian voters, Jakarta, 2007.

39. Aubrey Belford, "Son of Indonesian Dictator Gives Democracy a Shot," *New York Times,* 7 July 2011.

40. "Indonesia's Electorate Smells Graft," *Asia Sentinel,* 7 Oct 2011, http://www .asiasentinel.com/index.php?option=com_content&task=view&id=3834&Itemid=175, accessed Oct 2011.

41. Ibid.

42. Arienta Primanitha, "Indonesians Prefer Suharto to Yudhoyono: Poll," *Jakarta Globe,* 16 May 16 2011.

7. The China Model

1. "Why Grandpa Wen Has to Care," *Economist,* 12 June 2008.

2. Jason Dean, James Areddy, and Selena Ng, "Chinese Premier Blames Recession on U.S. Actions," *Wall Street Journal,* 29 Jan 2009.

3. Scott Snyder and Brad Glosserman, "Not Too Fast with China," 13 Nov 2009, Globalsecurity.org, accessed Sept 2010.

4. Deng Xiaoping, as quoted in Zhongying Pang, "China's Soft Power Dilemma: The Beijing Consensus Revisited," in *Soft Power: China's Emerging Strategy in International Politics* ed. Li Mingjiang (Lanham, MD: Lexington Books, 2009), 134.

5. Joshua Cooper Ramo, *The Beijing Consensus,* Foreign Policy Centre report, May 2004, http://fpc.org.uk/fsblob/244.pdf.

6. Author interviews with Chinese officials, Beijing and Washington, DC, Mar, May, and June 2005.

7. H. E. Fu Yuancong, "Why Does China Remain a Developing Country?," speech in Timor Leste, 6 Oct 2010, Ministry of Foreign Affairs of the People's Republic of China, http://www.fmprc.gov.cn/eng/wjb/zwjg/zwbd/t758927.htm.

8. Keith Bradsher, "In Downturn, China Sees Path to Growth," *New York Times,* 16 Mar 2009, A1.

9. U.S. statistics from Bureau of Economic Analysis, www.bea.gov/national /index.htm, accessed Nov 2010; Japan's statistics from Central Intelligence Agency, *The World Factbook,* https://www.cia.gov. /library/publications/the-world-factbook /geos/ja.html, accessed Nov 2010; China's statistics from "China's Economy Shows Strong Growth in 2009," British Broadcasting Corporation, 21 Jan 2010, news.bbc. co.uk/2/hi/8471613.stm, accessed Oct 2010.

10. "Major Foreign Holders of Treasury Securities," U.S. Department of the Treasury, www.ustreas.gov/tic/mfh.txt, accessed Nov 2010.

11. Roger C. Altman, "The Great Crash, 2008," *Foreign Affairs,* Jan/Feb 2009.

12. Thomas Friedman, "Our One Party Democracy," *New York Times,* 8 Sept 2009, A29.

13. Katrin Bennhold, "West Unready and Uneasy as China Boldly Emerges," *International Herald Tribune,* 27 Jan 2010, 13.

14. Mei Xinyu, "US Much Ado About Nothing," *China Daily,* 3 Nov 2010, www .chinadaily.com.cn/opinion/2010-11/03/content_11494163.htm, accessed Nov 2010.

15. For more on the central role of the CCP, see Richard MacGregor, *The Party: The Secret World of China's Communist Rulers* (New York: Harper, 2010).

16. Randall Peerenboom, *China Modernizes* (New York: Oxford University Press, 2007), 133.

17. For annual figures on direct investment, see UNCTAD's compilations of investment at www.unctad.org/WIR.

18. Author interviews with Obama administration officials, Washington, DC, Nov 2010.

19. Bloomberg News, "China Overtakes Japan as World's Second-Largest Economy," 16 Aug 2010, http://www.bloomberg.com/news/2010-08-16/china-economy -passes-japan-s-in-second-quarter-capping-three-decade-rise.html.

20. "Shenzhen Aims to Close to Singapore's GDP in Five Years," *Global Times,* 1 June 2010.

21. "China Country Overview," Ausaid, www.ausaid.gov.au/china/, accessed Nov 2010.

22. International Monetary Fund, "World Economic Outlook April 2009: Crisis and Recovery" (Washington, DC: IMF, 2009), 10.

23. Author interview with Thai official, Washington, DC, May 2010.

24. "China Urges Europe to Skip Nobel Ceremony for Activist Liu Xiaobao," Associated Press, 4 Nov 2010.

25. "Renminbi Banking Business in Hong Kong," www.hkma.gov.hk/media /eng/publication-and-research/.../fa3.pdf, accessed Nov 2011.

26. Joshua Kurlantzick, "Don't Bet on the BRICs," Bloomberg Businessweek, 3 Nov 2011, http://www.businessweek.com/magazine/dont-bet-on-the-brics-11032011 .html.

27. John Pomfret, "Obama's Meeting with the Dalai Lama Is Delayed," *Washington Post,* 5 Oct 2009, http://www.washingtonpost.com/wp-dyn/content/article /2009/10/04/AR2009100403262.html, accessed Oct 2011.

28. John Pomfret, "China's Strident Tone Raises Concerns Among Western Governments, Analysts," *Washington Post,* 31 Jan 2010, A1.

29. Author interview with State Department official, Washington, DC, Mar 2010.

30. Jeremy Page, "Tension Grows Between China and India as Asia Slips into Cold War," *Times* (UK), 12 Nov 2009.

31. John Glionna and David Pierson, "Tensions Between China, Japan Escalate," *Los Angeles Times,* 23 Sept 2010.

32. Peter Lee, "US Goes Fishing for Trouble," *Asia Times,* 29 July 2010.

33. Simon Roughneen, "Asean Sups with the Chinese 'Devil,'" *Asia Times,* 4 Nov 2010.

34. Stephen Halper, *The Beijing Consensus: How China's Authoritarian Model Will Dominate the Twenty-First Century* (New York: Basic Books, 2010), 15.

35. "Worldwide Military Expenditures," globalsecurity.org, accessed Aug 2010. Also, "The Fourth Modernization," *Economist,* 2 Dec 2010.

36. "Worldwide Military Expenditures," globalsecurity.org, accessed Aug 2010. Also, "The Fourth Modernization," *Economist,* 2 Dec 2010.

37. Zhang Haizhou and Cheng Guangjin, "China's Military Not a Threat: Major General," *China Daily,* 4 Mar 2010, http://www.chinadaily.com.cn/usa/2010 -03/04/content_11016513.htm, accessed Oct 2010.

38. "The Beijing Consensus Is to Keep Quiet," *Economist,* 8 May 2010, 41–42. Also, "Shanghai Bids Farewell to Massive Expo Fair," BBC, 31 Oct 2010, http:// www.bbc.co.uk/news/world-asia-pacific-11660298.

39. Peerenboom, *China Modernizes,* 9.

40. Bennhold, "West Unready and Uneasy as China Boldly Emerges," 13.

41. Author interviews with Thai, Vietnamese, and Chinese officials, Chiang Mai and Washington, DC, Mar 2007, May 2008, and May 2010.

42. Author interviews with Vietnamese and Thai officials, Washington, DC, Mar 2010.

43. Clifford J. Levy, "Russia's Leaders See China as Template for Ruling," *New York Times,* 18 Oct 2009, A6.

44. Sumit Ganguly and Manjeet S. Pardesi, "India Rising: What Is New Delhi to Do?," *World Policy Journal,* Spring 2007, 9–18.

45. "Cambodia and China Announced $1.6 Billion Deal," ChannelNewsAsia (Singapore), 5 Nov 2010, www.channelnewsasia.com/stories/afp...business/.../.html, accessed Nov 2010.

46. Author interview with Cambodian official, Phnom Penh, Mar 2007.

47. Anton Troianovski, "Xinhua in Times Square," *Wall Street Journal,* 30 June 2010, http://professional.wsj.com/article/SB10001424052748704334604575339281420753918.html?mg=reno64-wsj, accessed Oct 2011.

48. Xiaogeng Deng and Lening Zhang, "China's Cultural Exports and Its Growing Cultural Power in the World," in *Soft Power: China's Emerging Strategy in International Politics* ed. Li Mingjiang (Lanham, MD: Lexington Books, 2009), 151.

49. "The Confucius Institute Project," english.hanban.org/, accessed Sept 2010.

50. "Understanding Chinese Foreign Aid: A Look at China's Development Assistance to Africas, Southeast Asia, and Latin America," Wagner School, New York University, New York, 25 Apr 2008.

51. Geoff Dyer, Jamal Anderlini, and Henny Sender, "China's Lending Hits New Heights," *Financial Times* (UK), 17 Jan 2011.

52. "Chinese University to Expand Foreign Enrollment," Associated Press, 30 Aug 2010.

53. For more on this, see Joshua Kurlantzick, *Charm Offensive: How China's Soft Power Is Transforming the World* (New Haven: Yale University Press, 2007).

54. Zhang Weiwei, "The Allure of the Chinese Model," *International Herald Tribune,* 1 Nov 2006.

55. For more on this debate, see Afshin Molavi, "Buying Time in Tehran," *Foreign Affairs,* Nov/Dec 2004.

56. Ellen Lust-Okar, *Reform in Syria: Steering Between the Chinese Model and Regime Change,* Carnegie Papers, Middle East Series, Carnegie Endowment for International Peace, No. 69, July 2006, http://carnegieendowment.org/files/CEIP_CP_69_final1.pdf. Also, "Looking East," *Economist,* 21 Oct 2010.

57. Simon Romero, "China's Offer of $20 Billion in Loans to Venezuela Extends Needed Cash to Chavez," *New York Times,* 19 Apr 2010, A11.

58. Author interviews with Chinese officials, Washington, DC, Apr 2009, May 2009, and Dec 2009.

59. Ignatius Wibowo, "China's Soft Power and Neoliberal Agenda in Southeast Asia," in *Soft Power: China's Emerging Strategy in International Politics,* ed. Li Mingjiang (Lanham, MD: Lexington Books, 2009), 220.

60. Author interviews with Thai politicians and journalists, Chiang Mai, Feb 2010, and Bangkok, Aug 2007.

61. "More Views on Judiocracy in Thailand," Bangkok Pundit, 2 May 2010, asiancorrespondent.com/.../more-views-on-judiocracy-in-thailand/, accessed June 2010.

62. Ibid.

63. Yun-han Chu, "Third Wave Democratization in East Asia: Challenges and Prospects," *Asian 100* (July 2006), 13.

64. "World Poll Finds Global Leadership Vacuum," Program on International Policy Attitudes, June 2008, http://www.worldpublicopinion.org/pipa/pdf/jun08/ WPO_Leaders_Jun08_packet.pdf, accessed Aug 2010.

8. The Autocrats Strike Back

1. Anne Applebaum, "World Inaction," Slate, 8 Apr 2008, www.slate.com/id /2197155/, accessed Nov 2010.

2. "U.S.-Vietnam Relations," Embassy of the United States in Hanoi, http:// vietnam.usembassy.gov/relations.html, accessed Nov 2011.

3. Dmitri Trenin, "Russia Leaves the West," *Foreign Affairs,* July/Aug 2006.

4. Ibid.

5. "NATO Expansion Relapse into Cold War—FM Lavrov," RIA Novosti, 5 July 2007.

6. Author interviews with Indonesian opinion leaders, Jakarta, Mar 2007. Also, "Victims of 1998 Riots Still Silent," Reuters, 15 May 2008.

7. "Thai-China Friendship Now Not So Special," *China Post* (Taiwan), 29 June 2010, www.chinapost.com.tw/.../the.../Thai-China-friendship.htm, accessed Sept 2010.

8. "Thai PM Seeks Out Roots in Meizhou," *China Daily,* 4 July 2005, www .chinadaily.com.cn/english/doc/2005.../content_456688.htm, accessed Mar 2010.

9. Author interviews with staffers, Senate Foreign Relations Committee, Washington, DC, Mar 2010 and Aug 2010. David Barboz, "China Backs Away from Unocal Bid," *New York Times,* 3 Aug 2005.

10. Justin Blum, "Shareholders Vote in Favor of Unocal Acquisition," *Washington Post,* 11 Aug 2005, http://www.washingtonpost.com/wp-dyn/content/article /2005/08/10/AR2005081000986.html, accessed Oct 2011.

11. "Devastating Blows: Religious Repression of Uighurs in Xinjiang," Human Rights Watch, 11 Apr 2005, http://china.hrw.org/timeline/2005/devastating _blows.

12. Author interview with Uighur activist, Washington, DC, Feb 2010.

13. Edward Gargan, "Three Reported Dead in Latest Tibet Riots," *New York Times,* 6 Mar 1988.

14. Andrew J. Nathan, "Authoritarian Resilience," *Journal of Democracy,* Jan 2003, 6–17.

15. Charlie Szrom and Thomas Brugato, "Liquid Courage," *American,* 22 Feb 2008, http://www.american.com/archive/2008/february-02-08/liquid-courage.

16. Wayne Morrison, "China's Economic Conditions," Congressional Research Service report, 15 July 1998.

17. "Russia's Currency Reserves Exceed $500 Billion for the First Time Since 2008," Bloomberg News, 14 Oct 2010.

18. Charles Bremmer, "Vladimir Putin Wanted to Hang Georgian President Saakashvili by His Balls," *Times* (UK), 14 Nov 2008.

19. Author interviews with Russian opinion leaders, Washington, DC, and New York, Apr 2007 and May 2010.

20. Jeremy Page, "Who Poisoned Yushchenko," *Times* (UK), 8 Dec 2004, http://www.thetimes.co.uk/tto/news/world/article1974989.ece, accessed Oct 2011. "Yushchenko's Dioxin Level Second-Highest in History," Canadian Broadcasting Corporation, 16 Dec 2004, www.cbc.ca/world/story/2004/12/.../yushchenko-dioxin041215 .html, accessed Dec 2010.

21. "Who Poisoned Viktor Yushchenko?" *BBC Newsnight,* 22 Feb 2005, news. bbc.co.uk/2/hi/programmes/newsnight/4288995.stm, accessed Aug 2010.

22. Jeanne L. Wilson, "The Legacy of the Color Revolutions for Russian Politics and Foreign Policy," *Problems of Post-Communism,* Mar/Apr 2010, 23–36.

23. Yongding, "China's Color-Coded Crackdown," *Foreign Policy,* 19 Nov 2005, foreignpolicy.com/artiles/2005/11/18/china_s_color_coded_crackdown, accessed Sept 2007.

24. Jeanne Wilson, "Color Revolutions: The View from Moscow and Beijing," *Journal of Communist Studies and Transition Politics,* June 2009, 369–70.

25. Ibid., 370. Also, author interviews with Chinese officials, Washington, DC, and Beijing, Apr 2010.

26. Titus C. Chen, "China's Reaction to the Color Revolutions: Adaptive Authoritarianism in Full Swing," *Asian Perspective,* No. 2, 2010, 5–10.

27. "China Blogs Egypt on Top Twitter-Like Service," CBS News online, 29 Jan 2011, http://www.cbsnews.com/stories/2011/01/28/tech/main7295643.shtml, accessed Feb 2011.

28. Donald Clarke, "China's Jasmine Crackdown and the Legal System," *East Asia Forum,* 26 May 2011.

29. "Publics Want More Aggressive Government Action on Economic Crisis: Global Poll," Program on International Policy Attitudes, 21 July 2009, www.world publicopinion.org/pipa/articles/btglobalizationtradera/626.php, accessed Nov 2010.

30. Teresa Wright, *Disincentives for Democratic Change in China,* East-West Center, No. 82, Feb 2007, http://www.eastwestcenter.org/sites/default/files/private /api082_15.pdf.

31. "China Paper Blasts Middle East Protest Movements," Associated Press, 5 Mar 2011.

32. Rafaella Pantucci, "China's Slow Surge in Kyrgyzstan: A View from the Ground," *China Brief,* 11 Nov 2011.

33. Author interviews with Lao and Cambodian officials, Phnom Penh and Vientiane, Mar 2007 and Aug 2007.

34. Szrom and Brugato, "Liquid Courage."

35. Tania Branigan, "Purged Chinese Censor Behind Memoirs of Zhao Ziyang," *Guardian* (UK), 21 May 2009.

36. Yongding, "China's Color-Coded Crackdown."

37. Perry Link, "From Famine to Oslo, *New York Review of Books,* 3 Jan 2011, 56.

38. "China Restores Xinjiang Internet," British Broadcasting Corporation, news.bbc.co.uk/2/hi/8682145.stm, accessed Aug 2010. Michael Wines, "In Latest Upheaval, China Plies New Strategies to Control Flow of Information," *New York Times,* 8 July 2009.

39. Wilson, "Color Revolutions," 24.

40. "Another Year of Ramzn Kadyrov," Human Rights Watch, www.hrw.org /en/news/2009/03/31/another-year-ramzan-kadyrov, accessed Nov 2010.

41. Thomas Ambrosio, "Insulating Russia from a Color Revolution: How the Kremlin Resists Regional Democratic Trends," *Democratization,* Apr 2007, 232–52.

42. Thomas Ambrosio, *Authoritarian Backlash* (Burlington, VT: Ashgate, 2009), 42–44.

43. Ibid.

44. Thomas Ambrosio," Reacting to the Color Revolutions," presented at the conference of the International Studies Association, Chicago, 2007.

45. James Traub, "The World According to China," *New York Times Magazine,* 3 Sept 2006, http://www.nytimes.com/2006/09/03/magazine/03ambassador.html ?pagewanted=all, accessed Oct 2011.

46. For more on R2P, see responsibilitytoprotect.org.

47. See Theodore Friend, *Indonesian Destinies* (Cambridge, MA: Belknap), for more on this point.

48. *"What Did I Do Wrong?": Papuans in Merauke Face Abuses by Indonesian Special Forces,* Human Rights Watch, 24 Aug 2009, http://www.hrw.org/reports /2009/06/24/what-did-i-do-wrong.

49. "SBY's China Trip Dominated by Energy and Investment Deals," cable from U.S. Embassy Jakarta, Aug 2005, obtained through Freedom of Information Act.

50. *The Backlash Against Democracy Assistance,* National Endowment for Democracy, 8 June 2006, http://www.ned.org/docs/backlash06.pdf, 7.

51. Thomas Ambrosio, "Catching the Shanghai Spirit: How the Shanghai Co-operation Organization Promotes Authoritarian Norms in Central Asia," *Europe-Asia Studies,* Oct 2008, 1321–44.

52. Author interviews with congressional officials involved with OSCE, Washington, DC, Aug 2007 and Sept 2009.

53. Vitali Silitski, "A Year After the Color Revolutions," PONARS Policy Memo No. 376, Dec 2005, http://www.gwu.edu/~ieresgwu/assets/docs/ponars/pm _0376.pdf, 58–60.

54. Taras Kuzio, "Ukraine's Foreign and Security Policy Controlled by Russia," *Eurasia Daily Monitor* 7 (187), 18 Oct 2010, http://www.jamestown.org/programs /edm/single/?tx_ttnews%5Btt_news%5D=37043&tx_ttnews%5BbackPid%5D=484 &no_cache=1, accessed Nov 2010.

55. Ambrosio, *Authoritarian Backlash,* 56.

56. Ibid., 60.

57. Ibid., 245.

58. Author interview with Daniel Kimmage of Radio Free Europe, Washington, DC, Jan 2011. Also, "Russia Partying Abroad," Center for Security Studies, http://www.isn.ethz.ch/isn/layout/set/print/content/view/full/73?id=121806&lng=en, accessed Nov 2011.

59. Neil Buckley and Roman Olearchyk, "A Nation on Guard," *Financial Times,* 21 Oct 2010, 10.

60. Ambrosio, "Reacting to the Color Revolutions."

61. Erica Marat, "Russian Influence Intensifies in Kyrgyzstan After Elections," *Eurasia Daily Monitor,* 22 Oct 2010, http://www.jamestown.org/single/?no_cache=1 &tx_ttnews%5Btt_news%5D=37060, accessed Dec 2010.

62. Ambrosio, "Reacting to the Color Revolutions."

63. "Blasts Cut Georgian Gas, Electricity Supplies," CNN, 22 Jan 2006, http://articles.cnn.com/2006-01-22/world/russia.gas_1_gas-pipeline-natural-gas-gas-service?_s=PM:WORLD, accessed Nov 2010.

64. Kenneth Roth, "Despots Masquerading as Democrats," in *Human Rights Watch World Report 2008: Events of 2007* (New York: Human Rights Watch, 2008), 1–24, http://www.hrw.org/sites/default/files/reports/wr2k8_web.pdf.

65. "Undermining Democracy," 3. Also, Ambrosio, "Reacting to the Color Revolutions."

66. Clifford J. Levy, "In Siberia, Ruling Party Uses Clenched Fist," *New York Times,* 11 Dec 2010, A1.

67. Author interviews with European diplomats, Washington, DC, Jan 2010.

68. Vladimir Socor, "Russian Influence on the Upswing in Kyrgyzstan," *Eurasia Daily Monitor,* 23 May 2006, http://www.jamestown.org/programs/edm/single/?tx_ttnews%5Btt_news%5D=31703&tx_ttnews%5BbackPid%5D=177&no_cache=1.

69. Carl Gershman and Michael Allen, "The Assault on Democracy Assistance," *Journal of Democracy* 17 (2), 2006, 45, http://www.journalofdemocracy.org/articles/gratis/Gershman-17-2.pdf.

70. For example, "Human Rights Record of the United States 2001," issued by the People's Republic of China, www.china-embassy.org/eng/zt/zfbps/t36544.htm, accessed Aug 2010.

71. Ibid.

72. "ESC Rights and Authoritarian Distortions," Freedom House Countries at the Crossroads Governance (blog), 11 Nov 2010, http://blog.freedomhouse.org/weblog/2010/11/index.html, accessed Nov 2010.

73. Ibid.

74. Sophie Richardson, "Challenges for a 'Responsible Power,'" in *Human Rights Watch World Report 2008: Events of 2007* (New York: Human Rights Watch, 2008), http://www.hrw.org/sites/default/files/reports/wr2k8_web.pdf, 25–30.

9. Failure of the Emerging Powers

1. I have used a pseudonym to protect his identity.

2. Author interview with "Myo," Rangoon, Aug 2006.

3. Author interviews with Burmese exiles, Washington, DC, and Chiang Mai, Sept 2006.

4. Anil Raj, "Has India Abandoned Burma?" Amnesty International memo, 28 Sept 2010.

5. John Cherin, "Guarded Optimism," *Frontline* (Delhi), 6 Oct 2007.

6. Raj, "Has India Abandoned Burma?"

7. "Human Rights, What's That?" *Economist,* 14 Oct 2010.

8. Chris Kraul and Borzou Daragahi, "Lula Takes Risk in Welcoming Ahmadinejad to Brazil," *Los Angeles Times,* 23 Nov 2009.

9. See http://www.ccd21.org/warsaw.htm for more on the Council's meeting in Poland.

10. For more on the UN Democracy Caucus, see http://www.ccd21.org/Initiatives/undc.htm.

11. C. Raja Mohan, "Balancing Interests and Values: India's Struggle with Democracy Promotion," *Washington Quarterly,* Summer 2007, 105.

12. Ted Piccone and Morton Halperin, "A League of Democracies: Doomed to Fail?" *International Herald Tribune,* 5 June 2008.

13. Susilo Bambang Yudhoyono, speech, World Movement for Democracy, Jakarta, 12 Apr 2010.

14. "United States Supports Bali Democracy Forum," public diplomacy press release, Department of State, Washington, DC.

15. Liz Sidoti, "McCain Favors a League of Democracies," Associated Press, 30 Apr 2010.

16. Ibid.

17. Larry A. Niksch and Martin A. Weiss, "Burma: Economic Sanctions," Congressional Research Service report, 3 Aug 2009.

18. "The Friendlessness of Robert Mugabe," *Economist,* 21 Mar 2002, 43–44.

19. Wai Moe, "Thailand's Burma Policy Set to Change Under New Premier," *Irrawaddy,* 25 Dec 2008.

20. Lydia Polgreen, "Crackdown Provokes Fears for Sri Lanka's Democracy," *New York Times,* 17 Feb 2010.

21. Jorge Castaneda, "Not Ready for Prime Time," *Foreign Affairs,* Sept/Oct 2010, 114.

22. For more on the Sri Lankan abuses, see "Sri Lanka: New Evidence of Wartime Abuses," Human Rights Watch, 20 May 2010, http://www.hrw.org/news/2010/05/20/sri-lanka-new-evidence-wartime-abuses.

23. Simon Roughneen, "Thai-Burma Relations Through the Thaksin Prism," *Irrawaddy,* 10 June 2010.

24. Ibid.

25. "Deal Struck on Deep Sea Port," *Bangkok Post,* 10 Dec 2010.

26. "Behind Burma's Rising FDI," *Diplomat,* 31 Aug 2011, http://the-diplomat
.com/asean-beat/2011/08/31/behind-burmas-rising-fdi/, accessed Sept 2011.

27. Seth Mydans, "Thailand Begins Repatriation of Hmong to Laos," *New York Times,* 27 Dec 2009.

28. "Old Wars Never Die," *Economist,* 15 July 2010. Also, "Laos," in Freedom House, *Countries at the Crossroads 2011* (New York: Freedom House, 2011).

29. "Human Rights? What's That?" *Economist,* 14 Oct 2010.

30. Colum Lynch, "Russia, China Veto on Burma," *Washington Post,* 13 Jan 2007, A12.

31. "Zuma Says Zimbabwe's Coalition Government Is Working," *Mail and Guardian* (Johannesburg), 29 Aug 2009.

32. Ibid.

33. *False Dawn,* Human Rights Watch, 31 Aug 2009, http://www.hrw.org/reports /2009/08/31/false-dawn-0.

34. "Human Rights? What's That?"

35. "Dalai Lama Ban Halts Conference," *BBC Online,* 24 Mar 2009, news.bbc .co.uk/2/hi/7960968.stm, accessed Jan 2011.

36. "Wikileaks: Lula Asked Chavez to 'Low Tone' Against U.S.," Allvoices.com, http://www.allvoices.com/contributed-news/7691350-wikileaks-lula-asks-chavez -to-low-tone-against-us, accessed Nov 2011.

37. "Reason with Him," *Newsweek,* 21 Sept 2009.

38. "We Want to Join OPEC and Make Oil Cheaper: Interview with Brazilian President Lula," *Der Spiegel,* 10 May 2008.

39. "Lula da Silva Entangled in Controversy over Cuban Political Prisoners," *MercoPress,* 12 Mar 2010.

40. Andrew Downie, "Brazil Diplomacy on Iran Points to Larger Ambitions," *Los Angeles Times,* 22 May 2010.

41. "The Tehran Tango," *Economist,* 17 May 2010.

42. Will Englund, "Poland Sees Its Past in Belarus's Present," *Washington Post,* 22 Jan 2011, A5.

43. Ben Arnoldy, "Obama Presses India to Become Global Champion of Democracy," *Christian Science Monitor,* 8 Nov 2010.

44. "Suu Kyi Criticizes India's Ties with Myanmar Junta," Agence France Presse, 24 Nov 2010.

45. Author interview with Burmese exile, Chiang Mai, Feb 2010.

46. "Eva Golinger: US Using Democracy Promotion as Disguise for Regime Change," interview with *RT America,* 1 Dec 2010.

47. Joshua Kurlantzick, "What Qadaffi's Fall Means for His Evil Minions," *New Republic,* 26 Aug 2011.

48. Ted Piccone, "Do New Democracies Support Democracy?," *Journal of Democracy,* Oct 2011, 139.

49. "Turkish Prime Minister Slams Israel, Syria, and UN," *Huriyet Daily News,* 5 Oct 2011, http://www.hurriyetdailynews.com/mob_nx.php?n=prime-minister-slams -israel-syria-and-un-2011–10–05, accessed Nov 2011.

50. Piccone, "Do New Democracies Support Democracy?," 141.

51. Ibid., 148.

52. Ibid., 143.

53. Mohan, "Balancing Interests and Values," 101.

54. Ibid.

55. Christopher Munnion, "SA Poison Plan to Damage Mandela's Brain," *Irish Independent,* 11 June 1998.

56. Chris McGreal, "Mbeki Urged to Sack Ally over HIV Views," *Guardian* (UK), 7 Sept 2006.

57. Stewart Patrick, "Irresponsible Stakeholders?" *Foreign Affairs,* Nov/Dec 2010.

58. Patrick, "Irresponsible Stakeholders?"

59. "Northeast Rebels Are Shifting Base to Myanmar," Rediff News (India), 3 Sept 2010, news.rediff.com/.../northeast-rebels-are-shifting-base-to-myanmar.htm, accessed Jan 2011.

60. "Zimbabweans Rush to Avoid South Africa Deportation," BBC Online, www.bbc.co.uk/news/world-africa-12090722, accessed Jan 2011. Also, "Welcome Withdrawn," *Economist,* 15 Oct 2010.

61. Author interview with Thai official, Bangkok, Jan 2007, and Washington, DC, Apr 2010.

62. For more on Phao's narcotics business, see Alfred McCoy, *The Politics of Heroin in Southeast Asia* (New York: Harper, 1973).

63. Castaneda, "Not Ready for Prime Time," 116.

64. See, for example, Peter Maass, "A Touch of Crude," *Mother Jones,* Jan/Feb 2005.

65. "China's CNPC Starts Building Myanmar Pipeline," Agence France Presse, 3 Nov 2009. Also, author interviews with Chinese businesspeople in northern Burma, Feb 2007.

66. Michael Richardson, "Another Pearl in Beijing's String of Ports," *Japan Times,* 19 Aug 2010. Also, author interviews with Indian officials, Washington, DC, Apr 2010.

67. William Boot, "India's Support for Burmese Junta Pays Off," *Irrawaddy,* 24 Sept 2008.

68. Ibid.

69. Author interviews with Indian officials, Washington, DC, Sept 2010. On China's interests in Sri Lanka, see Vikas Bijaj, "India Worries as China Builds Ports in Sri Lanka," *New York Times,* 15 Feb 2010, B1.

70. Stephanie Hanson, "China, Africa, and Oil," Council on Foreign Relations Backgrounder, http://www.cfr.org/publication/9557/china_africa_and_oil.html, 3, accessed Jan 2011.

71. B. Raman, "India and Suu Kyi: Quo Vadis?" B Raman's Strategic Analysis, 17 Nov 2010, http://www.southasiaanalysis.org/%5Cpapers42%5Cpaper4173.html, accessed Oct 2011.

72. "Burmese, Chinese Traders Fight in Mandalay," *Democratic Voice of Burma,* 27 June 2011, http://www.dvb.no/news/burmese-chinese-traders-fight-in-mandalay /16321, accessed Sept 2011.

10. Failure of the West

1. Barack Obama, "Speech to the United Nations General Assembly," 23 Sept 2010, www.america.gov/st/texttrans.../2010/.../20100923103817su0.9430048.html, accessed Feb 2011.

2. Azar Gat, *Victorious and Vulnerable* (Stanford, CA: Hoover Studies, 2010), 3.

3. Thomas Carothers, *Critical Mission: Essays on Democracy Promotion* (Washington, DC: Carnegie Endowment, 2004), 47.

4. J. F. Carrión, P. Zárate, and M. A. Seligson, "The Political Culture of Democracy in Peru: 2006," Latin American Public Opinion Project (LAPOP), Vanderbilt University in Committee on Evaluation of USAID Democracy Assistance Programs, Improving Democracy Assistance: Building Knowledge Through Evaluations and Research (Washington, DC: National Research Council, 2008).

5. Beken Saatcioglu, "EU-Induced Democratization? The Case of Turkey on the Road to Membership" (paper presented at the 63rd Midwest Political Science Association National Conference, Chicago, IL, 7–10 Apr 2005).

6. Larry Diamond, "The Democratic Rollback," *Foreign Affairs,* Mar/Apr 2008.

7. "Egyptians Embrace Revolt Leaders, Military as Well," Pew Research Center Global Attitudes Project, Apr 2011, http://www.pewglobal.org/files/2011/04/Pew -Global-Attitudes-Egypt-Report-FINAL-April-25-2011.pdf, 2–17.

8. From my own analysis of *Phnom Penh Post* stories.

9. "Cambodia: 1997 Grenade Attack on Opposition Still Unpunished," Human Rights Watch, 30 Mar 2009, http://www.hrw.org/en/news/2009/03/30/cambodia-1997-grenade-attack-opposition-still-unpunished, accessed Jan 2010.

10. Joel Brinkley, *Cambodia's Curse* (New York: Public Affairs, 2011).

11. I have eaten at the Karzai family's restaurants in Baltimore, where I live, many times, but never personally have met any of the family members.

12. "Wise Council," *Economist,* 25 Mar 2010.

13. Gat, *Victorious and Vulnerable.* 11.

14. Charles Kupchan, "The Democratic Malaise," *Foreign Affairs,* Jan/Feb 2012, 67.

15. Author interview with State Department official, Washington, DC, Nov 2010.

16. Minxin Pei, "Corruption Threatens China's Future," Carnegie Endowment for International Peace policy brief no. 55, Oct 2007, http://www.carnegieendowment.org/2007/10/09/corruption-threatens-china-s-future/g4. Also, Liz Alderman, "Real Estate Collapse Spells Havoc in Dubai," *New York Times,* 6 Oct 2010.

17. Author interviews with PAD members, Bangkok, May 2006.

18. Author interview with David Schenker, Washington, DC, Nov 2011.

19. Tom Walker, "Revealed: The Terror Prison US Is Helping Build in Morocco," *Times* (UK), 12 Jan 2006. Also, Frederik Balfour, "Malaysia: A Surprising Ally in the War on Terror," *BusinessWeek,* 8 May 2002.

20. "Painting Democracy on Afghanistan," Council on Foreign Relations interview, 23 Oct 2009, http://www.cfr.org/afghanistan/painting-democracy-afghanistan/p20500.

21. Scott Worden, "Afghanistan: An Election Gone Awry," *Journal of Democracy,* July 2010.

22. Ibid.

23. Jon Boone, "Wikileaks Cables Portray Hamid Karzai as Corrupt and Erratic," *Guardian* (UK), 2 Dec 2010.

24. Ibid.

25. Ibid.

26. George W. Bush, "Second Inaugural Address" 20 Jan 2005.

27. Condoleezza Rice, "Speech to American University Cairo," 21 Jun 2005.

28. Andrew Kohut and Madeleine Albright, "An Iron Hand Is No Substitute for Democracy," *Financial Times,* 6 Dec 2011, A11.

29. Author interviews with democracy promotion specialists, State Department, National Endowment for Democracy, Washington, DC, Aug 2011.

30. Edward D. Mansfield and Jack Snyder, *Electing to Fight: Why Emerging Democracies Go to War* (Cambridge, MA: MIT Press, 2007).

31. Author interview with Tom Melia, Washington, DC, Nov 2009.

32. Tara McKelvey, "The Abandonment of Democracy Promotion," *International Journal of Not-for-Profit Law,* June 2011.

33. Author interview with Tom Melia, Washington, DC, Nov 2009.

34. Author interviews with Democrat Party leaders, Washington, DC, Aug 2010, and Chiang Mai, Dec 2010.

35. Author interviews with Thai opinion leaders, Bangkok, Oct 2006.

36. "Crucial 2007 Jakarta Governor's Race Taking Shape," U.S. Embassy Jakarta Cable, 12 Sept 2006, accessed through Wikileaks.org, Oct 2011; Ralph Boyce, "Thailand: My Meeting with General Sonthi," U.S. Embassy Bangkok Cable, 20 Sept 2006, accessed through Wikileaks.org, Oct 2011; and "Thailand Military Coup Leader Briefs Foreign Envoys, Promises to Appoint Civilian Minister Within Two Weeks," U.S. Embassy Bangkok Cable, 20 Sept 2006, accessed through Wikileaks.org, Oct 2011.

37. Tara McKelvey, "Is Democracy a Dirty Word?," *American Prospect,* 7 Dec 2009.

38. Author interviews with Obama administration officials, Washington, DC, Sept 2009.

39. Author interviews with Uighur activists, Washington, DC, Nov 2009.

40. John Pomfret, "Obama's Meeting with the Dalai Lama Is Delayed," *Washington Post,* 5 Oct 2009.

41. Walter Russell Mead, "The Carter Syndrome," *Foreign Policy,* Jan/Feb 2010, 1.

42. "Obama Proposes Cuts to Democracy-Promoting Programs Abroad, Despite GOP Rebukes over Egypt," Huffington Post, 14 Feb 2011, http://www.huffingtonpost.com/2011/02/14/obama-proposes-cuts-to-de_n_822861.html.

43. Author interview with Tom Melia, Washington, DC, Dec 2009.

44. Author interview with Elliott Abrams, Washington, DC, Jan 2010.

45. Biography of Michael H. Posner, www.state.gov/r/pa/ei/biog/27700.htm, accessed Aug 2010.

46. Michael Allen, "Time Is Ripe for European Endowment for Democracy," *Democracy Digest,* 18 Nov 2011, http://www.demdigest.net/blog/2011/11/time-is-ripe-for-european-endowment-for-democracy/, accessed Nov 2011.

47. "Ban Ki-moon Meeting with Suu Kyi a No-Go," Canadian Broadcasting Corporation, 3 July 2009, http://www.cbc.ca/news/world/story/2009/07/03/un-ban-suu-kyi-burma637.html, accessed Dec 2010.

48. Author interviews with GOP staffers, Washington, DC, Nov 2011.

49. Author interview with congressional staffer, Washington, DC, Dec 2011.

50. Matthew Alan Hill, *Democracy Promotion and Conflict-Based Reconstruction* (London: Routledge, 2011), 68.

51. Thomas Carothers, *Revitalizing U.S. Democracy Assistance: The Challenge of USAID* (Washington, DC: Carnegie Endowment for International Peace, 2009).

52. Hillary Clinton, "Remarks on Internet Freedom," Newseum, Washington, DC, 21 Jan 2010.

53. "Internet in Running for 2010 Nobel Peace Prize," BBC online, 10 Mar 2010, news.bbc.co.uk/2/hi/8560469.stm, accessed Jan 2011.

54. Thomas Friedman, "Censors Beware," *New York Times,* 25 July 2000.

55. Nicholas Kristof, "Tear Down This Cyberwall," *New York Times,* 17 June 2009.

56. Clay Shirky, "The Political Power of Social Media," *Foreign Affairs,* Jan/Feb 2011.

57. Angelique Chrisafis, "Ben Ali Forced to Flee Tunisia as Protestors Claim Victory," *Guardian* (UK), 15 Jan 2011.

58. Tara Bahrampour, "In Tunisia, First Steps Toward Democracy," *Washington Post,* 22 Mar 2011.

59. "Detained Google Exec Boosts Mubarak Protest," BBC online, 8 Feb 2011, www.bbc.co.uk/news/world-middle-east-12400128, accessed Feb 2011.

60. Author interviews with Google executives, Washington, DC, Feb 2011.

61. Author interviews with National Endowment for Democracy staffers, Washington, DC, Jan 2011.

62. Malcolm Gladwell, "Small Change," *New Yorker,* 4 Oct 2010, 45.

63. Evgeny Morozov, *The Net Delusion: The Dark Side of Internet Freedom* (New York: Public Affairs, 2011).

64. Author interviews with Thai human rights activists, Washington, DC, Jan 2011, and Chiang Mai, Feb 2010.

65. Andrew Marshall, "Thailand Discovers the Streisand Effect," Reuters (blog), 22 Aug 2010, http://blogs.reuters.com/archive/tag/censorship/page/2/.

66. Author briefing with Thai academics, Washington, DC, Feb 2011.

67. "New Survey Revives Spectre of Malaysian 'Green Dam,'" Malaysian Insider, 16 Aug 2010, http://www.themalaysianinsider.com/malaysia/article/new-survey-revives-spectre-of-malaysian-green-dam/, accessed Jan 2011.

68. Shanthi Kalathil and Taylor Boas, *Open Networks, Closed Regimes: The Impact of the Internet on Authoritarian Rule* (Washington, DC: Carnegie Endowment for International Peace, 2003), 78–80.

69. Cass Sunstein, *Republic.com* (Princeton, NJ: Princeton University Press, 2001).

70. Evgeny Morozov, "Is Russia Google's Next Weak Spot?," Net Effect blog, 10 Aug 2010, http://neteffect.foreignpolicy.com/posts/2010/03/26/is_russia_googles_next _weak_spot, accessed Jan 2011.

71. Morozov, *The Net Delusion*.

72. Ibid., 137.

73. Maziar Bahari, "The Regime's New Dread in Iran," *Newsweek,* 19 Dec 2010.

74. Author interview with Thai human rights activists, Chiang Mai and Washington, DC, Feb 2010.

11. Prescriptions for the Future

1. "Prachatai Editor Arrested," *Nation* (Thailand), 24 Sept 2010, www.nation-multimedia.com/ . . . /Prachatai-editor-arrested-30138684.html, accessed Mar 2011. Also, Ellen Barry, "Veteran Russian Journalist Beaten in Moscow," *New York Times,* 6 Nov 2010; and Maria Danilovs, "Belarus Opposition Complains of Dirty Tricks," Associated Press, 17 Dec 2010.

2. Author interview with former U.S. official, Washington, DC, Jan 2012.

3. Joel Simon, "International Institutions Fail to Defend Press Freedom," in Committee to Protect Journalists, *Attacks on the Press 2010: A Worldwide Survey by the Committee to Protect Journalists* (New York: CPJ, 2010), http://cpj.org/2011/02 /attacks-on-the-press-2010-introduction-joel-simon.php.

4. Scott Sayare, "Unesco Backs Dictator's Divisive Prize," *New York Times,* 8 Mar 2012.

5. Ken Silverstein, "Teodorin's World," *Foreign Policy,* Mar/Apr 2011, 54–62.

6. "Cambodia," in Freedom House, *Countries at the Crossroads 2010* (New York: Freedom House, 2010), http://www.freedomhouse.org/report/countries-crossroads-2010/cambodia.

7. Freedom Against Censorship Thailand, *Annual Report,* facdthai.wordpress. com, accessed Mar 2011.

8. Kenneth Roth, "The Abusers' Reaction: Intensifying Attacks on Human Rights Defenders, Organizations, and Institutions," in *Human Rights Watch World Report 2010: Events of 2009* (New York: Human Rights Watch, 2010), http://www.hrw.org/sites/default/files/reports/wr2010.pdf.

9. Author interview with Ralph Boyce, Washington, DC, Jan 2012.

10. Julie Schmit, "China Tops U.S. in Spending on Clean Energy," *USA Today,* 25 Mar 2010.

11. From my own analysis of Freedom House and Economist Intelligence Unit data.

12. Patricio Navia and Thomas D. Zweifel, "Democracy, Dictatorship, and Infant Mortality Revisited," *Journal of Democracy,* July 2003, 90–103.

13. Ibid., 100.

14. See earlier research on this topic by Morton Halperin, Joseph Siegle, and Michael Weinstein, *The Democracy Advantage: How Democracies Promote Prosperity and Peace* (New York: Routledge, 2005), 41–47.

15. Ibid., 33.

16. Ibid., 51.

17. Yasheng Huang, "The Next Asian Miracle," *Foreign Policy,* July/Aug 2008, 33–40.

18. Ibid., 39–40.

19. See also Halperin, Siegle, and Weinstein, *The Democracy Advantage,* 41.

20. Amartya Sen, *Poverty and Famines: An Essay on Entitlements and Deprivation* (Oxford: Oxford University Press, 1982).

21. Author interview with Ralph Boyce, Washington, DC, Jan 2012.

22. Charles Kurzman and Ijlal Naqvi, "Do Muslims Vote Islamic?," *Journal of Democracy,* Apr 2010, 50–63.

23. Author interviews with Philippine opinion leaders, Manila, Mar 2007, and Washington, DC, Sept 2010.

24. World Bank Group, "Doing Business Rankings," doingbusiness.org, accessed Jan 2012.

25. "Eurocham Paper Critical of China's Protectionist Measures," *China Briefing,* 4 Sept 2009.

26. Author interviews with U.S. policy makers, Washington, DC, Feb 2011.

27. Author interviews with Brazilian policy makers, Washington, DC, May 2011.

28. Ethan Kapstein and Nathan Converse, "Why Democracies Fail," *Journal of Democracy,* Oct 2008.

29. Ibid.

30. From my own analysis of Indonesian budget data.

31. "Top Singapore Ministers Face Pay Cuts of Up to 51 Percent," BBC online, 4 Jan 2012, http://www.bbc.co.uk/news/world-asia-16404935, accessed Jan 20120.

32. Peter Gelling, "East Timor Takes Steps to Avoid Pitfalls of Oil Wealth," *New York Times,* 21 Feb 2006.

33. Steven Levitsky, "International Linkage and Democratization," *Journal of Democracy,* July 2005, 20–34.

34. From my own analysis of Freedom House data.

35. "Haider's Freedom Party Wins Election," Associated Press, 7 Mar 2004. Also, "Gujarat Inquiry: Narendra Modi 'Partisan' over Riots," BBC online, 4 Feb 2011, www.bbc.co.uk/news/world-south-asia-12362891, accessed Feb 2011.

36. Author interview with former U.S. official in Thailand, Washington, Jan 2012.

37. "PAD Leaders Call for Power Seizure," *Nation* (Thailand), 20 Jan 2012.

38. Hilton Root and Bruce Bueno de Mesquita, "The Political Roots of Poverty: The Economic Logic of Autocracy," *National Interest,* summer 2002, 27–37.

39. From UN budget data.

40. Author interview with Win Min, Washington, DC, Nov 2010. Also, author interviews with Burmese analysts, Chiang Mai, Feb 2010.

41. Ben Arnoldy, "Chinese Warships Dock in Burma, Rattling Rival Naval Power India," *Christian Science Monitor,* 30 Aug 2010.

42. Indian Bagshi, "Turkey May Emerge as Regional Role Model," *Times of India,* 21 Feb 2011.

43. Ibid.

44. Landon Tomas, "In Turkey's Example, Some See Map for Middle East," *New York Times,* 4 Feb 2011.

45. Soner Cagaptay, "Arab Revolt Makes Turkey a Regional Power," *Hurriyet Daily News,* 16 Feb 2011.

46. "Prachatai Editor Arrested," *Nation* (Thailand), www.nationmultimedia .com/.../Prachatai-editor-arrested-30138684.html, accessed Feb 2011.

47. Seth Mydans, "Fighting for Press Freedom in Thailand," *New York Times,* 1 Nov 2010.

48. Author interviews with Thai academics, Chiang Mai, Feb 2010, and Washington, DC, Dec 2010.

49. Author interviews with Thai politicians, Washington, DC, and Bangkok, Feb 2010 and Dec 2010.

50. Author interviews with Thai journalists, Washington and Bangkok, Feb 2010 and Dec 2010.

51. Ibid.

Index